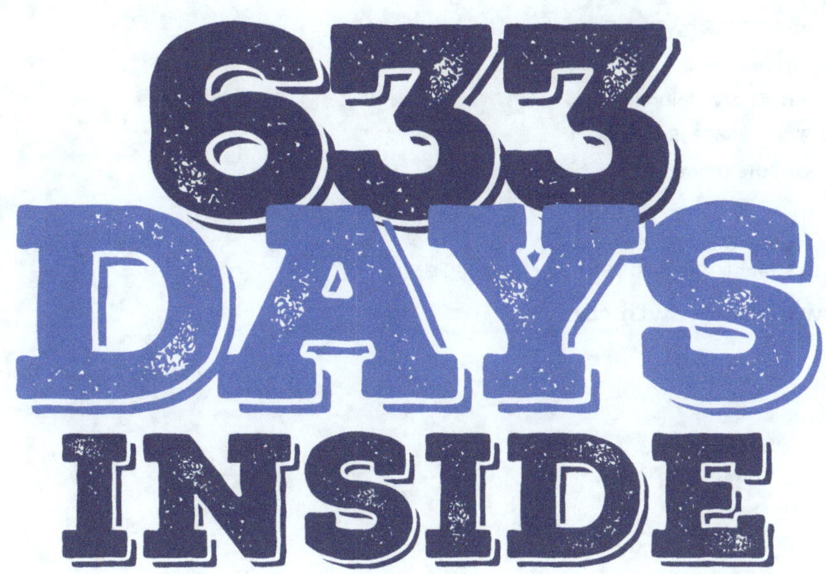

Lessons on
Life and Leadership

by Greg E. Lindberg

DEDICATION

*To my fellow prisoners at FPC Montgomery,
I thank you every day for your generosity,
humility, friendship, and perseverance.
I am lucky to have met you.*

ACKNOWLEDGEMENTS

I would not be here if it weren't for the kindness and generosity of thousands of people who have encouraged me and coached me along the way. My parents, teachers, coaches, fellow employees, lawyers, accountants, lenders, friends, family, and others too numerous to mention. Most importantly, I am eternally grateful to my fellow inmates at FPC Montgomery who taught me so much about life and leadership. And I am grateful to those members of the staff at FPC Montgomery who have a kind heart and a true mission to improve the lives of the inmates at the camp.

TABLE OF CONTENTS

TABLE OF CONTENTS

PART ONE: INSIDE

INTRODUCTION

My 633-day stay in a federal prison was the single most positive transformational event of my life. I turned around my health and regained some of my youth through the study of mitochondrial biogenesis. My gray hair literally turned red again, my memory improved, and my body now looks like I'm ten years younger.

The picture on the left in the gray shirt is me the day I checked into prison… the picture on the right in the black shirt is me 12 days after my release from prison. No photoshop.

I also discovered faith through the study of quantum biology. I made life-long friends, and I learned the power of gratitude. I became far more disciplined and focused and got rid of a lot of unproductive habits.

I would not trade my prison experience for anything. Yes, I sorely missed my family and friends. But the experience was a necessary part of my character development and a necessary part of my life plan.

On the day I checked into prison, I released a book, *Failing Early & Failing Often: How To Turn Your Adversity Into An Even Greater Advantage.* I did not know at the time what advantages prison would bring—but I had faith that I would find them. By the day I checked out of prison, I had concluded that prison was the SINGLE most advantageous experience of my entire life.

The key to all these advantages is the concept of hormesis.

Biologists use the concept of hormesis to explain how some things that can hurt us in large doses can make us stronger in smaller doses. We know this as "no pain, no gain" or "that which doesn't kill you makes you stronger."

According to *Aging and Mechanisms of Disease* (Mattson 2015) "Hormesis is a characteristic of many biological processes, namely a biphasic or triphasic response to exposure to increasing amounts of a substance or condition. Within the hormetic zone, the biological response to low exposures to toxins and other stressors is generally favorable."

The single most powerful lesson I learned in prison is the stunning power of hormesis. If you stress your body with fasting, cold temperatures, hard mental exertion, and extraordinary physical exertion—you will see extraordinary improvements in your mind and body driven by mitochondrial biogenesis.

The mitochondria are the powerhouses of every one of your cells. And they multiply and gain mass when they are challenged by hormetic influences such as starvation, freezing, and mental and physical exertion. And the more your mitochondria multiply and gain in size, the better every single one of your bodily functions works.

Prison itself was a hormetic experience. 633 days in prison was in the "hormetic zone" for me where the experience resulted in a biological and mental response that was favorable. If my prison time had been shorter—or a lot longer—this would likely have not been the case.

The lesson here: you must actively seek out painful challenges that make you stronger. Exercise is a well-known example of this. However, the same biological principles that work with exercise are also activated with fasting, hard mental challenges, and exposure to cold. All of these stressors activate mitochondrial biogenesis which can, over time, rejuvenate every one of your cells to a youthful state.

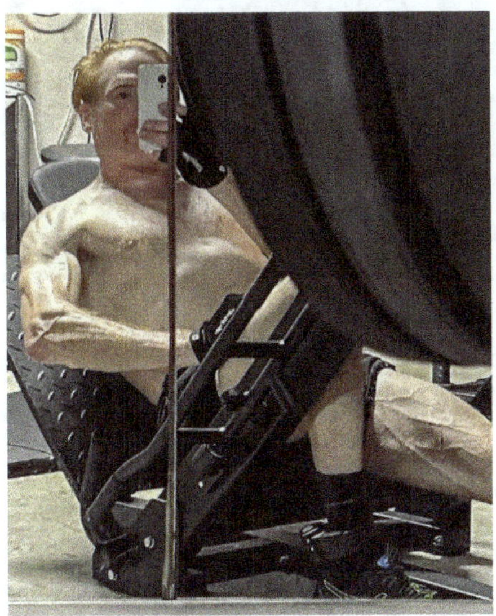

Left: Three weeks after release, doing leg presses—no photoshop, no photographer, a quick selfie in the mirror.

Above: Doing seated rows

Another powerful lesson I learned in prison is the power of focus. In prison, your email access is severely limited and you don't have a phone. You are forced to go back to pen and paper, and for me this was revolutionary. I found myself, for the first time, able to THINK and be far more proactive in my thoughts and actions. In the free world, where you are surrounded by constant electronic messages from all your devices, you slowly lose the ability to step back and think strategically.

> **Any legal system that requires spending a fortune to defend yourself is not a legal system at all—it's a prosecution system.**

Prison also taught me how broken the "justice" system is today in the U.S. I met countless fellow inmates who were in prison simply because they could not afford to fight. They took plea deals because they had no other good options. My own case cost me over $50 million in legal fees. Any legal system that requires spending a fortune to defend yourself is not a legal system at all—it's a prosecution system. It's no wonder there is a 97% conviction rate in the U.S. Very few people can afford to stand up to the federal government's prosecution machine.

I also saw the devastating effects that the over-criminalization of drug use has on African-American and Latino families. Well over half of the inmates at FPC Montgomery were there on some kind of drug charge. Some of the sentences were extraordinarily harsh—25 years for marijuana trafficking—when some states have legalized marijuana. These are good people whose lives are being thrown away because some people in Congress believe that harsh sentencing somehow can reduce drug use. There has been no evidence that this is the case, yet harsh drug sentences are still being handed down.

> **If you cannot command yourself to achieve a certain objective, to behave in a certain way, then you will wind up being forced to obey someone else.**

In prison, I also learned how commanding and obeying are two sides of the same coin. You cannot be a good commander unless you know how to obey. At FPC Montgomery, there are 1,001 rules and they are changing every day. I enjoyed the challenge of attempting to follow all the rules all the time. If you succeeded in following all these rules, which was no easy feat, the camp treated you well. Most importantly, you must be able to obey yourself. If you cannot command yourself to achieve a certain objective, to behave in a certain way, then you will wind up being forced to obey someone else. Obeying and commanding are the critical building blocks of any achievement in life—and prison reinforced this lesson for me in spades.

I also learned the power of how repeatedly doing the same thing over and over again can lead to mastery. By the end of my 21 months, I was one of the longest serving inmates in the Mobile unit at FPC Montgomery. I cleaned toilets up until the very last day before I was released. I did the same thing every day and had the same routine every week. By the end of my 633 days, prison for me was like clockwork: rise at 5.30am, workout for two hours, clean toilets, check email, take a nap, pick-up my mail, read mail, take a walk, sleep, and repeat. For the last year in prison, I only ate on weekends, which made my weekday routine very simple and uninterrupted.

I enjoyed the ascetism at FPC Montgomery. It was a good place to become singularly focused on my mission in life. I had far too many distractions in my life before I checked into prison. After 633 days of focus, I rebuilt my habits so that these distractions are no longer part of my life.

In prison I spent a lot of time teaching my fellow prisoners about goal setting, stress management, and career planning, and I learned from them in return. The teaching helped me hone the lessons I had learned building and turning around companies. It also brought me joy and inspiration, something I wasn't sure I would find in prison. I hope the lessons in this book help you find joy, purpose, and success in your own life.

What This Book Is, and What It Is Not

I've been battling unfair legal charges for over three years. The charges, the trial and my imprisonment have weighed heavily on my family, friends, and business partners. The biased news coverage has also been tough on them. I intentionally stayed under the radar for the first 30 years of business, hoping to create good while staying quiet. This silence allowed my detractors to define me. I look forward to setting the record straight in a future book when all legal proceedings are well behind me. You can read some of the publicly available documents on my case in the appendix to this book.

The U.S. Court of Appeals for the Fourth Circuit overturned my conviction in June of 2022 ruling that the district court unfairly violated my Fifth and Sixth Amendment rights. I was released from FPC Montgomery on July 15, 2022, after having served 633 days in prison. I missed my father's funeral and the birth of three of my sons. Those are things I can never get back. This book will focus not on the things I lost, but on the things I learned.

This book is an exploration of the leadership principles that I spoke about in my first book, proved by the crucible of 633 days in prison.

This is me, meeting my sons Max and Thor for the first time. In this picture I am about an hour out of prison. I am still wearing my $14 prison Timex watch. Notice my dark red all natural hair color. They don't give us hair coloring materials in prison. My head is down because I'm crying tears of joy. I get emotional every time I look at this picture.

I hope always to be a student, seeking self-awareness, but at the same time acknowledging who I am and what I have to offer to the world.

The purpose of this book is to help you turn any adversity, failure, heartbreak, or trauma into an even greater advantage. I have had a few failures and adversities of my own. I've been divorced, indicted, convicted, jailed, and have failed at numerous business ventures. I've made every mistake there is to make in business at least twice. I had a golf ball-sized brain tumor removed, which means I am half-deaf and had to learn to walk again. I've lost hundreds of millions of dollars on failed investments.

I am an entrepreneur, a leadership coach, an author, and a father. I have acquired and turned around more than 100 companies, each time finding people with the same commitment to hard work, entrepreneurialism, and a roll-up-your-sleeves attitude—and letting them lead.

Despite all the adversity I had faced in my life and career before prison, I had no way of knowing what I would encounter inside. I wrote this book in part to share that story, in hopes that it will help others faced with their own adversities.

I find that the most powerful lesson in navigating failure and adversity comes from Napoleon Hill, who wrote almost 100 years ago that "every adversity, every failure, every heartache carries with it the seed of an equal or greater benefit."

A warning before we start: This book is not going to give you the answers. Rather, this book will suggest a path that will lead to learning and wisdom through trial, error, and failure. Simply reading this book will not give you this knowledge; you must take the material in this book and turn it into daily action and habits that will ultimately form your character after many years of repetitive effort.

Nothing short of that will last. Nothing short of that will ultimately produce the greater advantage from your adversity.

Adversity will only make you stronger if you put the hard-earned lessons into action every day for the rest of your life. If you fail to put your newfound wisdom to work with new goals and objectives, you have wasted the experience.

Regardless of where you might ultimately find your advantage—in business, your career, art, sports, or your community—don't expect results quickly. Turning adversity into advantage can take years. But when the advantage does appear—and appear it will if you persist long enough—you will be overwhelmed by its power and wonder where it has been all these years.

> **The day you stop asking questions, relax and rest on your accomplishments is the day you start dying.**

Along the way, you will learn you must always be a student. The day you stop asking questions, relax and rest on your accomplishments is the day you start dying. Relaxations are dangerous in any field, from poetry to plumbing to politics.

And remember, I am not the teacher here. I am merely sharing my experiences as a fellow student. Your life experiences will teach you. This book will simply encourage you to have those experiences in the first place.

Don't be discouraged if your progress is slow in the beginning. Putting the principles from this book to work in your life is not easy. And this book is not meant to be an easy read—easy does not produce strength.

CHAPTER ONE:
Early Days in Prison

n October 2020, I reported to FPC Montgomery. Here is a note that I sent out after my first year there:

Dear Family, Friends, and Colleagues,

I hope you all have been well. I thought I would drop you a line to update you on how I'm doing here at FPC Montgomery.

As of tomorrow at 10am, I will have been down for a year. (In prison slang, "down" means how much time you have been in prison). With some luck it will be my last year in prison.

My life here in prison is normal, routine, and even comfortable. I read, I sleep, I work as a housekeeper, I work out, I eat, I fast, and I take long evening walks with my fellow inmates and talk about everything from almonds to quantum physics. I find brilliance among my fellow inmates every day.

There are hundreds of rules to follow and if you follow all of them all the time, the camp treats you well. I enjoy the challenge of following all the rules. Every few days you learn about a new one. For example, I was coming in from the rec yard this weekend after a workout and I had my shirt off. You don't need to wear a shirt on the rec yard. And you don't need to wear a shirt inside your housing wing. However there is about 25 yards of distance between the rec yard and your wing where it turns out you have to wear your shirt. I was made aware of this rule by the police and I quickly put my shirt on. (In prison slang, correctional officers are "the police.")

The discipline of mastering ever changing rules is a critical prerequisite to knowing how to command. Obeying and commanding are two sides of the same coin. You cannot be a good commander unless you know how to be a good soldier.

I am genuinely glad I came to prison. This experience has given me a monstrous amount of strength and energy that will last a lifetime. This experience has also given me an opportunity to build friendships and meet dozens of people that I would never have otherwise met. We lead fairly narrow lives on the street. ("On the street" is prison slang for being in the "free" world.) In prison, you are surrounded by hundreds of your fellow inmates and the population is constantly changing with new self-surrenders and new inmates "coming down from a low" all the time. "Lows" are higher level security prisons that often send their inmates to minimum security camps like FPC Montgomery as inmates get towards the end of their sentence.

I've had the opportunity to teach a number of classes to my fellow inmates on business, career planning, stress management, and entrepreneurship. I find great joy working with my fellow inmates to help them achieve their dreams. Many of them come from broken families where no one ever told them "you can do this." Sometimes that's all it takes for them to realize their talents can be applied in a legitimate career.

I've also discovered something I would have never discovered had I not come to prison: if you only eat on weekends—and give yourself a long 3-day weekend ;)—your body repairs itself and starts to get younger. When I was on the street, if someone told me to fast for 90 hours every week—I could not have done it. There is something about being locked up that hardens your resolve.

The science behind "intermittent fasting" is well known. When your body burns up all of its stores of glycogen—about 18 hours after eating—it starts to burn your triglycerides from your stored body fat. This in turn unleashes a whole cascade of survival genes and hormones that repair your body and help it grow stronger.

One of the most powerful effects of fasting is mitochondrial biogenesis. The mitochondria are the engines of the cell—producing energy via the "Electron Transport Chain" on their inner membranes. Mitochondria follow the same pattern: young, healthy, and energetic individuals have far higher numbers of mitochondria per cell than those who are not as healthy, young, or energetic.

Mitochondria are ancient bacterial organisms that combined with the cellular structure over a billion years ago. There are millions of billions of them in your body. If you learn to quiet your mind, you will hear them speaking to you. And they are hungry—for triglycerides digested from your body fat. If you only feed them glucose, they won't be happy for long.

When your mitochondria are happy, they multiply in droves. More mitochondria means more energy for every single part of your body. More energy means all parts of your body—including the stem cells which repair your body—perform better. After a 90 hour fast, human growth hormone goes up by 10x. Testosterone goes up (for men). Melatonin production goes up. Neural connections go up. Intestinal mobility goes up. Every single part of your body is re-energized.

Critically, fasting increases your Brain-Derived Neurotropic Factor (BDNF) by as much as 20x after a four day fast. BNDF is your brain growth hormone. After four days of fasting, your brain is on fire...absorbing, processing, and remembering information at several times its normal rate.

There is quite literally a force within each of us that, if awakened, will have the power to absolutely astonish you. If you listen to the ancient organisms that drive every ounce of energy you have, and you give these millions of billions of organisms what they want, they will generate literally thousands of gigawatts of additional energy for you along their Electron Transport Chain.

Last week I completed my 10th consecutive weekly 90+ hour fast. I am seeing dark red hair growing on my lower temples where the hair was previously gray. I've gained about 15 pounds of muscle and have lost enough abdominal fat to have a few defined ab muscles. Yesterday I noticed new hair growing on my arms that is far darker and more red than the hair that was there before.

My memory has improved. I can now walk through the TV room and remember the name of the actor in the show. This is a big change for me. In 2014, I went to a longevity clinic and they tested my memory. It was so bad that they asked, "Are you having trouble at work?"

I sleep like a teenager—up to 9 hours on some nights. I have not slept this well since the 1980s. My energy, focus, creativity, and organizational skills have all improved. I would gladly come to prison again to gain the knowledge of what a 90 hour weekly fast can do for the body —and build a habit of doing these weekly fasts that lasts a lifetime. In every adversity there are the seeds of an even greater advantage.

The lead prosecutor on my case told the court at my sentencing hearing that he wanted to "incapacitate Greg Lindberg." Well, I am far from incapacitated. My body, brain, and energy levels are growing. My family is growing (I have two baby boys on the way, due next year). And the team at the Global Growth group of companies is doing an extraordinary job delivering results and is making solid progress on all fronts.

My biggest challenge is that I dearly miss my family and friends. Visitation is behind a large Plexiglas wall and it's far from ideal for personal visits. The good news is that there is some chance that if my appeal goes well I could be home by year-end.

We received notification that the 4th Circuit Court of Appeals has tentatively scheduled my case for oral argument sometime this coming December 6th to 10th.

The National Association of Criminal Defense Lawyers (NACL), a large, well-respected group of former prosecutors and practicing criminal defense attorneys, has also filed an amicus brief in support of my appeal. According to NACL, "Permitting the district court to decide a disputed element of a charge under the guise of statutory interpretation flouts Gaudin and creates a dangerous precedent for criminal defendants in both white collar and street crime cases." Gaudin is a Supreme Court case that says a judge cannot instruct a jury on a finding of fact as the judge did in my case.

NACL explains that permitting my conviction to stand "would effectively permit judges to imprison defendants by entering verdicts on disputed elements as long as they only explicitly direct the element on one of the multiple overlapping charges."

There is a possibility if the oral argument goes very well that the 4th Circuit could issue a short judgment (ahead of their full ruling) shortly after oral argument that vacates my conviction. That would mean that, with some luck, I could potentially be released by year-end.

If the 4th Circuit doesn't vacate my conviction then we will take the case to the Supreme Court. And if the Supreme Court does not overturn the case, then I am well on my way to having a significant number of credits under the First Step Act, which allows early release for various activities such as earning my housekeeping apprenticeship certificate. Meanwhile, inmates are routinely sent home under the CARES Act when they reach the 50% mark on their sentence. With First Step Act credits, I could be at 50%—and potentially eligible for release—sometime next year.

If we don't win at the 4th Circuit, and we don't win at the Supreme Court, and I don't get First Step Act credits, and I don't get CARES Act early release, then it's possible I would qualify for up to 18 months of home confinement under BOP policies, which means I would be released in another two years or so. Regardless, I am prepared.

*I have this quote posted on my locker where I can see it all day long: **"The only thing that can prove today whether one is worth anything or not: that one endures."—F. Nietzsche.** I am eternally grateful to my parents for giving me the gift of extraordinary endurance.*

Meanwhile, I am grateful for each and every one of you—for everything you have done and are doing. I hope to see you soon.

I was used to living in a big house. I had indulged myself with a yacht. Life was good. Now I was living in a cell in a bunk room, sharing a small space and an even smaller bathroom with 21 other men. I missed my family. I worried about my friends and coworkers, and how my companies were doing. I was looking forward to getting a prison assignment so I could at least stay busy.

You learn a whole new terminology and whole new way of life. Being in prison, you are "down." When you are free, you are "on the street." The person who shares your cell with you is your "cellie." The surprising truth about prison is that your fellow inmates are incredibly supportive. They are a wealth of knowledge and wisdom, and you learn very quickly to listen. Prisoners support each other. That is one of the most important rules in prison. Inmates stick together. The support goes both ways: if you help an inmate get through a bad day, they will be there for you when your bad day comes.

> Enjoy the daily grind. Success starts with the discipline of daily execution and mastery.

Enjoy the daily grind. Success starts with the discipline of daily execution and mastery.

My first job in prison was cleaning toilets. I had hoped to do something that allowed me to use my philosophy or economics degrees, or my experience starting and turning around companies, but instead I was a janitor. I showed up every day and did an excellent job. After 5 months of working diligently, my efforts were noticed and I was promoted. I also got a second job as a teacher. I didn't ask for a promotion or a new job.

I just showed up and did my best and took pride in my work cleaning toilets. I did a good job. I was courteous, on time, respectful, and followed directions. Even in prison, hard work and good performance is rewarded. Some of my fellow inmates would say, "Lindberg, why are you working so hard?" and I would answer, "I take pride in my work." This is true for me regardless of what I do. There is no point in doing a job unless you give it everything you can. I believe that regardless of your position, you should show up and give it your best every day. I did not work hard to get a promotion. I worked hard cleaning toilets because that is my value system. The promotion was a by-product of those values.

My job cleaning toilets speaks to the power of incremental improvement. If you do your work 1% better every day, in 100 days you have doubled your productivity. I've seen this firsthand, in person, cleaning toilets. In the beginning, I was slow and inefficient. Over time, I learned the rhythm, the flow of the job and the optimal sequencing of steps to clean bathrooms quickly and efficiently. In 5 months of cleaning bathrooms, I was able to turn a three-hour job into a 45-minute job, simply with the right process, planning and daily maintenance. Every new day I arrived to clean the bathroom, I made incremental improvements on my previous day's work. It is very satisfying to see your skill set build over time, and the hard work at daily incremental improvement paid off when I was promoted. I was happy to clean toilets; the job fits very well with my core values of getting my hands dirty.

If this approach leads to a promotion at a prison facility, it can lead to a promotion anywhere. Don't be too proud to get your hands dirty with a frontline job assignment. Take the job, master it, and prove what you are worth. The meaning of life is to use your mind to its fullest extent. If you are cleaning toilets, engage yourself fully so that you are the best toilet cleaner your organization has ever seen. You can learn a lot starting at the bottom and, in most organizations, your efforts will stand out and lead to good things for your future. The teaching position I eventually got turned out to be one of the most satisfying experiences of my life. I taught goal setting and career planning to my fellow prisoners, and it became the best part of my week.

Prison was also a wonderful place to become socially immersed and to overcome any lingering social weaknesses that I might have had. I lived with 300+ fellow inmates. We sleep within 4 feet of each other and interact all day long. You can't walk more than a few steps in prison without running into another inmate. Social skills are developed quickly. My prison experience was like going to college all over again, except this time, unlike my college experience, I was not in the library studying all day long. I made numerous friendships that I would have never had time for "on the street."

Prison teaches perspective. Few things that happen "on the street" are as important as they seem at the time. And the things that are really important require reflection and thought, not a quick "fight or flight" response. Step out of the emotional roller coaster of instant communications and gain perspective, master the details, and study your markets, products, and opportunities. Be a philosopher for a while, and a student as well. As a result, you will be a better leader when it comes time to lead.

CHAPTER TWO:
My Mindset in Prison

Someday you might be faced with having to choose which prison you will lock up in, a prison of your own making or a prison run by those whom you have been bold enough to challenge.

I was prepared to do my time in prison regardless of how long it took.

Admiral Stockdale describes this mindset well: "You must never confuse faith that you will prevail in the end—which you can never afford to lose—with the discipline to confront the most brutal facts of your current reality, whatever they may be."

Admiral Stockdale was a prisoner of war in Vietnam for 8 years. He survived unspeakable conditions and cruelty. He talked about two groups of fellow prisoners who were unable to survive: those who gave up hope, and those whose hope was based on overly optimistic prognoses. Stockdale said the overly optimistic folks always believed they would be home by Christmas, by Easter, by their anniversary, by year end. When it didn't happen, their spirit was crushed.

Stockdale took the other route. He believed that, while they may not get out today, this month, or even this year, they would get home. While none of us are likely to be called upon to show the heroism of

Admiral Stockdale, we can learn from his experience. We must accept the facts before we can deal with them.

When I checked into prison in October of 2020, I was facing up to 87 months in prison. I resolved to continue my fight behind bars as long as it took to win. Yes, I hoped my prison time would be short. But I resolved at the time to learn how adaptable I could be to survive and thrive in this new environment. Humans are far more adaptable than we give ourselves credit for. Some of the greatest works in history have been dreamt up by people who were unjustly incarcerated.

In 1605, Miguel de Cervantes wrote the first volume of the groundbreaking literary classic Don Quixote while serving time in prison. French nobleman Marquis de Sade spent nearly all of his stints in prison writing, eventually completing 11 novels, 16 novellas, and 20 plays. Open editorial piece *Letters from Birmingham Jail* by Martin Luther King Jr. was written and published while he was imprisoned in Alabama. A direct criticism and call to action against the injustices of the U.S. court system, particularly its racial prejudices—an incredible work by an incredible leader whose significance can hardly be duplicated—was written in prison.

Humans can survive just about any adversity and turn it into a greater advantage. The first step is getting to the cold, hard truth about the adversity that you face.

Twenty years ago, everyone subscribed to print magazines and newsletters. The industry was bullish on print, even as circulation numbers began to fall. Publishers found articles entitled "Why Print Will Never Die" and circulated them among themselves. At every conference, there were feel-good presentations about how nothing would ever replace the weight of a book or magazine in your hands.

Some publishers faced the fact that print and mail were getting more expensive, while free content was becoming more and more readily available on the Web. Some of these publishers started testing workflow products and software. Others came up with creative ways to monetize Web content. Still others began using their content to sell products. Those companies look very different than they did 20 years ago. Some aren't even recognizable as publishing companies, but they are thriving.

The companies that spent their time telling each other that print would never die have failed. How were the successful companies different? First, they had leaders willing to face realities head on and who fearlessly tried and failed with many models knowing that one would prevail in the end. Second, they had a culture of reality.

"We must not lose our sense of proportion and thus become discouraged or alarmed. When we face with a steady eye the difficulties which lie before us, we may derive new confidence by remembering those we have already overcome."

--Winston Churchill, (Broadcast "Report of the War," April 27, 1941)

Winston Churchill personified resolve. He believed England would prevail against Hitler's war machine against all odds. He knew there were almost insurmountable challenges in their way. He knew his intelligence personnel were discovering new facts about Hitler's growing munitions factories and troop movements every day. He also knew he had a huge, challenging personality and few people would be willing to tell him bad news. So, he created the Statistical Office. This ministry existed outside the regular chain of command. Its sole purpose was to feed him unvarnished facts.

You want leaders with big personalities. You want strong, aggressive leaders. Those traits can also create an environment where people hesitate to come forward with bad news. That is why you must create a Culture of Reality where people are encouraged to speak up, no matter what.

Ask yourself: "How often do I get bad news before it shows up in the numbers? Do I get it early enough to act on it instead of reacting to it? How short is the path of information from the customer to my ear? How do I know what customers think about my products?"

Use these strategies to create a climate where brutal facts are shared:

- Make sure all employees are trained on your values
- Lead with questions, not answers
- Engage dialogue and debate, not coercion
- Conduct autopsies without blame
- Build red flag mechanisms
- Ensure a robust customer feedback loop

I saw the power of the Stockdale Paradox firsthand at FPC Montgomery. Those inmates who said "I'm going to get out by Christmas" because of some x, y, or z potential development in their case or new Bureau of Prisons policy were almost always disappointed. Some of them became bitter as a result and turned to unhealthy habits like overeating, etc. Those inmates who planned to be in prison the full length of their sentence did the best. They adjusted to the new life. They found happy places where they could find some contentment despite being locked up. They took on projects and found productive work that not only occupied their mind but made them stronger.

The survival formula for prison or for any major adversity and extreme circumstance you face is simple: *(1)* Accept the worst as a real possibility; *(2)* Find work and find daily productive tasks; *(3)* Set goals for improvement of your circumstances and measure your progress towards those goals. Every incremental improvement is a reason to celebrate. The Stockdale Paradox doesn't mean to give up optimism. It simply means to prepare for the worst while hoping for the best. And preparing for the worst means daily work and daily incremental improvements that will sustain you as long as it takes under the worst-case scenario to overcome your ordeal.

Get Better, Not Bitter*

It's natural to be angry at whoever has set you back, done you harm, and treated you with indignity. For some time, this anger is unavoidable for most of us. However, the faster you turn this anger into productive activity, the faster you can turn the adversity to your advantage.

After I was incarcerated, I started fasting for 44-48 hours in between meals. The stress of my legal battles and incarceration had already taken years off my life. I decided I was going to do whatever it took to get those years back. That's when I began researching intermittent fasting. Dozens of studies show numerous health benefits, including a potential 10x increase in ketone bodies which stimulate brain-derived neurotrophic factor (BDNF), which stimulates brain cell growth.

SPECIFIC DISCLAIMER: As I share my experiences with intermittent fasting and theories on quantum physics, I acknowledge that I am not a medical professional and that one should always consult with a physician before undertaking intermittent fasting and making other drastic changes to their diet and lifestyle. For independent research, see Appendix D for scientific studies, research and articles on the benefits of intermittent fasting.

Since I've started my fasts, my memory has improved dramatically, my sleep quality has improved dramatically, and my creativity, focus, and attention to detail have all increased. Fasting is quite possibly the hardest thing I've ever done. It is far harder than checking into prison. I would never have found the discipline to make such a life-changing step if I wasn't focused on turning my adversity to my advantage.

In the middle of my fast, when the hunger is the greatest, I tell myself, "If I don't succeed, they win." Bill Stetzer, one of the prosecutors in my case, said at my sentencing hearing that he wanted to "incapacitate Greg Lindberg." I am not going to be incapacitated. I am not going to let them win. I transformed the anger into productive activity. From the hundreds of medical journal articles I read, intermittent fasting is the single most powerful anti-aging treatment on the planet. And it's free and available to most of the 7.7 billion of us humans. The catch: intermittent fasting in a world of food abundance where 3 meals a day is socially acceptable is extraordinarily hard to do. I am thankful that I faced the challenges I've faced. They have given me the strength to do what I never would have done before. What strength can you find from your adversities?

Calm Under Fire

If there is anything that prison teaches you, it's calm under fire. "They've already locked me up; so what else could they do?" I see in the outside world enormous angst and fear over this and that. It's unproductive, and it undermines good leadership. The best leaders operate primarily in the cerebellum and have figured out how to disconnect the "fight or flight" emotion from their decision-making. They face indignities, insults, threats, pain, and failures with a calm determination. Their communications don't carry a negative emotional load that furthers the angst in the organization at the very time the organization requires rational and fearless thinking.

A simple technique: if you are facing a grave threat, start fasting. Your body will produce the brain-stimulating chemical compound "brain-derived neurotrophic factor" in substantially increased quantities after 24 to 48 hours of fasting. On that second day of fasting, your creativity, memory, confidence, and focus will multiply rapidly. You will become supercharged with energy to overcome the threats you face. Your heart rate will slow down, and a general calm will overcome you. These are all the traits we humans evolved over tens of thousands of years as hunter/gatherers.

When food was scarce, our bodies went into over-drive and produced extraordinary mental and muscular energy. The gene that produced this response to hunger very quickly came to dominate the human gene pool as those who became stronger and smarter about hunger lived longer and had more children. So stay calm under fire. Don't eat—drink only water. And take your leadership to a new level. The most amazing thing about intermittent fasting: the changes to your memory, speed of cognition, and vascular health are permanent because they occur via epigenetic changes, i.e. your genes are expressed differently and permanently after a period of intermittent fasting.

CHAPTER THREE:
Mitochondrial Biogenesis and Quantum Biology

In prison, I found time to read hundreds of medical journal and science journal articles. One of the most important that I found was a medical journal article on mitochondrial biogenesis and the power of fasting, "Thermodynamics and Inflammation: Insights into Quantum Biology and Aging" by Nunn, Guy, and Bell, published February 3, 2022, in the journal Quantum Reports.

The implications of Nunn et al.'s work [and all the 179 citations in his paper] are profound:

- The beginning of life on earth was directed by non-local intelligence. Single cell bacteria 4.5 billion years ago figured out how to use quantum tunneling to communicate and "self-organize" to survive. Scientists have no other explanation for how these bacteria—which are now our mitochondria—could have done this without direction from non-local intelligence. In other words, we were created by a creator.

- Billions of your cells are replicated every day, which appears to require quantum tunneling to non-local intelligence in order to accurately replicate your DNA. Ergo, our creator is creating each and every one of us every day—one cell at a time.

- After 4 or 5 days of fasting, your mitochondrial electron transport chain (ETC) ramps up in volume 20x, which massively increases the voltage generated on the ETC to around 600 million volts. Per basic quantum mechanics, this high energy of the "super excited" quantum wave function allows quantum tunneling of electrons and protons. Some physicists have suggested this quantum tunneling, which by definition is non-local, allows a connection to non-local intelligence. I believe this is why, during my 114+ hour weekly fasts, I can tap into non-local intelligence. At 600 million volts of power running on every one of my ten million billion mitochondrial electron transport chains, my quantum tunneling is off the charts after 4 to 5 days of fasting.

I believe quantum tunneling is a communication method among humans that increases dramatically after 4 to 5 days of fasting. In prison on the 4th and 5th day of my fasts, people that otherwise would not have approached me would come up to me and have conversations. I believe this is because the ultra-high voltage running along my electron transport chains allows long-range quantum tunneling—instant non-local communication with other people. I believe every one of us has these "quantum powers" if we chose to exercise them. Steve Jobs's "reality distortion field" was another example of quantum tunneling at work.

There are dozens of other profound implications in Nunn's work, but the above are some of the most powerful.

CHAPTER FOUR:
Infinite Intelligence

Eternal vigilance in the search for truth and self-awareness is the only key to lasting success.

I am more convinced than ever that my entire FPC Montgomery experience was part of the plan of infinite intelligence.

It can be difficult to find meaning and value in the more unpleasant and minutiae moments in life. I know this well. Here is a breakdown of your day when checking in at FPC Montgomery:

When self-surrendering, you arrive at the visitor center at the Maxwell Air Force Base. You enter the visitor center lounge and tell the officer on duty that you are there to report to FPC Montgomery as an inmate.

The officers at the visitor center take "custody" of you and will contact the camp, and they will send someone from R&D (Receiving & Discharge) to come and pick you up. The R&D officer will be driving a white van. They pat you down and place you in the van. They also ask you to sign paperwork stating that you are reporting on said date. They issue you a mask and escort you back to the camp. All newly arriving inmates are quarantined for 14 to 21 days—everyone is housed in a separate unit until they are released from quarantine.

When you surrender, you are not allowed to keep any clothing, unauthorized medications (even if over-the counter), or personal items. You cannot bring in any books with the exception of a Bible. All unauthorized personal items—including the clothes in which you present—you are given the option to have mailed to your residence via the United States Postal Service at your own expense or simply thrown away in the trash.

When you arrive at R&D, you will be placed in a waiting area either by yourself or with other inmates. You will be placed into a cell to wait to be processed for intake. You remain in the waiting area (cell) for a number of minutes or even up to an hour or more before being called out, depending on how busy the duty officers are at the moment. If you are held with other inmates, each inmate will be called out individually to undergo the initial intake process. There may be more than one R&D officer in the department at this time. During the entire process, you are asked many questions by the R&D staff. Questions about your crime, sexual orientation, marital status, general health questions, and if you are a witness against another inmate in a court case. The process is conducted in a very business-like manner, and it is very impersonal. It is humiliating and degrading, but it's important to remember that the staff is just doing their job. After an initial round of questions, the next step is the strip search.

Afterward, you are given khaki or green pants, shirts and a pair of black boots. The black boots are the most uncomfortable pair of footwear ever made—your feet will begin to ache within ten footsteps. Then you are taken back to the quarantine unit where the usual intake process will be completed. You will be seen by a nurse to determine whether or not you have shown up under the influence of drugs or alcohol, have exhibited suicidal ideation, or are otherwise so agitated that you may be a danger to yourself or others. They will take your temperature and you will be given COVID-19 and TB tests.

Afterward, you will meet one member of your team officially (i.e., case manager, case counselor, or unit secretary) who will sit you down in an office and go over your legal file, mostly having you sign myriad bureaucratic forms (e.g., forms about health care, indemnity, emergency contacts information, etc.). You will be taken to the laundry department where you will be issued a full set of clothing (from underwear to the uniform (green or khaki, multiple pairs) you will wear daily, a bedroll, pillow, towels, and a hygiene kit. You will also be provided your Admission and Orientation (A&O) handbook.

At this point, you are dropped off in quarantine to begin your prison sentence. In quarantine, you are not allowed to leave the unit and you are not allowed to have interaction with any other staff during the two-week incubation period.

I include all of this to highlight that a state change, even the most tedious and jarring, can be crucial to your development as a human. A simple way to handle such jarring transitions in your life: resolve to process the information and accept the information you learn as a necessary part of your life plan.

Melvin Vopson, in his recent paper, "Experimental protocol for testing the mass-energy-information equivalence principle," predicts that information is the 5th element of matter in the universe and that information has mass and energy like other forms of matter. This could then, in turn, explain the 90+ percent of the mass of the universe that physicists have called "dark matter."

By combining information theory and physical principles of thermodynamics, Vopson's theoretical proposals make specific predictions about the mass of information, as well as the most probable information content per elementary particle.

If the universe is primarily made up of information, then that information is ordered and has a plan. That is what information is by definition: an orderly syntropy-bringing force. And that syntropy-creating force is required for our DNA to replicate and thus is creating who we are every femtosecond.

In his July 2022 paper, "A possible information entropic law of genetic mutations," Vopson notes that the current scientific consensus is that genetic mutations are random processes. "According to the Darwinian theory of evolution, only natural selection determines which mutations are beneficial in the course of evolution, and there is no deterministic correlation between any parameter and the probability that these mutations will occur," Vopson says. However, taking into account information theory and the previously unobserved relationship between the information entropy of genomes and their mutation dynamics, one comes to a different conclusion, Vopson says. Specifically, "We are able to formulate a governing law of genetic mutations, stating that genomes undergo genetic mutations over time driven by a tendency to reduce their overall information entropy, challenging the existing Darwinian paradigm."

> **If you have sufficient information, you can reverse entropy and create syntropy.**

The implication of Vopson's latest work: our creator is creating us every femtosecond as our mitochondrial electron transport chains spin up highly excited electrons and protons that tunnel to non-local information, which in turn provides the information that adapts our DNA to the design of our creator. Evolution is not a random process of mutations and survival of the fittest. But rather, evolution is driven by advantageous adaptions sourced from non-local information that has the effect of reducing entropy and promoting syntropy. In this way, all living creatures adapt to their environments in the most efficient way to ensure syntropy. At the core, life is the process of accessing non-local information via quantum tunneling in order to bring order to entropy. And all entropy is simply missing information. If you have sufficient information, you can reverse entropy and create syntropy.

> In very simple terms: challenge yourself and your body will genetically alter itself to adapt to your new environmental conditions by accessing non-local information.

The practical implications for this principle are profound. The more you promote mitochondrial biogenesis through fasting, freezing, aggressive exercise and mental challenges, the more electrons you produce on your electron transport chain to power quantum tunneling. And the more power you have for quantum tunneling, the more non-local information you can access to reduce the entropy you encounter through quantum wave resonance. In other words, you adapt to your environment quicker with a higher mitochondrial copy number and greater mitochondrial mass. Some studies have suggested that over half of the human genome is expressed epigenetically—which means that you are literally creating yourself through interactions with your environment.

A portion of your brain and body exist in a state of quantum coherence that accesses information on a non-local basis. And when this quantum coherence is disturbed from various environmental perturbations, the decoherence of classical reality drives epigenetic changes to restore your quantum coherence. In very simple terms: challenge yourself and your body will genetically alter itself to adapt to your new environmental conditions by accessing non-local information.

I believe that in my 633 days in prison, my genes expressed themselves in an entirely new way, driven by the hormetic influence of the prison environment, my fasting, my freezing cold showers, and the aggressive physical and mental challenges I endured. All these changes were advantageous adaptations that helped me become stronger—and turn the adversity of prison into an even greater advantage.

Dirk Meijer, a professor emeritus at the University of Groningen in the Netherlands, suggests in his 2020 paper, "Water, The Cradle of Life via its Coherent Quantum Frequencies," that this quantum coherence of the body and mind is maintained by the harmonic frequency of pure water. "A new order parameter characteristic for water molecule assembly has been revealed, which implies quantum coherency and entanglement," says Meijer.

Specifically, "we may assume that water molecule assembly shows electromagnetic and electronic collective states that contain 'quantum imprints or molds' for living cells," Meijer says. Since water molecules have a comparable distribution of coherent electromagnetic field (EMF) bands to that of fluid assemblies in living cells, a resonant wave interaction is expected between the cytoplasm and surrounding water molecules, Meijer says.

In plain English: pure water exists in our cytoplasm and exists in a state of quantum coherence. This implies pure water is entangled with non-local information that is critical for the replication of every human cell. So, the more mitochondrial biogenesis you have through fasting, freezing, mental challenges, and physical challenges, the higher your rate of access to non-local

> So, the more mitochondrial biogenesis you have through fasting, freezing, mental challenges, and physical challenges, the higher your rate of access to non-local information, which is required to maintain your quantum coherence.

information, which is required to maintain your quantum coherence. The more quantum coherence you have, the more information you have to combat the entropy you encounter in the every-day world. And the more you counteract the entropy you encounter, the more syntropy you create and the more you improve the survival rate of your cells through advantageous adaptions.

Quite simply, by failing to challenge yourself with hormetic perturbations (i.e. pain), the weaker you become and the closer to entropy and death you are. Life is syntropy, death is entropy.

According to Meijer, consciousness resides in a field surrounding the brain and it shares information with the brain through quantum entanglement. Meijer says that this field of consciousness "transmits wave information into the brain tissue, that … is instrumental in high-speed conscious and subconscious information processing." In other words, the "mind" is a field that exists around the brain; it picks up information from outside the brain and communicates it to the brain in an extremely fast process, explains editor and reporter Tara MacIsaac.

Meijer described this field alternately as "a holographic structured field," a "receptive mental workspace," a "meta-cognitive domain," and the "global memory space of the individual."

Meijer's theory is similar to another theory called "orchestrated objective reduction," or "Orch-OR," that was developed by physicist Sir Roger Penrose and anesthesiologist Dr. Stuart Hameroff. Hameroff describes the theory: "... it suggests consciousness arises from quantum vibrations in protein polymers called microtubules inside the brain's neurons."

Penrose and Hamerof say "there is a connection between the brain's biomolecular processes and the basic structure of the universe." This ties to Vopson's theory of information as having both mass and energy as the 5th element of matter. If the universe is primarily information, and if your very consciousness requires a quantum coherence to create a non-local quantum wave resonance with that information, then you should take your quantum coherence very seriously.

Practically, what does this mean?

(a) **Be very careful with electronics,** since their harmonic frequencies may upset your quantum coherence.

(b) **Be very careful with negative people** who may likewise emit de-coherent quantum frequencies that can harm your access to non-local information.

(c) **Fast regularly, exercise regularly, and challenge yourself mentally.** All of these improve your quantum coherence.

CHAPTER FIVE:
Guiding Beliefs

Below is a list of the beliefs by which I live and lead. You may be familiar with some of them, as they are axioms, or widely accepted, generally true statements. Some of them I've formed myself based on my personal and professional experiences.

Collectively, these beliefs provide comfort and guidance. I encourage you to adopt any that resonate as true and meaningful for you.

AXIOMS

1. The leader in the room is the person closest to reality.

2. Helping others helps you.

3. Be relentlessly demanding at getting the right people in the right place on the bus.

4. Find what you can be the best in the world at and focus all your energy on it.

5. Enjoy the battles and welcome the fight.

6. "Next" is the most important word after any victory or failure.

7. Transmute your anger to positive daily habits to your goals.

8. Adversity will only make you stronger if you put the hard-learned lessons into action every day for the rest of your life.

9. The day you stop asking questions, relax, and rest on your accomplishments is the day you start dying.

10. Relaxations are dangerous in any field from poetry to politics.

11. The more diverse any society, the more tolerance for new ideas, failure, and the unorthodox.

12. The most diverse societies and organizations are the most successful in developing ideas that change humanity for the better.

13. Someday you might be faced with having to choose which prison you will lock up in. A prison of your own making or a real prison run by those whom you have been bold enough to challenge.

14. The essence of being human is the will to be free.

15. Goals create tension and give you a reason to live.

16. Accepting the status quo of your life is dangerous. It holds you back and gives you a false sense of security.

17. Love what you do.

18. Your subconscious is your fate.

19. Be prepared for a re-evaluation of all your values.

20. To think differently and to follow radically logical conclusions, you must eliminate the fear of where your logic might take you and what others might think about you.

21. Most people vastly underestimate the extent to which their free will is subject to subconsciously imposed limits.

22. Democracy is not the ultimate protector of freedom. Understandable rule of law uninflated by politics is more certain to protect freedom even in a monarchy.

23. In order to turn adversity into advantage, you must be fearless to the danger from those who will seek to stop you because they see you as a challenge or threat to established norms, ideas, practices, companies, competitors, and those in power today.

24. Make your goal an all-consuming obsession that puts everything else in perspective as less important.

25. True knowledge comes only from doing, learning, and failing in the school of hard knocks.

26. The greatest danger from education is believing you know.

27. Running a business requires experience and experience requires failure.

28. Getting good grades in a formal education environment has nothing to do with running a successful business.

29. The best business people assume they know nothing.

30. Get your hands dirty.

31. If you live your life with fear of others' opinions then you are not living your life.

32. Failure to turn adversity into an advantage is fundamentally a failure to break free from your comfort zone. Your ability to turn adversity into an advantage is directly proportional to your ability to endure pain.

33. Without gifts of adversity, you might slip into a most dangerous relaxation.

34. Hire people smarter than you and more talented than you and get the heck out of their way.

35. One "C" player on your bus can ruin your whole operation.

36. The amount of freedom you permit to those in your life will determine how accountable they are for upholding their commitment to you.

37. The core of your character is your ability to tell yourself you are going to do something—and then do it.

38. The rule of law in America is a mirage when one in five people is branded a "criminal."

39. Welcome pain. It makes you stronger. Truth is found on the far side of pain.

40. Love yourself enough to forgive yourself.

41. Thoughts lead to actions, actions lead to habits, habits form character, and your character is your fate.

42. Every human you encounter has something to teach you.

43. Big failure later is often caused by lack of failure early.

44. You can't predict where your next failure is going to come from.

45. There is no shame in failure, only in refusing to learn from failures.

46. Be proud of your failures.

47. Don't fear death. Instead, stake your goals on it.

48. The more you challenge established powers, the more people will try to take you down.

49. Pray. It's a powerful positive affirmation.

50. The caliber of your leadership is directly proportional to the distance in the future you can plan your actions and act consistently in the present with those plans.

51. The more you show gratitude and appreciation, the more it comes back to you.

52. The biggest act of humility for a leader is to accept and embrace the mistakes of those people on your team.

53. When the leader of an organization is afraid to make mistakes, everyone will be.

54. Forgiveness builds loyalty.

55. Eternal vigilance in the search for truth and self-awareness is the only key to lasting success.

56. If you find yourself easily achieving your goals, dream bigger.

57. It never gets easier: at every stage of growth, you have new and more powerful detractors.

58. Only decide to become a leader if you are prepared to attend the school of hard knocks for decades on end.

59. Leadership will increase your stress level and make you a target for everyone who wants what you have but doesn't want to pay the price.

60. If you aren't the first to be blamed, the first to take the negative attention, the first to face the risks of embarrassment, prosecution, and even death that comes along with leadership, then you aren't a true leader.

61. The stronger the leader, the less force they need to apply to achieve results.

62. Forced leadership is not leadership; it is the slavery of will.

63. Meaning in life comes from doing something well.

64. Your public narrative and persona will be created by someone; you will be far better off if that someone is you.

65. Succeed by doing the impossible.

66. When someone tells you it can't be done, prove them wrong.

67. Fail early & fail often. Failing late can be disastrous.

68. Be unreasonable if you want uncommon results.

69. The more feedback you get, the better leader you will be.

70. Master the warrior spirit; peace and comfort do not produce success.

71. People rise to your level of expectation or sink to your level of disregard.

72. Everyone has the seeds of something great inside them. Help them unlock it.

73. Getting the right people on your bus is 90% of success.

74. If you don't have people on your team capable of taking your job, you aren't building leaders.

75. Everyone you meet has experienced their own pain; understand it if you want to understand them.

76. Don't expect to ever find the truth. If you think you have found the truth, study quantum physics. That should convince you that you have a false sense of security.

77. If you are not scared, alone, and nervous, you have not stretched yourself far enough.

78. If people tell you that your idea is crazy, you might be onto something.

79. The cold and timid souls who know neither victory nor defeat will sit on the sidelines and criticize you to no end.

80. Set goals that drive your critics absolutely nuts.

81. You will never keep the critics happy, so don't even try.

82. The more responsibility you give to the people in your life, the more courage and accountability they will have.

83. Be the change you want to see in your organization.

84. The leader must create a necessity of learning.

85. Thank people who give you critical feedback. They have taken time from their day to help you improve.

86. Regardless of where you choose to make a difference, choose a path that will require you to use all your gifts.

87. The most important part of remaining humble is admitting you don't know.

88. Once a leader decides they have found the truth, the decline begins.

89. If you do not tolerate failure in your organization, you are wasting the tuition your organization paid to the school of hard knocks.

90. Your future & freedom depend on your ability to conquer your fear.

91. Your detractors whose power comes solely from their title know they are nothing.

92. There is danger in being the motivator—politically, socially, economically.

93. People who aren't able to achieve their goals will go out of their way to see that you do not achieve yours.

94. Seeking objective truth is not being afraid of what you uncover.

95. Be a philosopher first, and a leader second.

96. Your subconscious is your fate.

97. If you let society determine your goals, ultimately society can take away its approval.

98. Enjoy the daily grind. Success starts with the discipline of daily execution and mastery of the administrivia.

99. The 10,000 hour rule: you are not a master at anything until you have practiced for 10,000 hours (3-4 years working all day long). What are you practicing now?

100. 75% of the communication in the modern work environment is a waste of time. It's amazing how much is not important in today's communications.

101. If you are not afraid and alone sometimes, you are not going to grow.

CHAPTER SIX:
My First Impression of the Free World

My first impression of the "Free World" is that the lives of many Americans today are way too cushy and over-abundant. It's no wonder that people are not challenging the status quo—or thinking outside of the box—given how easy life has become. There is simply no reason to upset the established way of doing things. You have thousands of options for everything you could possibly want. Life out here in the "free world" is very comfortable—all too comfortable.

I ordered a prison bunk bed from Unicor to sleep in every night. I need the constant reminder of the austerity of prison. It brings me focus.

Another interesting psychological phenomenon: When I walked out of the front gate at Maxwell it felt as if I had been in prison for just a few moments. The entire experience was encapsulated in a separate part of space-time. It was a very strange experience. My perception of prison was so "unentangled" from the rest of space-time that it appeared to be just a few moments.

CHAPTER SEVEN:
My Charity

Helping others helps you.

I have a newfound appreciation of the enormous waste of humanity created by today's criminal justice system. I have found extraordinary talent in the ranks of the 70-plus million Americans who have a criminal record. (If you have a criminal record, you are welcome to apply for a position at one of our companies.)

Sadly, most employers don't see the opportunity of hiring people with a criminal record—despite the enormous tuition these people have paid in the School of Hard Knocks. That tuition is largely wasted by employers who refuse to hire people with criminal backgrounds.

In 2015, The Brennan Center for Justice published some shocking data*, some of which is represented in the chart below:

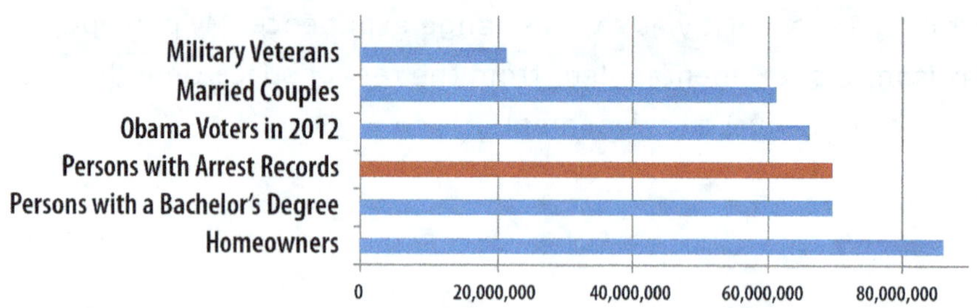

*https://www.brennancenter.org/our-work/analysis-opinion/just-facts-many-americans-have-criminal-records-college-diplomas, Matthew Friedman, November 17, 2015

There are just as many people in America today with a criminal record as with a college degree. There are more people with a criminal record in America than people who voted for Obama in 2012. Perhaps someone should start the "American Ex-Con Party"—its voter base would be the largest of any political party. Sadly, in many states, people with a criminal record can't vote.

Laws that prohibit felons from voting effectively disenfranchise a whole segment of the population. Perhaps this is intentional self-preservation by the existing elites. The practice skews elections to "law and order" voters—that is, voters who have not yet come face to face with the tentacles of the Leviathan. Over time, the more shakedowns there are of law-abiding citizens by the Leviathan, the more attitudes will change.

There are about 328 million people in the United States. When more than 70 million of them (21 percent, or one in five) have criminal backgrounds, something is gravely wrong. The rule of law in America is a mirage when one in five people is branded a "criminal."

With my new knowledge of and personal experience with the prison system, I am eager to launch a prison charity to supply welcome kits for Federal inmates. The kits may contain the following:

- high quality shower shoes (two sizes for the kits...large and extra large)

- a small book of positive affirmations and quotes

- a list of pro bono legal resources for inmates

- a list of First Step Act eligible classes via correspondence schools

On the last day I was in prison, the camp called me down to R&D, which is what happens when inmates are going to be released. This was a signal to the inmates that it was safe to "scavenge" my cube. I walked out the door and then came back a very short time later to find that someone had already taken my shower shoes. They went first.

I also will never forget one of my fellow inmates who said to me as I was walking out, "Don't forget us. You are one of the few people who can do something to help."

I won't forget them.

CHAPTER EIGHT:
The Quantum Physics of Leadership

Don't expect to ever find the truth. If you think you have found the truth, study quantum physics.

Quantum physics can teach us a lot about how to be better leaders. When I studied quantum physics, I realized that my thoughts, words, and actions shape my reality—and the reality of my company and employees—on a profoundly deep level. According to standard quantum theory, a quantum system exists in a "superposition" of all possible states, which collapses into a single state, or classical reality, only when someone or something observes or measures it (as Anil Ananthaswamy explains in the July 2021 edition of the *New Scientist*, which is a good primer on the subject). "However, this theory fails to define exactly what constitutes a measurement or an observer, and how exactly that collapse happens," Ananthaswamy says.

One theory that provides an explanation suggests that the "universe could have begun as a quantum system and continued evolving quantum mechanically until matter first became able to integrate information. This consciousness then started to collapse quantum reality, creating the classical reality we experience today," explains Ananthaswamy.

In short: quantum theory suggests that classical reality is created when matter integrates information from quantum reality.

In other words, by integrating information into your consciousness, you are creating classical reality. Napoleon Hill suggests that contagious positive enthusiasm generated by "high-level vibrations of the mind" powers people and leaders to success. Could this be a quantum phenomenon whereby the leader is quite literally collapsing the quantum superposition to create classic reality by integrating and observing information? This brings the fundamental success dictum of "if you can see, and you can believe, then you can achieve" to a whole new quantum level. Another implication is that a quantum system exists in a superposition of ALL possible states; so, quite literally, on a quantum level anything is possible as long as it obeys the laws of classical physics.

> By taking measure of the future by visualizing a specific future reality, the leader is quite possibly collapsing the quantum wave function to a specific version of classic reality in concert with the leader's vision.

The success of a leader is directly proportional to the "time span of management" of that leadership, i.e. the distance into the future that the leader can visualize the future and then take action today consistent with that vision. Perhaps the reason a long-time span of management is a successful management model is based in quantum physics. By taking measure of the future by visualizing a specific future reality, the leader is quite possibly collapsing the quantum wave function to a specific version of classic reality in concert with the leader's vision.

Another basic tenet of quantum mechanics is what Einstein called "spooky action at a distance." This is the ability of quantum particles such as photons to become paired or "entangled" and to remain paired even when separated by large distances and without any apparent means of pairing under the principles of classical physics. Quantum computing relies on this basic pairing of subatomic particles to store information. It's entirely possible that a leader creates a similar pairing at a subatomic level with those people who observe that leader's vision and consciousness. So, your vision could have a far deeper impact than simply conscious awareness in the minds of those who observe your vision. You could be creating a pairing of particles at a subatomic level with your team.

This suggests that the thoughts, actions, and visions that a leader permits to occupy their mind and permits others to observe can be far more consequential than a simple idea. The potential under quantum theory is that this observation and measurement by the leader, and observation and measurement by others, creates a pairing of particles at a subatomic level. Thus, the leader and the audience become "entangled" based on the amount of energy the leader has to power their quantum tunneling.

The implication: be extraordinarily careful with the thoughts and beliefs that you permit to occupy your mind for they will become your fate and the fate of the people around you. The old saying, "Don't put that thought into the universe," could be even more powerful that we think. If you pray, think carefully about what you pray for.

CHAPTER NINE:
My Philosophy on Failure

> There is no shame in failure, only in refusing to learn from failures.

We know failure is part of success—we have all seen the posters and put the quotes above our desks. Nevertheless, most of us think of failure as, well, a failure, and we do everything we can to avoid it. In society, education, and business, failure is a humiliating negative. Failing a class, putting on weight, getting wait-listed, dropping out, getting divorced, going bankrupt, being convicted, being sent to prison—all are considered failures in today's society when, in truth, these experiences can be the steppingstones for later, greater success in life. To quote the 2010 film based on the C.S. Lewis book *Voyage of the Dawn Treader:* "Hardships often prepare ordinary people for an extraordinary destiny."

We are often asked to dream of success, to imagine what life will look like when we win. But any such victory is likely to come only after agonizing failure and "practice shots."

Unfortunately, society does not prepare us for this failure. In fact, society abhors failure and teaches us from a very young age to avoid it. From the day our first grade is given in school, we are taught that failure is a problem.

We are taught not to fail on exams—let alone on something bigger, such as a business, a career, or a marriage. Fear of failure is driven into our psyche and culture at the deepest level.

As a result, for most people coming of age today the only safe route is to conform and to not make any waves.

This is a natural defensive mechanism driven by fear of opinion. Anyone who strikes out on their own runs the risk of embarrassment, being ostracized, being fired, and even prosecuted. In this kind of society, individualism and self-reliance are replaced with conformity and reliance on the accepted norms.

Unless we foster a willingness to fail, along with the courage to endure all manner of indignities and persecution, we might end up with generations of people living the life of the cold and timid soul who knows neither victory nor defeat.

The immediate feedback loop of today's social media world compounds this problem and makes people even more afraid of not getting enough "likes." The fact that everything you do will stay with you forever thanks to the internet is a heavy burden on people growing up today. The pressure to conform, not make waves and not take risks is enormous. Worse, you have no idea how culture will change in the future, and what is perfectly acceptable language or culture today may be grounds for ostracism later.

Instead of a world of cold and timid souls afraid of the slightest negative comment on Instagram, a much healthier approach is to learn to celebrate failing early and failing often.

A rethinking of our entire approach to failure is needed—especially if we are going to encourage the millions of people whose lives have been wrecked by COVID-19 to find the strength to turn their adversity into a greater advantage.

Failure is one of the most successful ways humans learn and society develops. When we don't succeed, we try again, each time moving forward with the knowledge we have gained from our past experience.

I am grateful that the failures and adversities I am facing now have come at a time when I have the energy and vigor to tackle them. Had these challenges come later in life, they could have been far more catastrophic.

Failure is a stigma in our society today, and that ultimately prevents people from recovering from failure. Failure should not be a stigma. Rather, it should be a badge of honor that you tried. You did your best, but it didn't work out. The tuition you paid was priceless. Put your newfound education from the School of Hard Knocks to work and try again.

We need to encourage learning through failure in school, business, relationships, and the justice system. Before we can learn from failure, we need to stop being frightened of failure and stop punishing failure so severely. We need opportunities to learn that failure isn't fatal and being right isn't the reward.

We need to celebrate being different just as much as being right. Our ability to learn from failure is in direct proportion to our ability not to fear the judgment of others and our ability to tolerate the unorthodox in our society.

Often, the right answer is simply a matter of our cultural perspective. The more diversity in any society, the more tolerance for new ideas and the more tolerance of failure and the unorthodox. The most diverse societies and organizations are the most successful in developing ideas that change humanity for the better.

We limit the growth potential of human ingenuity when we punish failure and ostracize and criticize those who are different. Ultimately, we all pay the price—with shorter lives and less prosperity.

///

The more diverse any society, the more tolerance for new ideas and the tolerance for failure and the unorthodox.

///

The leader who embraces the most radical diversity and who is the most inclusive will ultimately be the most effective. This is not just politically correct dogma; it's the only way true leaders get closest to the truth. Any prejudice weakens the leader's effectiveness. Mohammad, the founder of Islam, was perhaps the most effective leader in the history of the world precisely because of this tolerance and inclusiveness for all the different cultures and religions his armies encountered. He learned from them, absorbed them and welcomed them. Ironically, this led these cultures to adopt the Arab culture in a more lasting way than any other religious leader has accomplished. The most inclusive, diverse and adaptable culture is the most persuasive. Diversity in business brings increased creativity, higher innovation and faster problem-solving.

Plato had it right more than 2,000 years ago: "Nothing can be more absurd than the practice that prevails in our country of men and women not following the same pursuits with all their strengths and with one mind; for thus, the state, instead of being whole, is reduced to half."

A look at some of the most influential and creative Americans is a testimony to the power of diversity. Hamdi Ulukaya, the founder of Chobani yogurt, was a political refugee from Turkey. The creator and founder of Google, Sergey Brin, moved to the United States from Moscow with his family to escape persecution. Levi Strauss was born in Germany. Madeline Albright moved from Prague when she was a child. One of America's greatest architects, Ieoh Ming Pei, was born in China in 1917 and moved to the United States when he was 18. The founder of WhatsApp and the founders of YouTube? Immigrants. The diversity and life force that new people bring to a country or organization are powerful.

But, to make the most of these incredible talents, we need to promote a culture of openness and acceptance. It's no secret why California is the center of world innovation, from entertainment in Los Angeles to technology in Silicon Valley.

The culture of tolerance, diversity, and inclusion of the 1960s and 1970s in California provoked these engines of innovation because that culture welcomed truth-seekers. Steve Jobs came to Palo Alto because of the culture. He didn't go to Washington, D.C. or New York City, where he would face much stronger opposition from existing powers. Let in anyone who can help with progress.

Fear of failure, driven by fear of judgment, is the number-one reason people don't start a business, don't innovate on new medical technology, and don't seek new and more fulfilling relationships. Fear of failure is the only thing that can prevent you from recovering from any other adversity that you face.

CHAPTER TEN:
Historical Perspective on Failure

Running a business requires experience and experience requires failure.

We honor stories of heroic perseverance: Thomas Edison and his 10,000 attempts to find the filament that could burn inside a light bulb; Dyson's 5,126 attempts to make a bagless vacuum cleaner; and Helen Keller's determination to communicate, despite being deaf and blind. Steve Jobs was fired from Apple before he returned and made it the $2 trillion tech giant it is today.

We can only succeed if we embrace failure as our ally, as a badge of pride. We have to honor the effort, the struggle and not the result. We need to seek failure early. Not as a risk, not as setback, but as a moment of learning that offers us the momentum to propel us forward. When you fail early and often, you avoid catastrophic failure later.

The true innovators in our world—people such as Steve Jobs, Elon Musk, Patricia Bath, and Temple Grandin—place no value on the judgment of others. They succeed because failure isn't shameful for them. It isn't a humiliation. It's just a lesson learned.

The most rigid, top-down hierarchical societies, companies and cultures are the least innovative because they breed fear of failure and fear of judgment. It's a cycle that's hard to break. Rules become increasingly complex and convoluted as successive governments pass their own laws and regulations on top of previous laws and regulations.

In 1927, for example, all of the federal laws in the United States could fit into a single volume. By the 1980s, there were 50 volumes of federal laws comprising more than 23,000 pages. Between 1995 and 2014, there were more than 4,200 new federal laws enacted and more than 88,000 federal regulations enacted.

The more these complex rules multiply, the more people are taught to fear failure and the more ossified the entire society, company or culture becomes. This fear of failure is not unfounded. Most Americans have no idea what the tens of thousands of federal laws cover.

With a maze of tens of thousands of laws getting more complex every day, the individual has much to fear from running afoul of the power of the state. Socialism, in all of its forms, including National socialism, Soviet socialism, Chinese communism and Cuban socialism, is based on this single idea of dominating individuals through fear of judgment and reprisal. Socialist societies ostracize and prosecute those who do not conform in order to maintain their centralized power structure.

Socialist societies achieve this centralized power with tens of thousands of complex laws that all ensure that in order to be a law-abiding citizen, you must conform. The larger the government, the more the socialist tendency to quash the individual emerges, and the more self-reliant individuals are persecuted and shamed. This is the self-preservation instinct at the core of all socialist societies. Those in positions of power know that anyone who does not pay them homage, who challenges their power, ultimately challenges their legitimacy.

We are in the late stages of this in the United States today. We have become a nation steeped in the orthodoxy of millions of pages of indecipherable laws and even more complex social rules via which anyone can be charged with a felony. Our independent pioneer spirit has been quashed by the fear of failure. The American dream has become a straitjacket.

Complex laws proliferate everything we do. Government investigations abound in numerous directions, and with constant frequency. CEOs are routinely fired and careers are ruined for an ever-increasing list of "bad behaviors." Very few people are ever given a chance to learn from their mistakes—which, it turns out, is the only way to learn.

The United States today is an enormous "Leviathan" reaching into every aspect of our lives. Millions of pages of laws and regulations govern every aspect of our daily lives. If the FBI wants to investigate you or charge with you a felony, it can do so at will. Most Americans have no idea they could be charged with a felony for their routine business, tax, political, environmental, travel or recreational drug use activities.

It's not just U.S. citizens that are at risk. Even citizens of small towns in foreign countries can fall into the clutches of the tentacles of the Leviathan. Three U.S. senators recently sent a threatening letter to Fährhafen Sassnitz GmbH, which operates Mukran Port, alerting the company to its exposure to sanctions related to the Nord Stream 2 pipeline project. In the letter, the senators wrote, "This letter serves as formal legal notice that these goods, services, support, and provisioning risk exposing Fährhafen Sassnitz GmbH and Mukran Port, as well as your board members, corporate officers, shareholders, and employees, to crushing legal and economic sanctions, which our government will be mandated to impose."

I highly doubt the good citizens of Sassnitz, a small German fishing village, ever thought they could be hit with "crushing legal and economic sanctions" for their work on building a pipeline. Some Americans might think that the American model is the right model for the entire world. So, "Tough luck, small German fishing village. Do it our way," they say.

There is a different perspective to consider. With the United States being at the center of the global capitalist system, virtually anyone who touches a United States dollar anywhere in the world can be charged with a felony in the United States. This means maybe a billion people or more are unaware that they could be charged with a felony in the United States for something they had no idea was a crime. These people likely don't even speak our language, let alone understand our laws.

Even if your activity is not a felony, a federal prosecutor and an aggressive FBI agent can use their unlimited time and resources to build a case that a jury will believe because, after all, we are taught to conform from a very early age. And if you are the unlucky target of a federal prosecutor and the FBI, you don't stand a chance of winning unless you have $10 million to spend and can afford to not work at your "day job" for three or four years.

To paraphrase Rob Cary, if you need luck or money to ensure justice, we don't have much of a "justice" system at all. "Countless people have spent decades in state and federal prisons wrongfully convicted of crimes because of deliberate misconduct by prosecutors—none of whom have been held accountable for their wrongdoing," notes Sidley Powell and Harvey Silverglate.

As Daniel Medwed says, "Wrongful convictions tear at the tattered fabric of public confidence in the rule of law and the people chosen to enforce it. Without major repair efforts, the damage may soon be too great to restore faith in the idea of justice."

The rule of law requires that citizens be able to readily understand what is lawful and what is not. The rule of law requires that citizens be able to rely on law enforcement and government agents to tell them the truth about the law. The rule of law requires that citizens be able to trust law enforcement not to deceive them about the law. The rule of law requires that prosecutors and the judiciary be free from personal bias and political motivations. The rule of law requires that the law be applied equally to all, regardless of whether you can afford a defense lawyer or if your financial success makes you a "juicy" target for prosecutors.

Harvey Silverglate says it best: "When the feds appear on the scene, claiming to represent public interest by going after some citizen who had no reasonable way of knowing that his or her conduct could be deemed a felony, do not ask for whom the bell tolls. It tolls for all."

> **Democracy is not the ultimate protector of freedom. Understandable rule of law uninflated by politics is more certain to protect freedom even in a monarchy.**

Unfortunately for the Leviathan, the fundamental essence of being human is a desire for freedom. From the very beginning, we strive to earn the freedom to crawl, walk, and run. The fear of judgment that holds the Leviathan together is always overcome by brave risk-takers who are willing to fight for the truth, regardless of the cost. These first-movers inspire others to action.

Democracy is not the ultimate protector of freedom.

Understandable rule of law uninflated by politics is more certain to protect freedom even in a monarchy.

What happens if we continue to live in fear of judgment and fear of reprisal from the Leviathan? Or, for that matter, live in fear of reprisal from anyone in our lives? Those who fail to fight for the truth—and take action on that truth—out of fear of judgment remain in a prison of their own making. Their freedom is a mirage.

Someday, you might be faced with having to make a choice about which prison you will be locked up in—a prison of your own making or a real prison run by those whom you have been so bold as to challenge. If you find yourself in the latter, the good news is that it will make you stronger.

> # The essence of being human is the will to be free.

The essence of being human is the will to be free. This starts from the day we are born. My son, at the age of 11-months old, had one fundamental goal: to control his own destiny. At that point, that meant walking and talking. He had a lot to say, but no one could understand him just yet. He really wanted to walk and got annoyed that he couldn't.

We can only achieve our fundamental desire for freedom by developing a will, as well as a power behind that will.

Societies, companies, and families that empower people with the most freedom will see that trust returned in spades with accountability and responsibility. This, is turn, will produce results for that society, company, or family far in excess of its peers.

Ultimately, a Leviathan whose tentacles are so intertwined in the life of its citizens will collapse of its own weight. People stop taking initiative and stop delivering results. The elites have no one left to scalp. Ancient Rome, Soviet Russia and the British Empire all ultimately fell apart from myriad laws, taxes, and repeated scalping of anyone who was brave enough to stand out. Quite simply, the tentacles of the Leviathan reached too deeply into the life of the citizens and suffocated the very thing they were designed to protect.

With all due respect to political philosopher and author of *Leviathan*, Thomas Hobbes, he failed to see this coming when he waxed poetic about the power and utility of the Leviathan to administer the affairs of humanity. Karl Marx made similar errors. There is not a limited amount of power in society, as Karl Marx believed. There is an unlimited amount of power in the minds of each and every individual who chooses to harness it. All power is fundamentally derived from each individual's will to be free.

In Marxist-Communist societies, only the elites have any free will. At its most extreme in the Communist or Socialist dictatorship, the leader harnesses all the free will in the entire society. The society exists to serve the will of the leader alone. No one else is free.

CHAPTER ELEVEN:
Great Thinkers on Failure

f you are going to stand your ground, you need to know what you stand for. You are what you believe. Believe me, there are times when all you will have are your beliefs. In this section, I share with you the thinkers and philosophers whose ideas are critical to turning adversity into advantage.

Descartes

"A state is better governed which has few laws,
and those laws strictly observed."

—*René Descartes*

Is your fate determined by your culture, family, and media as they are embedded in your subconscious? Or do you have the analytical strength to start with Descartes' basic maxim, "Cogito ergo sum," and build your self-awareness consciously and knowingly, one thought at a time?

Descartes' statement of certainty is our guide to discovering truth. "I think, therefore I am." Boiling it down to its most basic, Descartes conceived "I know I exist because I know I can think." Thought, in fact, proceeds our knowledge of existence. As babies, we grasp at objects until we understand that our hands belong to us. As Descartes argued, we cannot trust our understanding of the world because we can only know the world from our own perspective. I can understand that someone's experience is different from mine, but I can't know it. What I do know is a combination of nature and nurture, my biological constructs and my learned understanding that together make my perspective.

Descartes teaches us that our view of the world is fundamentally shaded by our own experiences. To reach a level of self-awareness that allows you to capture your destiny in your own hands—that is, to turn adversity into advantage—you must separate this inherited world view from your own thought process.

For example, when I was a young child, I remember my parents suggesting that the Rockefellers (the descendants of John D. Rockefeller, the founder of Standard Oil) were somehow evil. My parents were just responding to basic human nature. After I started my business, I remember that my dad kept asking when I was going to get a job. For more than five years, every time he saw me, he would ask, "Greg, when are you going to get a job?" I would say "Dad, I have 12 employees. I don't need a job; I'm an employer."

My dad had a great career as an airline pilot. He loved to fly, and he was an employee all his working life. He had a good job, a good retirement, and wanted the same for his son. My dad gave me wonderful advice to "love what you do, and you'll never work a day in your life."

That was the best advice my dad ever gave me. He just never considered that "what you do" could be something other than working as a traditional employee. Being an employee is a wonderful thing, and it's a great move for most people—especially if you join the right organization that embraces failure and allows you to learn, grow, develop, and overcome adversity, all while riding the train of a larger group of people.

Regardless of your choice of vocation, that choice was likely heavily influenced by your family and cultural upbringing, which determine your subconscious mind. The subconscious mind determines what you think. And the way you think determines your actions. In turn, your actions determine the habits you form. Your habits form your character, and your character is your fate.

///

... your subconscious is your fate.

///

Quite directly, your subconscious is your fate. The subconscious determines the thoughts and actions you permit to occupy your mind. As Carl Jung said, "Until you make the unconscious conscious, it will direct your life, and you will call it fate."

Are you prepared to get out of your comfort zone and examine what unconscious beliefs are driving you to a fate that you might neither want nor deserve? Are you ready to embark on a path of self-awareness, of making the unconscious conscious, and to form new thoughts, new actions, new habits and a new character? These are critical steps toward turning adversity into advantage—and they must come first. You can't skip right to the end.

Plato

"We can easily forgive a child who is afraid of the dark; the real tragedy of life is when men are afraid of the light."

—*often attributed to Plato*

Plato's "Allegory of the Cave" tells the story of prisoners, chained to the wall of a cave from birth so they can only look forward at a blank wall. Behind them is a fire. Behind the fire, people and things move, casting shadows on the wall in front of the prisoners. That is reality for the prisoners.

When a prisoner escapes out of the cave and into the sunlight (or truth), he is dazzled and confused until he understands that this is reality. When he runs back inside to tell his fellow prisoners what he has learned, he is blinded in the darkness, and the prisoners turn on him and kill him, preferring the comfort of their known shadows to any stories of a world of three dimensions and sunlight.

This is a story about reality, about the force of our perception to shape our world, our reluctance to see the world differently and the power of it is the "red pill" from *The Matrix*. Morpheus says, "This is your last chance. After this, there is no turning back. You take the blue pill, the story ends, you wake up in your bed and believe whatever you want to believe. You take the red pill, you stay in Wonderland, and I show you how deep the rabbit hole goes."

Are you ready to take the red pill? Are you ready to separate perception, ego, bias, and intellect from your view of reality? Or are you entranced by the shadows of your mind? This is, perhaps, the most important step in turning adversity into advantage.

How to turn adversity into advantage

Those who successfully turn adversity into advantage force themselves to confront reality—however isolating it might be. Elon Musk has developed a method for separating perception from the truth, so he can access reality and help his team do the same. This skill has helped Musk's enterprises repeatedly turn enormous adversity (and what short-sellers believed was near-certain failure) into an even greater advantage.

Talking to *Rolling Stone* in November 2017, Musk outlined his process for assessing an idea:

1. Ask a question.

2. Gather as much evidence as possible about it.

3. Develop axioms based on the evidence and try to assign a probability of truth to each one.

4. Draw a conclusion based on cogency in order to determine: Are these axioms correct, are they relevant, do they necessarily lead to this conclusion, and with what probability?

5. Attempt to disprove the conclusion. Seek refutation from others to further help break your conclusion.

6. If nobody can invalidate your conclusion, then you're probably right, but you're not certainly right.

Musk explains, "Most people don't use it. They engage in wishful thinking. They ignore counter-arguments. They form conclusions based on what others are doing and aren't doing. The reasoning that results is 'It's true because I said it's true,' but not because it's objectively true."

> ## Be a philosopher first and an entrepreneur second.

Be a philosopher first and an entrepreneur second. The process starts with what Susan Scott calls "interrogating reality." She describes this as a "fierce conversation ... one in which we come out from behind ourselves into the conversation and make it real."

> **... seeking objective truth is about not being afraid of what you uncover.**

Fundamentally, seeking objective truth is about not being afraid of what you uncover.

Scott outlines three stages of interrogating reality: (1) Identify the issue on the table and your proposed solution, (2) Check to see that everyone understands, and (3) Check for agreement. "Be sure you get everyone's input and resist the temptation to defend your idea," she says. "Real thinking occurs only when everyone is engaged in exploring differing viewpoints."

In many companies today, you see the "The Corporate Nod." This occurs when people don't say what they are really thinking, according to Scott. "Companies and marriages derail because people don't say what they are really thinking." When people don't ask tough questions, everyone suffers. "The quality of our lives is largely determined by the quality of the questions we ask—and the quality of our answers," she points out.

While Scott outlines a logical path for fierce conversations, even more important to implementing such a logic is a lack of fear of opinion. Remember, in "The Allegory of the Cave," when the prisoner runs back inside the cave to tell his fellow prisoners what he has learned about the truth, they kill him. To think differently and to follow radically logical conclusions, you must eliminate fear of where your logic might take you and what others will think about you.

Socrates

Democratic Athens saw Socrates as a threat to its dogma. He was charged with corrupting youth when, in reality, he was teaching them to think for themselves. The guardians and the "herd" saw him as a threat. So, out of fear, they silenced him.

Many people today say democracy is the ultimate protector of freedom. As Socrates discovered, this is not the case.

Attorney General William Barr, who served under President George W. Bush and President Donald Trump, comments, "This criminalization of politics will only worsen until we change the culture of concocting new legal theories to criminalize all manner of questionable conduct. Smart, ambitious lawyers have sought to amass glory by prosecuting prominent public figures since the Roman Republic. It is utterly unsurprising that prosecutors continue to do so today to the extent the Justice Department's leaders will permit it."

The net effect of today's hyperaggressive extensions of criminal law is that the federal government is now determining what your "pursuit of happiness" means. There are tens of thousands of indecipherable federal laws on the books, and you never know when you might run afoul of one of them. The collective of the Leviathan has prescribed exactly what the options are for your happiness.

Author Ayn Rand said, "The Right to the Pursuit of Happiness means man's right to live for himself, to choose what constitutes his own private, personal, individual happiness and to work for its achievement, so long as he respects the same right in others. It means that Man cannot be forced to devote his life to the happiness of another man nor of any number of other men. It means that the collective cannot decide what is to be the purpose of a man's existence nor prescribe his choice of happiness."

Some people have chosen to build businesses and accumulate wealth. They are no better or worse than those who have chosen to be poets or surfers or to live off the grid with no material possessions. Despite this fact, billionaires are the "Socrates" of our generation.

Billionaires and innovators who have made their fortunes by refusing to accept the status quo are attacked in the media. Their vision, conviction, and determination make them targets for the 24-hour news cycle. George Soros, Elon Musk, and Jeff Bezos are relentlessly attacked in the media for their personal and professional decisions. For many, "billionaire" is a pejorative term, and Washington is very much interested in bringing tech giants to heel.

There is a danger in being the innovator—politically, socially, economically. You will be unpopular. You might be persecuted. The innovator challenges established thinking and established perceptions, which form the basis of the self-esteem and self-identity of the ruling class and the existing elites. This can be dangerous for the innovator.

Nietzsche

"I absolutely cannot see how one can later make up for having failed to go to a good school at the proper time. Such a man does not know himself; he walks through life without having learned to walk; his flabby muscles reveal themselves with every step. Sometimes life is so merciful as to offer this hard schooling once more later: sickness for years perhaps, that demands the most extreme strength of will and self-sufficiency; or a sudden calamity, affecting also one's wife and child, that compels one to a form of activity that restores energy to the slack fibers and toughness to the will to live."

—*Friedrich Nietzsche*

Nietzsche believed a good education from the "School of Hard Knocks"—not from any university—is a required form of character development.

Graduates of today's formal educational institutions have learned some tools for knowledge acquisition, but they haven't yet acquired true knowledge. True knowledge comes only from doing, learning and failing, preferably in the School of Hard Knocks.

Formal education, especially in a highly dogmatic and somewhat ossified society, is inversely correlated to truth-seekers. The more "education" you have, the more you believe you "know," when, in fact, true knowledge comes from doing.

Nietzsche notes that education is "essentially the means of ruining the exceptions for the good of the rule." And higher education is "essentially the means of directing taste against the exceptions for the good of the mediocre."

In other words, education is meant to fundamentally enforce the current culture, society, and the powers that be. It is meant to educate you to *prefer* the status quo. It is meant to give you the false premise that you know something. Such an education to induce conformity in our youth is highly corrosive to their free will and ultimately corrosive to an open society.

As Nietzsche stated, "The surest way to corrupt a youth is to instruct him to hold in higher esteem those who think alike than those who think differently."

Education in classrooms largely started with German Chancellor Otto von Bismarck, when he wanted to build a training system for soldiers in the Prussian army. If you want to train infantry soldiers for battle in 19th-century European ground wars, classroom training can be very effective. Bismarck's educational system worked well, and the Prussian army forced the unification of Germany and created the German Empire.

Today, we are thankfully not fighting infantry battles in Europe. Even if we were, the education of a modern warrior would involve little classroom training and lots of experience in the field. Yet, classroom training lives on and has largely outlived its usefulness.

Graduating with a Harvard MBA is dangerous in that you might be inclined to believe you know how to run a business. This is not the case. Running a business requires experience—and experience requires failure.

A reporter once asked Walmart founder Sam Walton, "How did you become so successful?" Walton answered, "I've made a lot of good decisions." When he was then asked how he learned to make good decisions, Walton replied, "By making a lot of bad decisions."

Formal education is about studying and learning from what is already known. It is about following rules, procedures, schedules, and pre-determined formats. Business is about navigating the unknown. It is about inventing and creating entirely in the absence of procedures and pre-determined formulas.

The best scholars in formal education know everything. The best business people assume they know nothing. In formal education, there is a clear demarcation between students and teachers. In business, the best leaders are always the students.

In 1872, Nietzsche presented a series of five lectures called "On the Future of Educational Institutions." He had no time for a higher education system determined "to make man into a machine by teaching him how to suffer being bored." He believed "the doer alone learneth," and "that which does not kill us makes us stronger."

If you are not doing, learning, and failing, you are not getting stronger. In fact, you might be getting weaker. Going to prison for up to seven years is not going to kill me; rather, it means, by definition, that it is going to make me stronger.

We learn so much from doing. And we stifle so much with formal education. Far too often, formal education is pampering and insulation from the experimentation and battles that build real knowledge and wisdom.

Thomas Edison (1847–1931), one of America's greatest inventors and businessmen, spent only 12 weeks in school. Edison was a sickly child. When he finally got to school, his teacher pronounced him "difficult." Edison's mother, an accomplished teacher, took him out of school and taught him from home. It was the perfect education for this curious, energetic child. He developed a love and ability for independent learning that would propel him through life.

Edison also had a great gift of learning from experience. As he famously believed, "Opportunity is missed by most people because it is dressed in overalls and looks like work." Edison "got his hands dirty." When he was 12, he was selling newspapers on the Grand Trunk Railroad line. He soon created his own paper, The Grand Trunk Herald, and sold it to passengers. By 15, he had learned to operate a telegraph. For the next five years, he traveled through the Midwest reading, studying, and experimenting with electrical science in his spare time.

At 19, while working the night shift at The Associated Press in Kentucky, he made the most of his time by developing a method of thinking without biases, proving things to himself through objective examination and experimentation. By 22, he sold his first invention and earned enough money to devote himself to discovering needs and creating solutions. It is an education that is unthinkable for so many of us now, but we can see so clearly the lessons of perseverance, inquiry, experimentation, and innovation that Edison learned on the road.

Steve Jobs is another example. His formal education looks like a mess. He was labeled as "difficult" in elementary school, although his parents stood by him. He was a loner who was bullied in middle school. In high school, he was equally fascinated with electronics and literature. Jobs dropped out in his first semester at Reed College without telling his parents. He attended classes—famously, Robert Palladino's calligraphy class—slept on the floor in friends' dorm rooms, got money from returning Coke bottles and ate for free at the Hare Krishna temple. Formally, not a lot going on. Informally, Jobs was learning about electronics beside his father, a machinist, making personal connections that would found Apple, exploring ways of thinking, learning about digital technology and finding out what products sell.

Bill Gates, the founder of Microsoft, dropped out of Harvard in 1975 after a year to pursue his passion for coding. By 1981, Microsoft had a revenue of $16 million. It was what Gates learned from his own initiative and inquiry that made all the difference to his life. You know this for yourself. When you think back over the lessons you have learned in life, so many of them were in the doing; so many were outside formal classrooms and lessons.

Hegel

"It is solely by risking life that freedom is obtained...
the individual who has not staked his or her life may,
no doubt, be recognized as a Person; but he or she has
not attained the truth of this recognition as an independent
self-consciousness."

—*Georg Wilhelm Friedrich Hegel, The Phenomenology of Spirit*

For Hegel, life is a process, not an end. We reach a point of understanding; that state is challenged; we reach a new understanding, and the process begins once again. Once we stop questioning and working toward synthesis, we stagnate. It is so important to keep learning and keep doing what you love. The minute you feel life is at an end, that you have nothing more to learn, that there are no more surprises, it's over and you die. If you are always growing, you are always learning, you are always stretching, you are always alive—right up to the day you physically die.

Three of the men I most admire are working and learning into their 80s and beyond. The chairman of the Global Growth board, George A. Vandeman, challenges himself every day at the age of 80.

George's career has been one of constant learning, striving, and growth. Before coming to Global Growth, George was chairman of the board and a director of MPG Office Trust (a Southern California-based office property REIT) until its sale in late 2013. From April 2006 to November 2008, George was a member of the board of directors of ValueVison Media, Inc., operator of the cable shopping channel ShopNBC. He also served as vice chairman of the board of Genelux Corporation, a San Diego-based biotechnology company. And, until recently, he was a member of the board of directors of Symbio Pharmaceuticals, Limited, a publicly traded, Tokyo-based biotechnology company. In addition to serving on these boards, as an attorney George advised hundreds of boards of directors, including boards of some of the world's largest companies.

From 1995 to 2000, George was senior vice president and general counsel of Amgen and a member of its operating committee, a company with revenues of $23.75 billion in 2019. Before joining Amgen, George was a senior partner and head of the mergers and acquisitions practice at the international law firm, Latham & Watkins, where he worked for nearly three decades. His client list at Latham comprised a "who's-who" of American business and entertainment, including Marvin Davis, Ted Turner, Merv Griffin, John Forsythe, Aaron Spelling, Hard Rock Café, Holiday Inns, Michael Jackson, Imagine Films, and Nestlé USA.

George was also the founding shareholder of KHNR, an all-news station featuring CNN Headline News Radio, in Honolulu. He was the architect of and a principal in the acquisition of Los Angeles television station KTLA, Channel 5 in 1983 by Kohlberg, Kravis, Roberts and the subsequent sale of that station in 1985 to The Tribune Company. He was also a founder of Cinema Group, an independent motion picture production company, and VideoNet, the first live-via-satellite teleconferencing company. George was a member for many years and past chair of the board of councilors at the University of Southern California Law School.

My oldest employee, Stan Sanoff, was born in 1926. That's right—1926. He works for us five days a week as our assistant general counsel in California. Stan is the epitome of someone who has never stopped learning. As a young man, he left school before he matriculated to play jazz clarinet in New York. When his family moved west, he set up a credit collection bureau. From 1954 to 1963, he grew his business.

Nearly 10 years in, Stan was getting "bored of the business world." When a client of Stan's confided he was about to leave his job to start practicing law, Stan was shocked. "I didn't even know you could go to law school!" It was a life-changing revelation. Stan enrolled in Southwestern School of Law. He had never been considered a "natural student" but in the second week, he knew he was exactly where he should be. He graduated *magna cum laude* despite having to juggle his studies, two young children, and running a business. Apart from his seven holes-in-one on the golf course, his graduation honors are his proudest achievement.

Stan has worked in law ever since. At 96, he jokes that "red wine and good genes" are his fountain of youth. I know from working with Stan that his strong life force is also because he never stops learning. California labor law changes every year, every week; it's very complicated. Stan is up on all the laws. That's my inspiration—to be 96 and still learning.

I met Les Sufrin in 2001, when he helped Global Growth with the acquisition of The Coding Institute. Les has been like a father to me ever since. He introduced us to our first lenders, helped us close our first acquisitions and provided wise counsel on myriad life and business matters. Global Growth would not exist today if it weren't for Les Sufrin.

In 1975, Les left his comfortable job with a big accounting firm to start out on his own. From day one, Les had clients who recommended him to other clients, and so his firm grew. Thirty years later, he sold his business to a French firm and kept working for Global Growth.

Les' success has been founded on consistently providing the best possible client service. The lesson he passed on to his staff was that "the most important thing in client service is your work ethic. You have to be fully committed, 24/7, to the work ethic. There's a need for balancing home and professional life, but when you are engaged in doing the work, you should be 24/7 in that engagement and totally focused on service."

From this work ethic, Les built a professional business he is rightly proud of. "My greatest thrill has been taking a start-up professional accounting practice from nothing and building it into a very reputable firm that enjoys an international reputation and also being able to provide a livelihood and professionalism to all my employees over the years."

One of Les's other great joys is bringing together an insight into the numbers and an understanding of the business. He calls it "marrying the words and music." Born in 1941, Les is aged 81. You can hear his enthusiasm for people, their stories, and their work in his voice.

"Every client represents an opportunity to learn more about another business, another industry. Every new client is like an additional graduate degree." Les' other tips for success include: "You have got to stay in touch with everyone. You can't stand on ceremony. And try to do the right thing, always. I like to help people, which comes from my work. You want to help people succeed and support them through adversity." In between working and connecting with existing and new clients, Les fits in time to visit museums, galleries, and the opera with his wife. Les has lived a life that is rich with risk, reward, and return. His dedication to learning and constantly extending his knowledge is a quality I admire deeply.

Jim Collins

"Great vision without great people is irrelevant."
—*Jim Collins*

In a 2009 profile in *The New York Times*, Jim explained that when his wife, Joanne Ernst, announced she thought she could win an Ironman triathlon, Jim resigned from his job at Hewlett Packard and devoted himself to her training, sponsorships, and well-being. Joanne won the Hawaiian Ironman Triathlon in 1985.

For his 50th birthday, Jim's gift to himself was 18 months of training for an attempt to climb El Capitan in fewer than 24 hours. Jim made it to the top. In 1995, he founded a management laboratory in Boulder, Colorado, where he conducts research and engages with CEOs and senior leadership teams. Jim is also a Socratic advisor to leaders in the business and social sectors and, according to *Forbes* (2017), he is one of the "100 Greatest Living Business Minds."

One of Jim's most foundational concepts is "First Who, Then What." He discovered great leaders who build organizations from the people up. He described it as "getting the right people on the bus" and making sure those people are in the key seats before you figure out where you are going to drive. Business is unpredictable. You can't possibly know what challenges you are going to face, but you can know that your team can handle anything while adapting and continuing to perform at their peak under any circumstances.

Collins is right. The right person in your business can be a transformational game-changer, and the wrong person can cause you endless misery. The biggest failures in my life can be traced back to one simple decision: allowing the wrong person on my bus.

Unfortunately, there is no way to learn how to bring the right people into your life without failing with the wrong people first. Once you learn who is right for you, your friends, your organization and your career, give them the respect of their own freedom. They are critically important to you, and you must treat them with utmost care.

In business, hire people who are smarter than you, more talented than you, and then get the heck out of their way. If you hire the second best instead of the best or a "C" player instead of an "A" player, you are going to get your butt handed to you on a silver platter.

If I had hired better people to help with government relations, I wouldn't be writing this book. I had a VP of compliance. I had a consultant. I had a head of government relations. I had a general counsel. I had outside counsel. But I didn't have the right people on my team. None of these people ever gave me even the slightest warning something might have been amiss. A better team would have done better.

On the flip side, I have seen how the right business leader can transform a money-losing business into one of the most successful businesses. I bought Beckett Collectibles in 2008 and went through two CEOs to find the right one. At the time, it was losing millions of dollars a year. Today, it makes more than 10 million dollars a year. Had I not persisted in finding the right leader for Beckett, the business would likely have died.

This lesson applies to every relationship in your life—your love life, your spouse, your friends, your business associates, your partners, your co-workers, your lawyer, and your accountant. Just one wrong person on your bus in any one of these areas can mean the difference between misery and a beautiful and rewarding life.

Napoleon Hill

"Whatever the mind can conceive and believe, it can achieve."
—*Napoleon Hill*

Napoleon Hill's *Think and Grow Rich* is my all-time favorite book. I must have listened to it on tape more than 1,000 times. Early in my career, it helped me set and achieve my goals and find my burning desire. Hill believes the art of success is simply setting an objective and turning it into a burning desire, with daily focus on the goal. Business and success are by-products of setting a goal and achieving it. It could be a goal to lose weight or to fast 22 hours a day. It could be a goal to raise a family, a goal to climb a mountain, master electric car repair or to live off the grid for a year with your family.

The core of your character is your ability to tell yourself you're going to do something—and then do it. That is the agreement we make with ourselves. That is internal integrity. For me, that is what success means. "I said I was going to do it, and I did it." Your free will depends on it.

I said I was going to build a billion-dollar business. I said I was going to get into the insurance business. I said I was going to do acquisitions. I said I did nothing wrong with my campaign donations, and I intend to win my case, regardless of how long it takes. I made a commitment to myself and a commitment to other people. Your ability to keep your own word is the core of your character.

This was perhaps Hill's greatest advice: "In every adversity, there are the seeds of even greater advantage." I have seen the power of this firsthand.

My indictment and trial have together been the most powerful learning experience. I wouldn't give it up for anything. My education in the School of Hard Knocks has been priceless. You can't buy this kind of education anywhere at any price. You have to go through it. You have to live it.

Humans have three responses to adversity: It makes us weaker, it has no impact, or it makes us stronger. Thankfully, thanks to my parents, adversity and failures make me stronger. The more intense the adversity, the greater the strength. Napoleon Hill understood this, too. His son was born deaf. He kept telling his son, "This is an advantage. You're deaf; it's got to be an advantage." He had no idea how being deaf was going to turn into an advantage for his son; he just knew it would. His son later built a successful hearing aid company.

Ray Charles faced similar adversity. He was born poor and black in the Jim Crow South. He lost his eyesight by age 7. His father abandoned his family. Despite these challenges, Charles became one of the greatest modern musicians. He turned his lack of sight into a greater advantage of mastering sound.

You've got to keep looking for the advantage in adversity because, at first, you won't see it. It might take years to emerge. But emerge it will, if you persist long enough. After the indictment, we found a new chairman, a new legal team, and a new CFO. We discovered wonderful new leaders. Our team is more disciplined and more focused than ever. I have had an amazing education about the machinations of politics and law enforcement in the United States. I have a new passion for helping people who don't have the means to fight injustice. There are all kinds of advantages coming from this adversity. The light of this advantage is very clear to me. It's coming straight at me.

PART TWO:
MY FAILURES AND ADVERSITIES

"If there is no struggle, there is no progress.
Those who profess to favor freedom, and yet depreciate
agitation, are men who want crops without plowing up
the ground. They want rain without thunder and lightning.
They want the ocean without the awful roar of its many
waters. This struggle may be a moral one, or it may be a
physical one; or it may be both moral and physical; but it
must be a struggle. Power concedes nothing without a
demand. It never did and it never will."

— Frederick Douglass

CHAPTER TWELVE:
Early Business Failures

Fail early & fail often. Failing late can be disastrous.

I was born in a working-class family. My parents (who were children of a plumber and an auto mechanic) taught me that hard work and discipline were rewarded with success. I remember looking at a ledger book my grandfather kept.

He made 8 cents an hour and recorded every penny of income and expense. My dad never took a day off when I was growing up.

I started a business in 1991 with $5,000. I was an undergrad at Yale at the time and saw an unmet need in the home care market for regulatory compliance information and launched a home care newsletter.

By 1998, my business consisted of 12 people working out of one room full of folding tables and computers. We were struggling to meet payroll and pay our printing bill.

During the 1990s, we built products in the healthcare space and started looking at acquisitions. My first acquisition was for $17,000 in the travel ticketing space just before it disintermediated. That first failed acquisition taught the group a lot about how not to acquire companies.

We survived a major adversity in 1998, when changes in regulations for home care agencies led to the loss of over half of our customers in fewer than six months. We learned from this adversity how to maintain a strict discipline in cutting costs as revenues decline.

I have enormous empathy for the pain of tens of thousands of small business owners who have lost their life's work because of COVID-19.

Sometimes, a "near-death experience" makes you stronger. My business almost died in 1998, and we were able to diversify our revenue streams and rebuild cash flow. By 2002, we were able to close a "stretch" acquisition for $8 million, which gave us a foothold in the medical coding space.

In 2006, we acquired a health care business with $4.8 million in EBITDA. We put into place new management and implemented our core values using lessons from several prior turnarounds.

We then launched over a dozen product lines. Fourteen years later, that business has multiplied its customer base and has EBITDA of more than $74 million.

In 2007, we opened our first offshore office in Faridabad, India. It became a center for excellence in software development, finance, and leadership. It allowed us to buy companies under stress, cut costs, and invest in development at the same time. Today, we have more than 1,800 employees in India.

In 2009, I survived a brain tumor. I was fortunately able to return to work within a few days after the successful surgery.

During the 2008–2009 timeframe, we perfected a turnaround expertise. Private equity groups noticed the success and started reaching out to the group when they had a business in trouble. We looked for companies that were stuck in a rut.

We developed a turnaround strategy based on core values. At acquisition, the team went into each company and spoke about our unique culture. The team offered flexibility, meritocracy, and unlimited opportunity for growth. In exchange, the team demanded that each employee grow and stretch. "A" players would have their roles expanded, and "C" players needed to go.

The team wanted a company comprising only people who were passionate about what they were doing. Using this turnaround management expertise, we acquired more than 100 companies between 2009 and 2019. Priceless. You can't buy this kind of education anywhere at any price. You have to go through it. You have to live it.

CHAPTER THIRTEEN:
My Most Public Failure/ Commissioner Story

Every human you encounter has something to teach you.

I ask all my employees to do personality charts. My personality chart reflects that I am low on social, have a high preference for autonomy, am low preference for social interaction, and show very high detail orientation. And detail orientation at a very high level becomes paranoia. I write everything down. Every single thing I do is written down on my to-do list and then crossed off and checked. I have spreadsheets on everything I do. Being detail-oriented has been an important part of success in business because, after all, you've got to watch your business. As it turns out, I wasn't paranoid enough.

With a low social preference (and thus low social ability), I often miss important cues from social interactions and tend to take statements by other people at their analytical face value rather than understanding the social implications of the conversation.

Perhaps subconsciously feeling this social weakness early on, I hired Bridgett Hurley as a "master of all things people related" in the late 1990s. She has been instrumental in building the people side of Global Growth with a social awareness and people related talent that far exceeds anything I've been able to develop.

In 2016, I became politically active during the 2016 general election for North Carolina's Commissioner of Insurance. I exercised my First Amendment right to support former Commissioner Wayne Goodwin's campaign. This ultimately set off a series of unfortunate events that lead to my indictment, conviction and imprisonment.

In March of 2018, the North Carolina Commissioner of Insurance sent me an email stating that I was doing "an outstanding job" answering "hardball questions" from insurance regulators. Being somewhat socially (and thus politically) naive, I took this statement at face value.

Little did I know, at that very same time the NC Insurance Commissioner had convinced the FBI to help him entrap me in a bribery scheme by recording my conversations with him where he repeatedly and aggressively demanded donations while I told him that "everything we do must be fully compliant with North Carolina law."

Had Bridgett been a part of the meetings with the NC Insurance Commissioner, she would have immediately realized, as she often does, that "something is off" about the way the NC Insurance Commissioner was behaving. I didn't see the snake in the grass, and she would have.

The lesson: Surround yourself with people who excel at your areas of weakness. In the early years, Bridgett and I sometimes clashed because we are very different people. But unless you welcome differing views, you are not going to make the right decisions. Conformity and homogeneity on a team is a recipe for failure.

Given my low social orientation and my low level of social and political awareness, I never suspected that the NC Insurance Commissioner was lying to me in his email. I never suspected that he was lying to me in his conversations with me in order to set me up and execute his entrapment scheme. This entrapment ultimately led to me being sent to prison after the judge in my case ordered the jury to find me guilty in what was essentially a directed verdict.

Throughout this battle, I learned what extraordinary strength our business philosophy brings to our group of companies because our companies deliver quarter after quarter of record results. Amid the worst legal battles we have ever seen, and amid the worst economic environment in decades, our group of companies produced record results.

My parents were always so supportive of me. I don't think it ever crossed their minds that some people resent success and will try everything they can to ruin you. That was the single biggest surprise in all of this. My parents were always proud of me—during both my failures and successes. "Just do your best" is all they ever said. I (naïvely) never expected the hatred from all quarters for being "successful." My parents were honest, hard-working people.

Turning adversity into advantage does not require a formal education. It does not require a particular background or heritage. It does not require any particular talent or skill. It does not require connections, lots of friends, or even any current opportunities.

Turning adversity into advantage only requires your undying faith and commitment to yourself that you can, and will, turn your adversity into an advantage, or that you will die trying. Without the commitment to achieve this advantage or die trying, you might not get there.

PART THREE: LESSONS FROM PRISON

CHAPTER FOURTEEN:
Never Ever Give Up

> Your future and freedom depend on your ability to conquer your fear.

Transcend Fear

I met a fellow prisoner who was originally sentenced to life in prison. He was a young man, maybe 30 years old. He had won several appeals, all done on his own, and was now facing another 5 years instead of the rest of his life in prison. Being sentenced to life in prison puts this in perspective. This fellow inmate had no choice: he was going to win his legal battle, or he was going to die trying.

I was inspired by him. If you can learn to face death in the way that this inmate does, or a solider does—as a possible sacrifice for the goal you are fighting for—death simply becomes one of the potential sacrifices you must make to achieve your goal.

Whatever you are fighting for will live on as energy even if you are not around anymore. Your family, your business, your art, your community, your life's work comprises the energy you bring to the world.

A simple statement I say to myself when I set a goal is, "I am going to achieve this goal, or I am going to die trying." It is a simple binary outcome. You can rest assured of one or the other outcomes.

- I am going to win the case pending against me, or I am going to die trying.

- I am going to build the business I want to build, or I am going to die trying.

- I am going to raise wonderful children, or I am going to die trying.

- I am going to cure aging, or I am going to die trying.

- I am going to survive my brain tumor, or I am going to die trying.

Love Yourself

In prison, you encounter people who had the unfortunate accident of birth to be born in an unloving and hostile environment. At a very early age, this negative energy instilled self-doubt and a lack of self-esteem. In the class I taught for my fellow inmates, I emphasized the mantra, "I love myself." Self-appreciation and self-esteem are the keys to not tolerating a life you don't want to live. Self-love is the key to demanding what you think you are worth from life. If you think you are nothing, life will give you nothing.

> Love yourself enough to forgive yourself.

The day before I checked into prison my mom said to me, "Son, I am so proud of you." I credit this unconditional love from my mother as one of the key reasons I have found the fortitude to persist through adversities to find the advantage they can bring. My father died while I was in prison, and I miss him greatly.

Success begins with faith in yourself. If you find yourself lacking faith in yourself, discover what subconscious beliefs are lurking unexamined and examine them. It's likely that, at some point, someone put a belief into your subconscious that you weren't good enough or weren't worth loving. Surface that subconscious belief and relentlessly rewrite it with a new belief: "I am worthy, I am loved." Drill this into your subconscious with emotion. Emotionalizing new beliefs is the only way they can travel into the reptilian brain, which stores your subconscious beliefs.

Andrew E. Budson, M.D. explains in *Psychology Today*, "Automatic routines which, over time, we have learned to do without thinking about them, such as playing tennis and even driving, are largely performed by our reptilian brain. So, when we are driving and, at the same time, engrossed in a conversation with a friend, we may find that we have driven somewhere with no memory of how we did it—that's because the reptilian brain was doing most of the driving."

The scary part of life is that a lot of what we do is done without thinking, governed by our reptilian brain. Our fundamental beliefs, for starters, if they are not excavated, challenged, and potentially revised, are then governing our life from their position in the reptilian brain.

If you do not have total and utter faith that you can keep your own word and achieve your goals or die trying, then someone, somehow, has put the wrong belief into your reptilian brain. If you cannot rewrite this faulty belief to give yourself new faith on your own, seek professional help.

> The more you show gratitude and appreciation, the more it comes back to you.

Appreciate the Small Things

Prison teaches you to value the small things. When I broke my fasts, I loved to eat peanut butter and jelly sandwiches. One day, one of my fellow inmates gave me a bag of peanut butter, and it was the best part of my week. Regardless of how bleak your situation may be, there is always something you can appreciate, and always something that can bring you joy.

Everything is a matter of perspective. That bag of peanut butter, which had a dozen or so individual packets in it, was enough for 10+ peanut butter and jelly sandwiches, which I enjoyed just as if they were a 5-course meal at a Michelin star restaurant. A simple sandwich can bring enormous joy in prison.

"On the street," people are far too dismissive of the simple joys and rewards in life. We pass them over without thinking. On the street, far too often we end up failing to show gratitude for our sustenance. What are some small things you may overlook that fuel you?

75% of the communication in the modern work environment is a waste of time.

Set Aside Time for Reflection

One of the things prison taught me was how important setting aside time for reflection is. In the world outside of prison, you are bombarded with electronic messages constantly. Each one of these triggers a brief emotional response as the very first response to all stimuli: fight or flight. Once your brain understands this new plea of information is not a threat, it relaxes, and your cerebellum takes over. Constant stimulus from new information in the new electronic age puts us into a constant "fight or flight" mode which burns out our adrenal glands and causes all manner of health problems. In prison, I can check email once every 45 minutes. There is usually a line since we only have three computers for 100 inmates in my unit. I tend to check email two or three times per day. So, I only have two or three "fight or flight" moments where my adrenaline goes up as I review new emails to see if there are any threats. The rest of the day is far more relaxing. I take a daily nap. I think, ponder, and reflect. I find myself to be a far better decision-maker.

Constant electronic communication harms our ability to think, which is, after all, the most important job of a leader. In prison, given the very limited access to email, I tend to think about a response for several hours before sending anything. I also have long periods with no new information stimuli which allows my brain to stay in a reflective vs. reactive mode. It's highly productive to step back and think.

Nurture Growth

I loved to see my fellow prisoners get excited about starting a business. Most of them had to fight for everything in life and were never given any inspiration or positive feedback that they could, in fact, succeed in business. Many were born into families where drug use was common, and they turned to the drug trade. I saw an enormous amount of talent in my fellow inmates for business success —what is missing in many of them is the encouragement and someone to simply say "I believe in you." Sadly, many of them never had anyone who believed in them. It brings tears to my eyes just thinking about it. You can turn a life around by helping someone change their beliefs about themselves and helping them put new positive affirmations into their daily thoughts. I saw it firsthand every day in class and it was one of the most rewarding experiences of my life. I've printed here in this book some letters from my fellow inmates so you can see for yourself what my classes meant to them.

> Everyone has the seeds of something great inside them. Help them unlock it.

The biggest lesson I learned from my fellow prisoners is what resilience really means. I mentioned a young prisoner who was originally sentenced to a life sentence for a nonviolent drug crime. He had fought a legal battle over several years and now had less than 5 years left to serve. Many others endured deaths of children, divorce, and abandonment by loved ones. They just kept going. You can, too.

Over the years, we have acquired a number of companies that no one wanted, and no one had the expertise to turn around. Just about every company can be a great company with the right people in the right place on the bus. Likewise, there is enormous value in taking the time to find the right place on the bus for employees who may not otherwise be valued.

I believe there is greatness in every human being. Every one of us has a special gift. In prison, if you get to know an inmate well enough, you will find their special talent. It may be poetry. It may be art. It may be leather craft. It may be cooking. I saw an amazing range of talent in prison and there is an amazing range of talent in everyone on your team. One of my fellow inmates who had been down for many years had composed and memorized hundreds of poems. He wrote them on greeting cards in the most perfect handwriting I had ever seen. This was his greatness.

If you get to know someone well enough, you can find their inner greatness. And if you are a leader, you can find a place for them on your bus. Most importantly, you must keep an open mind and believe there is greatness in everyone—if you are patient to look for it and nurture it.

Every one of us is a descendant of Mitochondrial Eve—the most recent common matrilineal ancestor for all modern humans that lived around 155,000 years ago. Mitochondrial Eve gave all of us our mitochondrial DNA. We are all brothers and sisters, part of the same big family. Every one of us has the same mitochondrial DNA from Mitochondrial Eve. And every one of us has a greatness within that is powered by our mitochondria, even your worst detractors and those who want to "incapacitate" you. They, too, have a greatness within if you look hard enough and forgive them for what they have done.

Welcome Pain

> Are you willing to face the most pain and danger of anyone you lead? The leader must always be willing to face the most pain and the most danger.

Many of us have heard of PTSD (post-traumatic stress disorder). Less well-known is post-traumatic growth, or PTG. Developed by psychologists Richard Tedeschi, Ph.D., and Lawrence Calhoun, Ph.D., in the mid-1990s, PTG is the understanding that people who endure a psychological struggle following adversity often experience positive growth afterward.

PTG is different than "resilience." People who are resilient rarely experience PTG. It is people who struggle to bounce back who often grow the most after a traumatic experience. Tedeschi and Calhoun developed a "Post-Traumatic Growth Inventory" which measures growth in seven areas:

- Greater appreciation of life
- Greater appreciation and strengthening of close relationships
- Increased compassion and altruism
- The identification of new possibilities or a purpose in life
- Greater awareness and utilization of personal strengths
- Enhanced spiritual development
- Creative growth

There is a great book by Dr. Bruce Perry and Oprah Winfrey called *What Happened to You?* (2021) about trauma and resilience. Dr. Perry helped Oprah set up her leadership school for girls who had experienced sexual violence and abuse as children. Here, he uses the term Post Traumatic Wisdom or PTW. The text, using this concept, offers a great way to look at the adversity—you aren't less because of the trauma that happened to you. When you experience it, pull through and thrive, you have a wisdom that others may never have.

It is possible to thrive after a disaster. Given that 61 percent of men and 51 percent of women report at least one traumatic event in their lifetime, we need to develop a new attitude to pain. As with failure, we are taught to avoid pain from the earliest age. Pain, however, is not only unavoidable, it is essential.

COVID-19 has presented all manner of trauma for millions of people. Lives have been lost, businesses ruined, relationships torn apart, and careers ruined. If you are fortunate enough to be alive to be reading this, then this trauma can turn into an even greater advantage.

I do not know of a single great artist, musician, entrepreneur, religious leader, or military commander, personally or by reputation, who avoided pain. You must know you can endure pain to be a leader. It is by withstanding pain that you find the truth and break free from the constraints that put you in danger—moral, physical or emotional—in the first place.

The types of pain most people want to avoid include:

- Physical pain (lack of exercise)

- Mental pain (lack of disciplined thought)

- Emotional pain (fear of loss of love)

- Social pain (fear of failure)

- Financial pain (fear of financial risk)

- Pain that keeps us locked in the prison of our comfort zone (fear of life)

Sam Chand spells it out beautifully: "Do you want to be a better leader? Raise the threshold of your pain. Reluctance to face pain is your greatest limitation. There is no growth without change, no change without loss and no loss without pain. Bottom line: If you're not hurting, you're not leading."

Until recently, most of my pain was self-inflicted, giving up a social life to work, dedicating my time and energy to my business. The greatest test of my life has been my trial and public accusations of wrongdoing. I was fortunate to have the funds to fight a battle in court, but my money would have been worthless if I hadn't been prepared to suffer through the pain of this battle. The measure of the strength of your character is your ability to endure pain. This translates into your ability to seek the truth and escape the prison of your comfort zone and mediocrity. Quite directly, your free will is dependent on your ability to endure pain.

The amount of pain and trauma you can endure and turn into an equal or greater advantage is the measure of your ability to connect with your fundamental will to be free. Each of us has that fundamental will, and each of us can identify, surface and connect with that will through making the subconscious conscious.

To understand how enduring pain can free your will, become an art and music lover. Most great art and music comes from a place of great pain.

Hegel said it best: "If we are in a general way permitted to regard human activity in the realm of the beautiful as a liberation of the soul, as a release from constraint and restriction, in short, to consider that art does actually alleviate the most overpowering and tragic catastrophes by means of the creations it offers to our contemplation and enjoyment, it is the art of music which conducts us to the final summit of that ascent to freedom."

If you want to succeed, you must study the masters in your field. This might seem obvious, but the most successful people make it an obsession.

If you find your happiness in business, start by memorizing the Forbes 400. You have to read every single scrap of information you can find about people who are successful. You need to read and emulate. Then, most importantly, put your own ingredients in the mix. I learned the hard way that you cannot simply emulate someone else's success; you must always innovate.

Many savvy investors have admired the Berkshire Hathaway (BRK) model that provides $118 billion in insurance "float" for investment, primarily in affiliated equity. Competing buyers, like private equity funds, must pay equity returns to their investors, whereas BRK's cost of funds is based on underwriting losses and annuity crediting rates—a far lower cost than private equity LPs demand or even corporate debt markets.

Under insurance laws in many states, and under the NAIC Model Holding Company Act, affiliated investments are permitted without limitation, provided they are fair and reasonable. So, why is BRK the only insurance company with the majority of its assets invested in affiliates? The answer: Regulators in various states don't like the model of affiliate investment.

The BRK model was first approved by the Nebraska Department of Insurance in the late 1960s and 1970s. Now, this approval is effectively grandfathered, and further approvals for new entrants into the market are not welcome.

Senator Ben Nelson was appointed the director of the Nebraska Department of Insurance in 1975. He made the wise decision to support the growth of

BRK's National Indemnity's affiliate investments. Policyholders win when their premiums are invested by a long-term, patient and savvy investor with a reputation for investing in inflation-protected investments.

Through no fault of his own, Warren Buffett has an additional enormous moat around his business: regulatory approval for an incredibly intelligent and profitable investment strategy that no one else can replicate. Today, BRK still invests the majority of its assets in affiliated investments.

BRK has become the backstop for the entire P&C world, and has lowered the cost of insurance worldwide with its large balance sheet. It has also provided stable capital for a long-term buy and hold approach protecting the jobs of hundreds of thousands of employees. It's the right model of capitalism—long-term and people-focused.

Numerous investors have pondered how to replicate this model. I tried to replicate it. Some critics might say, "well, you aren't Warren Buffett." True, I'm not.

My group of companies was founded with $5,000 in 1991 and has a fair value net worth in excess of $1 billion today—a CAGR in excess of 50 percent. This corporate annual growth rate is a significantly better performance than BRK and most family offices, private equity funds, hedge funds, and publicly traded conglomerates. Other critics might say, "Well, you don't have Warren Buffett's reputation." True, but where was Warren Buffett in 1980? Our equity returns are better.

Some other reasons our model was superior to BRK include:

- BRK typically puts its acquisitions on the balance sheet as "wholly owned subsidiaries," which means these assets are less liquid than our middle market loans. Refinancing a loan is easier than selling a company.

- BRK is primarily a P&C insurance company, which has more volatile liabilities and needs more liquid reserves than a life insurance company.

- Our portfolio is more 21st-century oriented, with a focus on health care, technology, and financial services. And, our investment track record is superior to what Buffett was able to achieve at the same age.

- We added two layers of disaffiliation to provide third-party oversight in a downside scenario: stock holdings in trusts and affiliated assets managed by third parties. BRK doesn't have these protections. If things "go south," the largest shareholder can call all the shots—which could lead to a conflict between the shareholder of the parent company and the policyholders of the subsidiary insurance companies.

It wasn't until March 2018 that the Nebraska Department of Insurance told us it would never allow anyone to repeat what Warren Buffett did. Through no fault of his own, Buffett now has an ironclad regulatory monopoly on investing insurance reserves in affiliates. No one else need apply. Warren Buffett made his $100 billion and single-handedly lowered insurances rates worldwide. But don't try to emulate his success because the door is firmly closed to new entrants.

CHAPTER FIFTEEN:
Maintain Discipline

Thoughts lead to actions, actions lead to habits, habits form character, and your character's your fate.

Discipline in Your Emotions

Prison teaches you how to stay calm under emotional situations. "They've already locked me up, so what else could they do?" I see in the outside world enormous angst and fear over this and that. It's unproductive, and it undermines good leadership. The best leaders operate primarily in the cerebellum and have figured out how to disconnect the "fight or flight" emotion from their decision-making. They face indignities, insults, threats, pain, and failures with a calm determination. Their communications don't carry a negative emotional load that furthers the angst in the organization at the very time the organization requires rational and fearless thinking.

A simple technique: If you are facing a grave threat, start fasting. Your body will produce the brain-stimulating chemical compound "brain-derived neurotrophic factor" in substantially increased quantities after 24 to 48 hours of fasting. On that second day of fasting, your creativity, memory, confidence, and focus will multiply rapidly. You will become charged with energy to overcome the threats you face. Your heart rate will slow down, and a general calm will overcome you. These are all the traits we humans evolved over tens of thousands of years as hunter/gatherers.

When food was scarce, our bodies went into overdrive and produced extraordinary mental and muscular energy. The gene that produced this response to hunger very quickly came to dominate the human gene pool as those who became stronger and smarter about hunger lived longer and had more children. So, stay calm under fire. Don't eat. Drink only water. And take your leadership fame to a new level. And most amazing about intermittent fasting, the changes to your memory, speed of cognition, and vascular health are permanent because they occur via epigenetic changes, i.e., your genes are expressed differently and permanently after a period of intermittent fasting.

Discipline in Your Thoughts

In prison, there are generally two categories of inmates—those who are getting bitter, and those who are getting better. Those who are getting bitter spend their time complaining, finding fault, and engaging in all kinds of bad habits and unproductive activities. They are angry at the Bureau of Prisons and angry at the system as a whole. It's natural to be angry at whoever has set you back, done you harm, and treated you with indignity. By staying in an angry and emotional state, however, they are failing to move their thought process to the cerebellum where they can develop positive work habits and goals to turn their adversity into an advantage.

For some time, this anger is unavoidable for most of us. Anger can be an extraordinarily powerful motivator, but only when you channel the anger into productive activity towards a specific goal for self-improvement. However, the faster you turn this anger into productive activity, the faster you can turn the adversity to your advantage.

The inmates who are getting better see prison as an opportunity to gain strength and perspective on all levels. I've met several prisoners who have been down for 10+ years and have used that time to completely transform who they are. They are positive, optimistic, and focused on improving their mind, body, and soul.

Build your discipline by repeated warnings to yourself that if you don't achieve your goal, if you don't become stronger from this adversity, then "they" have won. If anger is driving you, ponder this: What is the one thing that would mean you win, and your distractions lose?

Your adversities are likely to fall short of the adversity that these prisoners face. Are you going to turn it into a productive advantage by improving yourself, or let the opportunity go to waste?

Thoughts lead to action. Action leads to habit. Habit forms character and your character is your fate. So quite directly, the thoughts that you permit to occupy your mind will become your fate. Do you intentionally select the people in your life based on the positive thoughts that they will put into your mind during your interactions with them? Inevitably, the thoughts of those with whom you surround yourself will ultimately become your own thoughts, even if only subconsciously. In prison, it's clear that many people are there because they simply allowed the wrong people into their life.

One wrong person in your life can determine your fate. Who do you permit to occupy your mind? Do you take the people you allow into your life seriously enough? And likewise with the employees you hire?

Discipline in Your Actions

I was born in a working-class family. My grandfather on my mom's side was an auto mechanic; on my dad's side, a plumber. Both were hardworking, everyday people. A generation prior to that, my ancestors were German and Swedish peasants who immigrated to the United

States in the late 1880s. I remember looking at the census documents of my great-great grandfather, Peter Frederick Lindberg. He was listed as a "day laborer." His own great grandfather worked to dig the Gota Canal in Sweden, living in a hut alongside the great dig.

My ancestors lived a long, hard, grueling life. I feel an extraordinary obligation to not waste the hardship they lived through. I am grateful for their struggles and grateful for the gifts of perseverance I inherited from them.

Instead of dating a lot in my 20s, I built a business. By 2000, when I was 30 years old, I had built a $5 million business from scratch with no outside capital. I bootstrapped it. By the year 2001, the business was making about $1 million in profit a year. That could have afforded me a very good life in 2001. Even so, I didn't take that money out of the business and start spending it.

I paid myself just enough to live on: $40,000 a year for the first 10 years. Everything else went back into the business. I kept reinvesting and reinvesting. We bought more companies and grew the business. And, we became more successful. It can look like luck, magic, or being in the right place at the right time, but when I look back at those early years, it was simply discipline and focus.

When I say "discipline," I don't mean a cold, heartless monotony. Rather, I mean building your dream into a fiery passion and allowing that fire to consume you at the expense of all else. Inside, you get a "burning" and nothing else matters except keeping your word for achieving the goal you set for yourself.

To paraphrase Nietzsche, your passion must be great enough to extend your will across great stretches of your life "and to despise and reject everything petty including even the fairest, divinest things in the world."

Are you prepared to live the life a monk, rejecting all earthly and petty pleasures for the sake of keeping your word? Sometimes, that is what it takes. That's exactly what I learned in prison.

Prison teaches you the power of the ascetic. Everything there requires discipline, and the more discipline you apply, the better the results. Our commissary purchases were limited to $90 per week. We got two rolls of toilet paper per week. We were issued one towel. This, and many other examples, did not simply encourage the practice of self-discipline, they required it. Each makes you stronger by forcing an ascetic in virtually everything you do. Nothing is wasted. Everything has value. I remember when I got my first pen. I remember when I found my first paper clip. The ascetic teaches you to value the smallest of forward advances and appreciate with sincere gratitude the smallest of gifts. The best part of prison is the generosity and support from my fellow man as I see from my fellow prisoners every day.

All discipline comes from a place of emotional fortitude where you don't break discipline in times of stress, fear, anger, and depression. The more you adhere to your long-term goals with daily discipline, the more effective your leadership will be. The more support from your friends, the more confidence you will have to avoid breaking discipline when things are not going your way.

When you share your stress with your friends, their support can help you overcome the challenge without turning to bad habits, whatever they may be. Knowing this, I have been amazed by, and grateful for, how supportive my inmates are of each other.

Part of the ascetic is being a scavenger. We throw away so much that is valuable. Once, at Montgomery Federal Prison Camp, I found a half-eaten bag of almonds in the trash. I fished them out. We were limited to $90 a week at this commissary, and a bag of almonds was $1.70. When an inmate is sent home, the items he leaves behind are scavenged by fellow inmates in a matter of hours. My tennis shoes must have been worn by three or four other inmates before me. To buy new shoes costs $90 at the commissary, which means I would have no commissary food for a week. So, I wore a worn-out pair of tennis shoes. Everything there is important: plastic bags, tape, paper clips, etc. There is enormous value to "trash" in the right place at the right time.

Are you paying enough attention to what other people consider trash?

One of the most important leadership lessons is the art of obeying commands. Obeying and commanding are two sides of the same coin. The best commanders are likewise the best at obeying. We all encounter a higher power. Your ability to obey when you encounter a higher power is a testament to your leadership strength—particularly the humility and self-awareness to recognize when you are not the leader. Failure to obey at the right time is a failure to see reality, and the right leader is always the person closest to reality. So, by failing to obey, you are no longer the leader.

Being locked up in prison presents dozens of opportunities to obey every day. Now several months into my prison sentence, I find these opportunities to obey a tonic to the soul. Knowing I can obey with the same enthusiasm as I can command makes me stronger. Wake up at 5:30 am. Clean toilets. Stand up for count. Wear uniform as prescribed. Keep cell neat and tidy. Address the guards formally. Obeying builds character and character builds leaders.

Discipline with Your Eating

I turned 52 this year and I feel like I'm 25 years old. I have never felt better, slept better, and never had better memory and physical strength. Most think that the whole prison experience is terrible. But the truth is, it has made me stronger. The key: prison has given me the discipline to do an intermittent fasting routine where I fast for 114 hours, then eat 54 hours, on a rotating basis. I would have never had the discipline to do this fasting routine had I not come to prison.

There are numerous recent medical journal articles which show that when you fast for more than 48 hours, your body repairs age-related damage (via autophagy) and generates new tissue for your brain, skin, and muscles (via mitochondrial biogenesis). Also, after 48 hours of fasting your body produces 20 times the level of Brain-Derived Neurotropic Factor (BDNF), which creates new brain cells and synaptic connections via neurogenesis. I can now remember the names of employees from 20 years ago. My flexibility has improved to the point where I can now touch my toes, which I was never able to do. I am also putting on muscle mass for the first time in my life.

The medical studies on intermittent fasting with animal models suggest that intermittent fasting can increase life span by up to 40%. Numerous studies indicate that intermittent fasting is the most powerful anti-aging treatment on the planet, and it's available free to everyone. Note that almost all the major anti-aging drugs in development are calorie restriction mimics. However, it's far better to simply restrict your calories for intermittent periods.

Calorie restriction has been around for a while, but it has major drawbacks—the body needs a "feast" period after fasting. Intermittent fasting produces epigenetic changes so that the genes expressed during fasting carry over into the "feasting" state. Intermittent fasting literally changes how your genes are expressed.

Leadership is a never-ending increase in your stress level as you reach toward your goals. Every one of the 30+ trillion cells in your body must be prepared for that stress. Intermittent fasting does exactly that: it increases the stress resistance of every cell in your body by improving mitochondrial biogenesis and activating autophagy. The effects on your creativity, focus, detail orientation, and determination are profound.

> As soon as you achieve a goal, the most important word is "next". What is your next goal?

Discipline with Your Goals

Success can be defined simply as setting goals and working toward meeting them. Success and goal achievement are often confused with monetary success, but it is not. The process of setting goals for a poet, plumber, or surfer are the same: Do you have the internal integrity to keep your own word and do what you say you are going to do?

Author Ayn Rand says it best: "Achievement of your happiness is the only moral purpose of your life, and that happiness, not pain or mindless self-indulgence, is the proof of your moral integrity, since it is the proof and the result of your loyalty to the achievement of your values."

Your happiness comes from being the best you can be in the plumbing trade, the most creative poet, or the most talented surfer. All of these require goal-setting and an extraordinary dedication to rational and consistent effort. True happiness can only be achieved with such effort.

Happiness cannot be achieved by escapism and pure pursuit of pleasure.

"Happiness is not to be achieved at the command of emotional whims," according to Ayn Rand. "Happiness is not the satisfaction of whatever irrational wishes you might blindly attempt to indulge. Happiness is a state of non-contradictory joy—a joy without penalty or guilt, a joy that does not clash with any of your values and does not work for your own destruction, not the joy of escaping from your mind, but of using your mind's fullest power, not the joy of faking reality, but of achieving values that are real, not the joy of a drunkard, but of a producer. Happiness is possible only to a rational man, the man who desires nothing but rational goals, seeks nothing but rational values and finds his joy in nothing but rational actions."

I grew up in California. My dad was an airline pilot, and he found his happiness to be a "damned good stick." My mom found her happiness in her six wonderful children.

Despite their modest income, my parents ponied up the cash and sent me to a private high school, Crystal Springs Uplands School. I was really lucky to go. However, it was a school of mostly wealthy parents and their kids. My parents were working class. Everyone would drive up to the school in their Beamers and Porches. My mom dropped me off two blocks away because she was so embarrassed by the 1979 Honda Civic (she called it "Tin Lizzie") that she drove. I would walk the rest of the way to school. My parents couldn't afford a nice car because they were putting all their money into tuition. It never occurred to me at the time that my mom was embarrassed about her old Civic. I only knew her as a fearless and dominant woman who could handle anything that came her way.

It was at that point I started dreaming about a nice car. The car I got was a 1969 hand-me-down Chevy Malibu that my sister gave me. It was totaled and then refurbed. California is a car culture. Some people put more into their cars than their houses. All the girls liked nice cars. I wanted to have a nice car. What did I have to do to get one? Clearly, my parents weren't going to buy it for me. I had to make some money. That was the first goal I set in life.

The very first thing I did when I started my own business was to lease a new Mercedes 190E. I washed that car three times a week. My rent payment was less than my car payment. It was a labor of love. It was a beautiful, shiny, low-end, entry-level Mercedes. My life was very basic. I had that car. I slept in the office. I built my business. And it worked. Within five years, I had a turnover of $1 million and a staff of 12.

It was time for the next goal.

In 2002, I bought a business in Naples, Florida. I would fly into Fort Myers and drive to Naples (there weren't any commercial flights to Naples back then). In Naples, I would stay at the Inn on 5th Avenue—right on the approach path for the private airport. Every five minutes, a private jet flew over my head. I would sit there, working, looking up at these planes flying over. I watched these guys fly right into Naples's municipal airport on their own jets. I thought that was pretty cool, and I dreamed about having my own plane for many years.

The cost of operating one's own plane is astronomical. The cheapest private jet is at least $1 million a year. My entire business at the time was making a couple of million a year. I couldn't afford it. But, I put that dream in my goal book (Napoleon Hill 101: "Set a goal and achieve it." See it, believe it, and achieve it.). I imagined myself flying on that plane every day. I did the math and realized that the company would need to probably get to $50 million of EBITDA before we could afford a private jet. So, I set the goal to achieve $50 million in EBITDA.

When I started going to Naples, we had a few million dollars of EBITDA. By 2014—when I leased a plane—our EBITDA came in right at

$50 million. I worked 12 hours a day, six or seven days a week, for 12 years for that dream. I built a business so that I could afford a plane. I loved every minute of the business. It wasn't as if it was hard labor, but I worked hard to achieve my long-term goal. First is the dream. Second is years of hard work. I leased that plane in 2014. I started the business in 1991. That is a long time.

After you achieve your dream, the most important thing is to immediately set a new goal. Don't linger on being proud of yourself. Take yourself out to dinner, take your friend out to dinner. Then ask, "What's next?"

If you find yourself easily achieving your goals, dream bigger.

Every chosen field—from auto mechanics to poetry to plumbing—has a need for people who dream big. My grandfather was a plumber. You might think of that profession as somewhat traditional—until your toilet doesn't work, your water bill is unsustainable or you find out there is lead in your pipes (in fact, some historians say that lead pipes were one of the primary contributors to the decline and fall of the Roman Empire, one of the greatest empires in the history of humanity). Don't underestimate the importance of "workman-like" jobs such as plumbing or auto mechanics. Your entire world is based on them. The people who work in these professions can achieve greatness at the same level as any other.

Regardless of where you choose to make a difference, choose a path that will require you to use all your gifts. As Descartes says, "It is not enough to have a good mind; the main thing is to use it well."

CHAPTER SIXTEEN:
Success as a Leader

Be the change you want to see in your organization.

Hi-Vis Leader

You need to own your public profile. If you are anonymous in today's world, your enemies get to define who you are. It's scary and it's risky, but you have got to control your public persona or your opponents will do it for you. My personality is "very low social." My best day is Sunday, when no one is around. I prefer to be alone with my thoughts; that is just who I am. Publicity is all a distraction. I avoided publicity. And that was a mistake.

"If I was down to my last dollar, I'd spend it on public relations."

—*Bill Gates*

Plato talks about the hierarchy of the soul. His "Allegory of the Cave" reflects the different hierarchies of the human soul. At the bottom are people motivated by gluttony and feeding themselves. Next are people motivated by glory and honor. At the top is the person motivated by the truth. I just want to know the truth. I don't want the glory. I don't want the honor. That is why I was off the record for many years. I know now it was a mistake. You can't be anonymous in this world. My business philosophy was, "We don't brag about our success; we just succeed." At any age, in any career, at any point in life, you need to create a public persona for yourself.

I have done this recently, so I can share my tips with you. Write down your own story and share it with others. Film yourself being interviewed and post it on a YouTube channel. Offer free advice to your peers. Write articles and publish them. Accept all requests for interviews and promote yourself in local media outlets. Make the most of Twitter, Instagram, LinkedIn, and Facebook.

Of course, you should be judicious, but you need to be out there, where the public can see you. Attend local events, sponsor local charities, give speeches at local schools. Turn up for the church bake sale and pack up the lemonade stand—and make sure someone takes your photo while you are doing it. I used to think these strategies were bragging, but I now know the consequences of modesty: You are vulnerable if you can't be seen. Your public narrative and persona will be created by someone; so, I recommend it is you, and you should start today.

Develop Self-Awareness

In order to gain self-awareness, you must have the emotional fortitude to deal with criticism and learn from your mistakes and failures.

- Emotional fortitude is the key to self-awareness, effective coaching, and surviving failure.

- Coaching and self-awareness are the keys to achieving performance through others.

- Energy is the key to enthusiasm, generating forward motion and imagination, and it is the key to doing better and better every day in every way.

- Personal organization is essential to mastery of details and business processes.

- Details are the key to engagement with the business and effective financial management, financial modeling and metrics-based coaching.

- Engagement with business is the key to building reality-based strategies.

- Reality-based strategies are key to facing the brutal facts, maintaining our competitive advantage.

So, quite literally, emotional fortitude is a requirement to maintain your competitive advantage and win in any walk of life. Each person on the team must have the fortitude and ability to take ownership of the customer relationship.

Emotional fortitude means you must be open to criticism from your coach, your employees, and your customers. Peter Drucker suggests that every leader engage in feedback analysis. "Every time you make a decision, write down what you expect will happen. Nine or 12 months later, compare the results with what you expected," he says.

You should also be getting feedback from your employees, peers and customers. The more feedback you get, the better a leader you will be.

How do you know if you're self-aware? How easy was it for you to list your failures and weaknesses? When was the last time you got criticism from your coach and acted on it? When was the last time you were criticized by your direct reports? If you have the emotional fortitude to open yourself up to criticism and to truly hear and act on it, you will gain self-awareness.

So, if you haven't done a 360 review, why not?

Set Your Standards

In my family, we have a set of standards; we call them the "Lindberg Family Values." They comprise the following:

1. Love what you do, and do what you love.

2. Mistakes are OK. The only question is, what did you learn?

3. You are expected to pay your own way and earn your own way. No handouts.

4. Big dreams are GOOD and to be encouraged. If you think big, you get big.

5. Self-reliance and self-sufficiency build character, and dependency destroys it.

6. Struggle and challenges build character.

7. Humanity has unlimited potential. You CAN. End of story.

8. Happiness is using your mind to its fullest extent and power.

9. Master the warrior spirit; don't seek peace and comfort.

10. Think for the very long term.

11. Objective reality powers success, whereas blind faith leads to persistent failure.

12. Respect our family heritage; the struggles of our ancestors have created us.

13. It's your life. Don't let anyone make you feel guilty for living it your own way.

I encourage you to have a similar list for yourself, both personally and professionally. Of course, there should be a high degree of crossover between the two, but your professional values should focus on the work and results you intend to deliver.

Some core behaviors that are essential in any successful group of people include:

- **Accountable and responsible.** You are able to manage the entire process, work independently without supervision and deliver on time without excuses.

- **Adaptable and flexible.** You don't get hung up on things that don't matter to the core objective or core principles; you can handle change.

- **Demanding.** You are assertive, aggressive when appropriate, won't accept a lack of response or lack of results and you hold yourself and your team to a high standard.

- **Dogged and determined.** You are able to fail early and fail often without losing faith in ultimate victory. You are also able to accept criticism without an emotional response.

- **Precise and fastidious.** You are able to master details and careful operating practices and hold others to the same high standard.

- **Systematic and methodical.** You are able to master a process by repeated practice and effort; you don't jump to conclusions without necessary buildup.

- **Workmanlike.** You are informal, non-hierarchical, not too proud to fail, connected to your team and focused on execution and results—not just ideas and strategy.

These values are summed up in our Global Growth Code of Conduct:

- **Hire the best.** Don't tolerate "C" players on your bus.

- **Expect the best.** Don't tolerate mediocre performance.

- **Keep climbing.** Don't tolerate people who rest on past accomplishments.

- **Never stop learning.** Don't tolerate people who aren't coachable.

- **Get your hands dirty.** Don't tolerate prima donnas and people who don't do real work.

Do You Measure Up?

At whatever stage you are in your career, it is important to regularly ask yourself the following questions. You might not tick all the boxes every time (remember, it's important to fail often), but keeping these challenges in your sights helps you stay on track and keeps you close to reality.

- **First "who," then "what."** Do you work overtime to get the right people on the bus and the wrong people off the bus? Are your team members accountable, responsible, disciplined people who take their goals and their commitments seriously?

- **Do you constantly inject a continuous stream of "A+" talent into the organization?** You must have a relentless focus on hiring and recruiting to make sure you get attract and keep lots of new A+ players who will energize every business unit.

- **Do you train relentlessly?** Model the masters and then train relentlessly so everyone can learn. Leadership training and development, when done right, is continuous, ongoing and never-ending.

- **Does your team get regular coaching, ranking and talent reviews?** Everyone on the team has a different level of capability. Make sure you customize the minimum standards of performance to each individual.

- **Do you receive effective coaching?** You should coach from the field, not the locker room. There is no shame in your areas for improvement—tackle them head-on every day. If you don't have an effective coach, find one.

- **Do you face the brutal facts head-on without flinching?** There are no secrets, hidden agendas or politics in a well-run company. If you are not getting critical feedback and unwelcome news, there is something wrong.

- **Do you set clear goals and achieve them?** Start with the end in mind. Then work backward to determine what you need to do today to get there. All your goals should be in writing, and the expectations must be clear. Accountable people welcome clear goals. When we miss goals, we are accountable for the miss, and we don't just move the goal line.

- **Do you promote strong leaders who are self-aware and willing to admit their mistakes?** The true leader is the person closest to reality, who is not too proud to admit failure and asks, "How can I help you succeed?" If there isn't someone on your team good enough to take your job, you need to spend more time on leadership development.

- **Are you workmanlike?** As a leader, you need to roll up your sleeves and get things done.

- **Are you a visionary strategist?** Do you have a seven-year plan for every business you are involved in? Do you think ahead? Be prepared for tomorrow's problems. When there is no way forward, invent one.

CHAPTER SEVENTEEN:
Success as an Organization

"You shouldn't go through life with a catcher's mitt on both hands. You need to be able to throw something back."

—*Maya Angelou*

Define Your Offer

As you think about your "burning desire" in life while you think about what you want to achieve, start first with how you are doing good. Global Growth starts with Global Good.

What is "good"? Abraham Maslow was a psychologist who studied positive qualities and the lives of exemplary people. In 1954, he created his "Hierarchy of Human Needs."

In Maslow's hierarchy, each need must be met before you can move on to the next. It starts with physiological—breathing, food, water, sex, sleep. Next is safety—whether that is employment, health, family, or property. Next are love and belonging—family, friendship and intimacy. Esteem is next—confidence, achievement and the respect of others. At the top is self-actualization—morality, creativity, acceptance of facts, and lack of prejudice.

What are you going to offer that meets one or more of people's needs? When I think of acquiring a company, I always consider what need it meets:

- Food, water, shelter, health

- Energy, education, ICT

- Health span, freedom

The success of Global Growth was based on a significant percentage of investments related to healthcare. Healthcare is an infinite good and will consume an ever-greater portion of the world economy in the future. Within 50 years, healthcare will quite possibly be north of 50 percent of the GDP of advanced economies.

What kind of return will this bring for your business, and what kind of return will this be for the world? This is not just an altruistic concern; companies that add value attract the best people, and they are more likely to thrive.

- Cure blindness

- Provide healthcare

- Conduct research to increase healthy lifespan

- Ensure freedom of the press

- Make personal information secure

- Protect financial security

- Make healthcare more efficient

- Improve the quality of healthcare

- Advance people's careers through training and certification

- Encourage investment in the environment

- Share technological advancements

Each Global Growth company must contribute to its humanitarian impact by creating value and social good. Before I acquire a company, I ask, "How does this company add value?" And this is not only because I believe it is important to contribute to improving the world; companies that make the world a better place are more likely to thrive.

Each Global Growth company must seek out and contribute to social good in order to have a positive humanitarian impact on the world. Global Growth companies and their affiliates have donated millions of dollars to causes and provided many hundreds of volunteer hours. Here are just a few examples of the work we do—outside of work hours:

- We have committed to providing one million meals worldwide to areas affected by the global pandemic. Our companies operate in more than 20 countries, and our giving program must do the same. We have delivered meals via nonprofits in the United States, Europe, India, the Philippines, Costa Rica, and the Ukraine.

- We have partnered with the Akshaya Patra Foundation in India and the Food Bank of Central and Eastern North Carolina.

- We also invest in eye care and eye surgery for underserved populations. Through sponsored free clinics and events, adults and children who would otherwise go without the means to maintain and correct their eyesight can get proper care and eyeglasses.

- In 2019, Special Olympics North Carolina (SONC) officially received recognition as a "Healthy Community"—a distinction from Special Olympics, Inc. that denotes a year-round focus on advancing the health of people with intellectual disabilities. SONC's nutrition-focused health programs and resources provide opportunities for athletes to learn about the benefits of healthy eating. We support these initiatives of this distinction through "Gold" partnership status. Our contribution as a Healthy Communities partner helps promote nutrition education among SONC athletes, as well as allow for engagement opportunities among Global Growth employees.

- We provided startup funding for Interrogating Justice, which since 2021 has helped more than 400,000 people facing prosecution understand their rights under the law and the resources available to them. They have done so with a staff composed mostly of people who have spent time in prison.

Embrace 'And' not 'Or'

In *Man and Superman*, George Bernard Shaw wrote, "The reasonable man adapts himself to the world: the unreasonable one persists in trying to adapt the world to himself. Therefore, all progress depends on the unreasonable man."

All progress belongs to the unreasonable person. We are taught to be reasonable, to accommodate, to be polite and negotiate. But, there are times when you must demand the unreasonable. You must ask for more than anyone thinks is possible.

- Turning a bankrupt publishing company into a thriving online business that makes $15 million a year.

- Delivering record results, despite COVID-19, legal battles, and pending incarceration.

- Growing organically at over 15 percent per year over 15 years straight.

- Keeping the team together and motivated, despite all manner of adversities, false allegations, and negative media attention.

I can't tell you how many times over the past 29 years I have heard "You can't" and gone on to prove the doubters wrong. I've been told:

- You can't launch a newsletter company from your dorm room.

- You can't start a company without outside investment.

- You'll never be able to buy that company because the big players want it.

- You can't just buy an insurance company.

Fundamentally, when someone tells you, "You can't," and this conflicts with a commitment you have made to yourself, you have a choice: honor your own word, or listen to their feedback. If you have made a commitment to yourself to achieve the goal you have set out or die trying, you have no choice but to prove the doubters wrong.

Often, doubters will say that you must make a choice. Instead, Jim Collins encourages us to embrace "and" not "or." Here are some "ands" that we embrace:

- **Profitability and growth:** Most managers say they can turn a profit or invest in growth. I ask all my leaders to do both. Get creative. Figure out how you can get your development done cost-effectively while keeping costs down elsewhere.

- **Customer-focused and employee-centered:** The customer should be the focus of every business decision. Where does that leave the employees? It leaves them working as part of a customer-focused, thriving organization that offers them almost unlimited opportunities for growth.

- **Fearlessness and compliance:** We are aggressive. We are also compliant. We push boundaries but understand that we must do so in compliance with applicable laws and regulations. We can develop game-changing products while maintaining a robust quality system that ensures we still meet the letter of the law.

- **Strategic thinking and execution:** We always plan for the future but insist on operational excellence. We break molds and try the impossible, but we are still workmanlike in our pursuit.

- **Organic growth and acquisitions:** We grow through acquisition, but that should never be the only way. When we acquire an asset or company, we expect its leader to show sustained growth as well.

Acquisitions are exciting, but they cannot take a leader's eye off the mandate for the strategic growth of existing companies.

Do the Impossible

I began in 1991 as a 21-year-old student reading a newsletter and thinking, "I can do better." My main competitor didn't take me seriously until it was too late. My newsletter, *Home Care Week*, became a significant competitor in the industry.

By 1998, my company, Eli Global, comprised 12 people working out of one big room full of folding tables and computers. We published *Home Care Week* and *Rehab Report* and had just launched *Home Care Compliance Alert*.

That same year, cuts to home care funding from the Balanced Budget Act of 1997 hit us hard and made us grow up. We let go of quality people. We worried about meeting payroll and paying our printing bill.

We built up our products in the healthcare space and started looking at acquisitions. Our first acquisition was the Travel Research Bureau in 2000. We bought the company for the price of taking over the owner's debts and cleaning out his office. My IT director and I rented a U-Haul and came back with a pile of files, furniture, a glass pumpkin candy dish, and a microwave. The microwave was a handy addition to our poorly-equipped break room. However, the most valuable thing we got from the acquisition was a tough lesson. The Travel Research Bureau addressed the complex connection between travel agents and ticketing entities—just as companies such as Travelocity were transforming the industry.

Our next big step was buying The Coding Institute in 2002. We had to deal with prima donna writers who were extremely expensive and modestly talented. They left the company, thinking they had dealt us a fatal blow. We then hired brilliant people with great attitudes and gave them two weeks to master material that took most people a year. Ninety percent of them succeeded and became the core of Global Growth's editorial excellence. Some of these writers are millionaires today because of the stock appreciation rights in our group of companies that they received.

Our third big step was completing a $40 million acquisition in 2006. We'd had our eye on the company for years, as did several other suitors. But we were scrappier. We found the owner's contact information from a colleague of a colleague. We e-mailed him to say, "We are going to be on your front doorstep Monday, and we will do what it takes to buy your company."

Our first India office was a real game-changer. We found a new way to live by our "and, not or" philosophy. Opening our Faridabad office in 2007 allowed us to cut costs while investing in growth and product development.

After Faridabad, our globalization strategy really took off. We opened offices in the Philippines and Malta. We bought our first non-U.S. company in Ireland. In the meantime, our publishing business was faltering. Workflow products and information in real time were replacing newsletters. So, we transitioned our products into software that integrated into the customers' daily activities.

Our health care business grew, while our print-based competitors faltered.

In 2012, we saw we had a knack for growth. We were successful in taking "okay" businesses and making them great. Our growth was limited by two factors: access to great leaders and access to capital. We invested in leadership development, bringing in robust executive coaching to grow internal leaders while creating an aggressive recruiting team to find them externally.

I learned some hard lessons during those early years:

- Have the financial discipline to run your company as if there is about to be a recession.

- No matter how good the deal, you must look at long-term market-drivers.

- Build a loyal community, and you have built a barrier to entry for your competitors.

- Ignore people who tell you that you won't succeed. Just prove them wrong.

- Roll up your sleeves and get your hands dirty.

- Embrace a location-agnostic business philosophy, or you will get left behind.

- Innovate or die.

PART FOUR:
HOW TO WIN IN BUSINESS

CHAPTER EIGHTEEN:
Focus on People

> "We found instead that [great companies] got the right people on the bus, the wrong people off the bus, and the right people in the right seats. And then they figured out where to drive it."
>
> —*Jim Collins, Good to Great*

Be relentlessly demanding at getting the right people in the right place on the bus.

Get a Great Team

Getting the right people on your bus is 90 percent of the business. You have people who want to grow. They want to make a career for themselves. They want to make money. They want to run a business. They want experience. Providing growth opportunities for exceptional people is fundamentally my business strategy.

Your growth as a company is limited only by the number of great people ("A" players) in the right positions. Jim Collins, in *Good to Great*, says that truly great companies focus on "First who, then what." He says you must start by getting great people and then decide where they will take the company.

It is hard to hire the right people, and it takes a long time. The only thing more costly in the long run is not hiring the right people. Hiring the right people allows you to move on to tomorrow's opportunities without having to micromanage yesterday's problems.

If you hire people with the potential to grow and hire other great people, you've unfettered your potential for growth. The biggest mistake most leaders make is not hiring people who will challenge them. If you don't find the right person at first, keep looking or try another recruiting firm. Don't settle.

Here are some questions to ask about yourself and anyone you are considering bringing onto your team:

- **How long into the future can you work and plan without any guidance?** The best leaders have the longest time span.

- **How long into the future can you hold your vision while simultaneously acting on short-term steps that will get you there?**

- **What is your span of control?** The highest-level leader can keep a maximum number of complex parallel and conditional initiatives operating simultaneously and integrating each as necessary.

- **What caliber of people do you hire?** Are you afraid of hiring people who can replace you?

- **What is your level of emotional fortitude in making decisions?** Do you react emotionally in times of stress, or do you react analytically?

- **How close to reality are you?** Do you face the brutal facts, regardless of consequences, or play politics?

- **What is your level of self-awareness?** Do you accept critical feedback as a gift to make you better, or are you defensive and do not listen to the feedback?

Even when you do everything possible to hire the right person, sometimes they will turn out to be the wrong person. As soon as you know someone can't thrive in a position, let them go or move them to another place on the bus.

Ask yourself: Would I hire this person again? If you wouldn't hire them again, they should not be on the team.

You are what you tolerate. If you tolerate people who don't fit your values, your values don't matter. If you keep people who are mediocre, excellence doesn't matter. Think about the times you've had to let people go. How many times have you said, "I should have done it sooner?" Almost never do people say, "I really should have waited to let that person go."

The biggest obstacle to adding "A" talent and removing "C" talent is that it takes hard work and persistence in the short run. However, if you get it right, your job is a lot easier in the long run. You now have time to tackle new opportunities. The most common way to stop growing is to stop hiring "A" talent and people who challenge you.

Ask yourself, "Would you hire this person again?" If not, move them off the bus or to a different spot on the bus. Also ask yourself, "If they quit and came back a week later, saying they had made a mistake, would you emphatically rehire them?"

Once you've decided you have the wrong person, no one benefits from delaying action. The employee in question is under great stress and will become a negative, toxic influence on the culture.

Develop Independent Leaders

"Hierarchy is an organization with its face toward the CEO and its ass toward the customer."

—*Jack Welch*

Management is a fallacy. Most management activity justifies the existence of management instead of focusing on results. That is why, in the aggregate, small businesses grow faster, are more profitable and create more jobs than larger ones.

At the core of the fallacy of modern organization management—in business, government, the nonprofit sector and even the family unit—is a lack of trust. The theory of leadership common in most organizations today is that followers must be told what to do. This theory of leadership is expressly based on a lack of trust and a lack of confidence in the followers. That lack of confidence and lack of trust will become a self-fulfilling prophecy.

People will either rise to your level of expectation or fall to your level of disregard. If you expect those whom you lead to be independent, they will be independent. If you expect them to be dependent and disregard their talents, most will comply and become dependent.

I've made this mistake numerous times by assuming that someone on our team is not capable of making the next big step in their career development. When some of these people were turned over to another leader in our organization who had a more open mind regarding their potential for growth, they thrived.

In organizations without such enlightened management that gives people opportunities to become independent leaders in their own right, layers of hierarchical control develop to accommodate for the fact that no one feels comfortable making a decision.

If your child is empowered to make their own decisions early in life, your job as a parent will be a lot easier. The same is true in any organization.

In big corporations, over-management is a much bigger leadership problem than under-management. This is why, in aggregate, small businesses soundly outperform large ones. Likewise, "over-parenting" is a much bigger problem in families today than "under-parenting." Kids are raised to be dependent and obedient.

This doesn't mean you abdicate. Empowerment requires very clear accountability and authority. What you will deliver as a leader each year is the most important conversation you will have with your team—the "Accountability Conversation." This is not an easy conversation, especially if the person is afraid of failure or afraid of commitment. Once this conversation is done, step back and allow people the freedom to achieve.

This "federation of independent businesses" has been at the core of the Global Growth operating philosophy since day one. We kept adding businesses to our group and gave them a wide latitude to perform. The worst move you can make when you are growing is to layer-on top management hierarchy that adds self-justifying overhead.

In the past, when I was more hands-on with the business units, I would tell people, "If things are going well, and you are on-plan and building your business for the long term, you won't hear much from HQ unless you ask for help. No news is good news. Meanwhile, if I show up at your office and tell you I'm your new co-pilot, this is not a good sign."

> **When values are clear, and knowledge flows freely, behaviors don't need to be controlled.**

These have been the foundations of running a federation of associated businesses, and they apply to leading an organization of any size. Don't force leaders to become "part of a big company." Ego and empire-building, which in the end is seeking glory, are always trumped by the fundamental truth that answers are found on the front lines—with customers and those who serve them—not at HQ. The leader in the room is the person closest to reality, and reality starts with the customers and the market in which you operate.

The right role for any centralized leadership function, from family to business, is sharing knowledge and values. When values are clear, and knowledge flows freely, behaviors don't need to be controlled. They are prescribed by shared values and shared knowledge. This approach avoids the demotivating effects on the human psyche of not being trusted and being told what to do. Children want to be trusted and everyone on your team wants to be trusted.

> How many cultures have been destroyed by a bureaucratic focus on rules and processes instead of giving people freedom to think and do for themselves what is right?

After the end of World War II, new governments in many Western democracies were formed, with rules and regulations that were simple and straightforward for everyone to understand. As successive governments passed more and more regulations, these rules have become ever more complex and indecipherable. The message of the millions of pages of laws and regulations that entrepreneurs must navigate is simple: the government is going to tell you what to do and how to do it.

This "movie" always ends in the collapse of the Leviathan under its own weight. People simply stop taking the initiative because of their learned helplessness and constant reminders from the Leviathan that they are unworthy of making their own decisions. It is similar to a child who was raised by a domineering parent and was told constantly they were not permitted to make decisions. This child will ultimately give up. The Leviathan, through all of its rules, regulations and "programs," is saying it owns the problems. And, if you own someone else's problem, they can't own it.

Instead of a complex set of rules and regulations, what works is a simple set of values and shared best practices. Western democracies all start off with this simple set of core values. Successful families and businesses do the same.

"If you try to change it, you will ruin it. Try to hold it, and you will lose it," Lao Tzu notes. His advice is relevant for any relationship you have in life—your friends, your family, your lovers, your co-workers and your employees. The tighter you hang on to something, the more likely you are to lose it. Global Growth has done a lot of acquisitions, and one of the most important reasons we are successful is that we work very hard to preserve and enhance the original essence of the business we acquired. Often, this starts with keeping the business and its brands intact and not attempting to integrate the company.

What works instead is a simple set of shared values and expectations:

- You must achieve your earnings targets.
- You must have a coach and be on a continuous path of self-improvement.
- You must build your business for the long term.
- You must be growing faster than your market.

Global Growth's "federation of associated businesses" model will always beat the "central planning" model of many large companies.

Good leaders need coaches, not bosses. The more you can empower your leaders to do their best without interference from a boss, the better they will do. The more you can empower anyone in your life to do their best without your interference, the better they will do. People almost always rise to your level of expectation.

Ownership thinking and empowerment generates leaders at all levels: salesperson as leader, telemarketer as leader, customer service rep as leader. You might think this would lead to too many bosses and not enough workers—but the opposite happens. You have a team of independent, confident, scrappy workers who are determined to deliver their best and know it is their responsibility to do that. And that is the attitude you want everyone on your team to have.

At every stage of the development of the Global Growth group of companies, we faced the same challenge: Control or let go. Early on, I edited every single newsletter issue that went out and every single marketing piece. I learned to let go and trust that the people I hired would produce high-quality content.

> At every stage ... we faced the same challenge: Control or let go.

At one point, we were running diverse companies under one management structure. We could build a more complex management structure, or we could let go. We chose to let go. We brought on competent CEOs and gave them the reins. Our oversight consisted of enforcing company policies, compliance reviews and strategic planning reviews.

Then, we realized we were assessing strategic plans for businesses for which we had never met a single customer; and we were enforcing compliance rules in countries we'd never lived in. We could create more comprehensive strategic review and compliance teams, or we could let go. We let go. We hired competent, entrepreneurial portfolio leaders to drive the strategy for their portfolios and enforce compliance.

It might seem that the lesson here is that strategic reviews and compliance aren't important. The lesson is just the opposite. They are so critical that they should be tackled by experts, not dilettantes. Each leader must have accountability and authority. Every organization and every person in each organization must understand clearly what they are accountable for delivering, even as they are given flexibility in how to deliver it.

How to Build Confidence in Others

Empowering your staff, children, or other people in your life to be more independent requires that you help them first build confidence. Here is a tangible way to do that:

Have them pick a positive affirmation, such as, "I speak my mind every day, regardless of what people think about me." Then, repeat it every day. It becomes a habit, and this habit forms part of your character.

A few suggestions: "I am disciplined, rigorous, relentless, dogged, determined, diligent, precise, fastidious, systematic, methodical, workmanlike, demanding, focused and consistent, accountable and responsible, adaptable, and flexible, and I act with ferocious resolve to achieve my goals."

The credit for this list of affirmations goes to Jim Collins, who lists them as attributes of the culture of companies who make the leap from good to great. They help me overcome fear every day. I must have recited these affirmations a thousand times before I went into the nine-hour surgery that successfully removed my brain tumor.

As I prepared for a seven-year prison sentence, these affirmations guided me and strengthened my resolve to win my case or die trying.

Create your own positive affirmations today, and help your staff create theirs. Write them down. Recite them daily, out loud, with conviction, confidence, and passion. Visualize yourself acting in this way. Visualization is the most important part.

Three basketball teams were studied over a two-week period: **Team #1** was told to practice daily as normal for two hours. **Team #2** was told not to practice at all. **Team #3** was told to visualize practicing daily for two hours.

The results: **Team #3** (the team that practiced mentally) achieved nearly the same improvement in results as **Team #1**, the team that practiced physically. **Team #2** performed substantially worse.

Your action item: Create a clear vision of who you are after you have achieved these positive affirmations. Then, review this vision daily and in detail until you can see your success as clearly as your current reality. Then, the most important step: emotionalize these affirmations in times of great fear so they become part of your reptilian brain, which can only be programmed via emotional input.

I emotionalized these affirmations going into surgery, preparing for prison, and numerous other circumstances for which I would normally be overcome by fear. These affirmations are so far- driven into my reptilian brain that I get teary-eyed just thinking about them. Auto-suggestions as positive affirmations can help you overcome any fear, especially the fear of opinion.

A Simple Way to Build the Right Culture Through Meetings

Politics and social climbing have no place in any effective organization. Team members who are wasting time on politics aren't producing results. Results

Politics and social climbing have no place in any effective organization.

are the only thing you should value. One effective way to reinforce this culture is through how you run meetings.

At Global Growth, we suggest a meeting code along these lines:

- **Face the real issues directly;** that is, the elephants in the room that no one wants to talk about.

- **Participate.** If you are quiet in a meeting, why are you there?

- **Praise and criticize publicly.**

- **Share financial information.**

- **Bring all issues to the group.** No subgroups, private conversations, etc. Ask yourselves, "What are we afraid to talk about?" Then, address those issues.

- **Offer analysis.** Not just numbers, raw data, or speculation.

- **Be inclusive.** Ensure the meeting is equally productive for all participants, regardless of location.

- **Listen attentively.** Don't hold side conversations, and don't interrupt.

- **Be accountable.** When action items are discussed, agree on who will do what and by when.

- **Be respectful of the group's time.** Only hold detailed discussions of issues relevant to the group as a whole.

- **Be prepared.** Have an agenda, send out information beforehand when possible and bring all information necessary for the scheduled discussion.

Susan Scott, author of *Fierce Conversations*, suggests you ask these questions in your meeting:

1. What has become clear since we last met?

2. What are you trying to make happen in the next three months?

3. What is the most important decision you are facing?

4. What topic are you hoping I won't bring up?

5. What part of your responsibilities are you avoiding right now?

6. What do you wish you had more time to do?

7. If you were hired to consult with our company, what would you advise?

Use these principles in EVERY conversation you have, especially ones you think are "private."

The true culture of an organization will show up in what you say when no one is looking or, in my case, when I didn't know someone was looking. As C.S. Lewis said, "Integrity is doing the right thing when no one is watching." Not knowing I was being recorded, here is what I said: "We're gonna do it right, and we're gonna do it with every single piece of law out there."

What are you going to say when you think no one is listening? Your freedom may depend on it. Stick to your internal integrity—regardless of the pressure from people who hold power over you.

When I was indicted in 2019, my belief in the value of independent leaders faced the ultimate test: I stepped aside and handed management of my businesses to my "A-player" leadership team. During my absence, my businesses grew both top and bottom line. That is test that I hope you never face, but it reinforced my belief in finding leaders who challenge you and act independently.

Get Close To Reality

"You must never confuse faith that you will prevail in the end—which you can never afford to lose—with the discipline to confront the most brutal facts of your current reality, whatever they may be."

—*Admiral Jim Stockdale, eight-year Vietnam POW*

"Bad news isn't wine. It doesn't improve with age."

—*Colin Powell, 16th U.S. National Security Advisor, 12th Chairman of the Joint Chiefs of Staff, 65th U.S. Secretary of State*

The leader in the room is the person closest to reality, the person who does not rely on hope as a strategy.

To continuously improve, we must receive continuous feedback on the good, bad and ugly. Managing without feedback is like bowling without seeing the pins.

In *Good to Great*, Jim Collins refers to the "Stockdale Paradox:" "Never confuse faith that you will prevail in the end with the discipline to confront the most brutal facts of your current reality."

Humans can survive just about any adversity and turn it into a greater advantage. The first step is getting to the cold, hard truth about the adversity you face. This means I am preparing daily for a lengthy prison sentence. Prepare for the worst, aim for the best.

Leaders are truth-seekers, not commanders.

Twenty years ago, everyone subscribed to print magazines and newsletters. The industry was bullish on print, even as circulation numbers began to fall. Publishers found articles entitled "Why Print Will Never Die" and circulated them among themselves. At every conference, there were feel-good presentations about how nothing would ever replace the "weight" of a book or magazine in your hands.

Some publishers faced the fact that print and mail were getting more expensive, while free content was becoming more and more readily available on the web. Some of these publishers started testing workflow products and software. Others came up with creative ways to monetize Web content. Still others began using their content to sell products. Those companies look very different than they did 20 years ago. Some aren't even recognizable as publishing companies, but they are thriving.

The companies that spent their time telling each other that print would never die have failed. How were the successful companies different? First, they had leaders willing to face realities head-on and who fearlessly tried and failed with many models, knowing that one would prevail in the end.

Second, they had a culture of reality. Winston Churchill personified resolve. He believed England would prevail against Hitler's war machine against all odds. He knew there were almost insurmountable challenges in their way. He knew his intelligence personnel were discovering new facts about Hitler's growing munitions factories and troop movements every day. He also knew he had a huge, challenging personality and that few people would be willing to tell him bad news. So, he created the Statistical Office. This ministry existed outside the regular chain of command. Its sole purpose was to feed him unvarnished facts.

You want leaders with big personalities. You want strong, aggressive leaders. However, those traits can also create an environment in which people hesitate to come forward with bad news. That is why you must create a "culture of reality" via which people are encouraged to speak up, no matter what.

Ask yourself, "How often do I get bad news before it shows up in the numbers? Do I get it early enough to act on it instead of reacting to it? How short is the path of information from the customer to my ear? How do I know what customers think about my products?"

Use these strategies to create a climate where brutal facts are shared:

- Make sure all employees are trained on your values.

- Lead with questions, not answers.

- Engage dialogue and debate, not coercion.

- Conduct "autopsies" without blame.

- Build red-flag mechanisms.

CHAPTER NINETEEN:
Focus on Results

Stay Focused on Results

In many organizations, titles are on every door. Titles are what everyone knows. However, in a results-driven organization, titles are not prominent. Your results are what everyone knows.

Categorizing people based on their titles is like watching the shadows that come from the fire inside the cave. They aren't the truth. The truth is the reality of what each individual has produced. In a results-driven organization, everyone on the leadership team can answer every one of these questions:

- What is your revenue year to date as compared to goal?

- What is your strategy for the next five years?

- How will you beat your competitors?

- What are your leading indicators?

The results-driven organization goes beyond the top level of leadership. Every person in the organization should know their make-or-break metrics. They should know your company's goals for the next five years. They should know how their successes and failures affect the company's bottom line.

Stay Scrappy

In a healthy, apolitical company, the leader isn't "too good" to do any job in the company. A leader connects with employees and customers, signs for packages, and gets in the trenches. Titles don't matter, results do. The best leaders put customers and employees first, which inspires loyalty. That customer and employee loyalty translates into business results. Your results do the talking for you.

In my first office, leaders worked from cubicles, and the frontline staff, such as customer service, billing and sales, worked in offices. It's a balance I maintain today. The most important employees are the ones who face the customer. The rest of the organization is there to provide strategy and make them successful.

At first, our offices were ugly because we couldn't afford anything better. We spent money on marketing, great people, gym benefits, and technology (and good coffee), but not on office furniture. As the company became more profitable, we kept the ugly office furniture, especially in the interviewing room. We realized some people were turned off by the folding tables and bare walls. Those people would never succeed at our company. If we lost a candidate because of office décor, good riddance.

For the longest time, we kept an old shopping cart in our conference room that was from our in-store advertising business. We also kept a desk that I used in 1991. On first impression, the conference room looked like a lot of junk. This was intentional. It scared away people who were not going to get into the trenches, roll up their sleeves and focus on results over titles and the size of their office.

How do you know you are scrappy?

- You don't care about titles.
- You don't care about offices.
- You don't tolerate bureaucracy.
- You keep administrative personnel to a minimum.
- Your internal communications are direct, simple and straightforward.

How scrappy are you?

- If you ask anyone in my organization what their make-or-break metrics are and how they affect the company's bottom line, can they answer?

- How often do people ask about titles? How many administrative personnel are in your organization? Is it over 5 percent?

- How often do I and other leaders have conversations with customer-facing employees?

- How long is my employee handbook? Is it more than 10 pages?

- Does everyone in the organization know the company's strategic plan and mission?

And ask yourself:

- When was the last time I spoke with a customer?

- Do I have administrative staff between me and my employees who schedule my phone calls or send my emails?

- When was the last time I signed for the mail or took out the trash?

> ## Make your goal an all-consuming obsession that puts everything else in perspective as less important.

Creative Destruction

What is your long-term transformational vision for your company? Every company must have one. It's not enough to do the same things well. Simply doing more of the same thing is neither visionary nor transformational. It's often a recipe for marching straight off a cliff.

In 2005, 90 percent of our revenue came from print newsletters. It wasn't enough to strive to be the best print newsletter company in the world. We had to transform, so we launched software products and bought a certification company. We transformed before the newsletter market crumbled at our feet.

Capitalism is the process of creative destruction. How do you make sure you are transforming ahead of your industry? How do you make sure you are the one creating the destruction and not the one being destroyed? Only the paranoid survive. Use threat analysis to build a bomb-proof company.

Ask yourself:

- Where will my industry be in five years? What is its strategic direction?
- What are my top five external business or competitor threats?
- What are the top five political, governmental, and regulatory threats to my business?
- What are my top five internal threats?
- What are my top five tech threats?

Ask yourself:

- What kind of business could put me out of business?

Then, become or acquire that business. In his book, *Traction*, Gino Wickman uses an image to help leaders visualize the importance of effective goal-setting:

Imagine you have a pile of rocks, a pile of pebbles and a pile of sand. You are asked to put them into the glass container that matches their total volume. If you start with the sand and then the pebbles, the rocks will spill over the top. However, if you start with the rocks and then add pebbles and then sand, you will be able to fit them all in. Do what is most critical first, and let the rest fill in around it.

Once you have decided what kind of disrupter you need to be, it's time to use your fearlessness of failure we've talked so much about. Don't be timid: If the change you are envisioning is not out of your comfort zone, you aren't stretching far enough. It's time to set what Jim Collins calls your "Big, Hairy, Audacious Goal (BHAG)"—a future that cannot be achieved in a straight line from your current reality. Then, make it happen.

Remember your commitment to achieve your goal or die trying. Genius is divine perseverance. Creativity is a function of discipline and focus over a long period of time. Strategic thinking sets the course, but operational excellence from daily perseverance is what achieves results.

CHAPTER TWENTY:
Focus on Mindset

"It's not that I'm so smart: It's just that I stay with problems longer." —*Albert Einstein*

Always Keep Learning

Global Growth has gone through numerous transformations over the past 30 years:

- From print newsletters to online software

- From coding to entire revenue cycle

- From a single company to a federation of independent businesses

- From a U.S. company to a global company

- From revenue cycle to health care technology

- From a health care company to a company diversified across many industries

- From third-party debt to a mix of third-party debt and insurance asset funding

"Character cannot be developed in ease and quiet. Only through experience of trial and suffering can the soul be strengthened, vision cleared, ambition inspired, and success achieved."

—*Helen Keller*

- From a federation of independent businesses to a federation of independent portfolios of businesses.

- From insurance asset funding back to third-party debt funding

Adversity will only make you stronger if you put the hard-learned lessons into action every day for the rest of your life.

One of the greatest advantages that has come from our legal battles has been the recruiting and hiring of new leaders at Global Growth. Our new chairman, new chief financial officer, and new legal team all are direct results of the lessons from our legal battles. These are all "first who, then what" hires, and the transformational effect on the business is immediately apparent when you bring on talented, new leaders.

Over the next 40 years, we will go through many more transformational changes. Sustainable greatness requires the never-ending personal growth of everyone in the organization. All our leaders must stretch and grow to survive.

To be sustainably the best requires the continual growth of the competencies of all the people in the organization. This means putting yourself in situations for which you have to stretch and grow to survive. If you aren't afraid, you aren't nervous and you aren't stretched. Therefore, you aren't learning. As we have discussed, comfort and relaxation together equal your eventual weakness and downfall.

Leadership is about taking your team places they didn't think they could go—because they were too afraid, nervous, or uncomfortable to go there. Some people are prisoners of their comfort zones. Criticism leads to growth and success. Fear of criticism prevents timid souls from achieving greatness. Leaders must learn by doing and experimenting. Real credit goes to those who are willing to bear the risk of failure by venturing into the unknown and unproven.

Develop a Growth Mindset

A strong desire to learn and grow leads you to:

- Embrace challenges and welcome hardship as a learning experience. Never avoid challenges.

> Master the warrior spirit; peace and comfort do not produce success.

- Persist in the face of setbacks. Fail early, fail often, but don't give up, and never surrender.

- Understand that daily workmanlike effort is the key to mastery. There are no shortcuts or easy ways out. Don't be cynical about the benefits of extra effort.

- Welcome criticism from others. Get the bad news first; it's the only way you can do better.

- Always welcome useful negative feedback.

- Find lessons and inspiration in the success of others. Celebrate and learn from the success of others or the success of people you hire.

Good leaders are demanding because they refuse to allow people to default on their commitments to themselves. Those who develop themselves and keep their word get support. Those who can't or won't develop themselves will be gone. The leader must create a necessity of learning. This means forcing people into situations during which they must learn to survive in the organization. There is no steady state.

Complacency kills life. Growth enlivens. You must be the change you want to see in your organization. As Nietzsche notes: "If only we could foresee the most favorable conditions under which creatures of the highest value arise, we can increase courage, insight, hardness, independence, and the feeling of responsibility; we can make the scales more delicate and hope for the assistance of favorable accidents." The more responsibility you give to people in your life, the more courage and accountability they will have. The less responsibility you give to people in your life, the less accountable they will be.

Think Long Term

One of the biggest mistakes American companies make is favoring quarterly earnings over long-term, strategic results. Yes, quarterly earnings are important, but not when they come at the expense of long-term results. A focus on public share price is largely what drives the quarterly earnings-focused mindset of the typical American CEO.

Time and time again, public companies cut corners to drive quarterly earnings and ultimately face a write-down or write-off or other business adversity because of persistent short-term thinking. Our most important daily action is to prepare for the next 40 years. I constantly ask myself, "What will Global Growth look like 44 years from now?" For example, in 1970, Berkshire Hathaway had $32 million in insurance assets and similar amounts of sales and net worth. Today, it has $78 billion in insurance assets and hundreds of billions in sales/net worth.

Our long-term thinking shows up in our behaviors:

- Global Growth comprises a buy-and-hold group of companies.

- We have only sold a handful of companies.

- We have a 40-year plan for each business we operate.

- We build long-term relationships with our employees and customers.

- We invest in people for the long term.

- We focus on those who are coachable, who can grow beyond their comfort zone and who don't rest on past accomplishments.

- We focus on the "A" players and move the "C" players off the bus.

- We have no outside common equity investors, which allows us to focus on long-term growth.

- The founder and the employees own 100 percent of the common equity of the company.

- We are driven by a passion for excellence, not big offices or big titles.

- We are quietly confident. We stay below the radar, and we don't shout about our success.

- We have strong cash reserves, strong cash flow, and we invest for the future.

- We are building a diversified group of businesses worldwide.

- We aren't afraid of turnarounds and getting our hands dirty with hard work.

PART FIVE: EXPERT COACHING

The caliber of your leadership is directly
proportional to the distance in the future
you can plan your actions and act consistently in the
present with those plans.

CHAPTER TWENTY-ONE:
Lagging and Leading Indicators

When you consider your competition, there are two key questions to answer: What would a well-funded competitor do to put you out of business? Why would you fail? If you know the answer to these key questions, act on them.

You have some insights. Now, how do you act on them? Well, you need to make decisions based on metrics. Decisions based on intuition, or guessing, will never be confident decisions. Metrics and key performance indicators give you the ability to predict the future with a high level of confidence. It is not guesswork; rather, it is understanding the data, applying your vision and creating strategy from your experience and knowledge.

> A leading indicator looks forward at future outcomes and events. A lagging indicator looks back at whether the intended result was achieved.

It is vital to understand your leading and lagging indicators. Simply put: leading indicators influence your future performance. Lagging indicators analyze your past performance. Both are important but, too often, we look to the past because it is in our comfort zone. A leading indicator looks forward at future outcomes and events. A lagging indicator looks back at whether the intended result was achieved.

Apply the concepts of leading and lagging indicators to a car. Leading indicators look forward, through the windshield, at the road ahead. Lagging indicators look backward, through the rear window, at the road you have already traveled.

A financial indicator such as revenue, for example, is a lagging indicator. It tells you what has already happened. Strictly speaking, last year's revenue does not predict future revenue (although it has been used to do just that by many businesses in the past). But an indicator such as customer satisfaction does point to future revenue. Satisfied customers are more likely to repurchase and tell their friends about your company.

Lagging indicators are typically "output" oriented—easy to measure but hard to improve or influence—while leading indicators are typically input oriented—hard to measure and easy to influence.

A great example is weight loss. The amount you weigh is a clear lagging indicator that is easy to measure. You step on a scale, and you have your answer. But, how do you actually reach your goal? For weight loss, there are two leading indicators: calories taken in and calories burned. These two indicators are easy to influence but hard to measure. You can restrict what you eat and exercise for three hours a day, but when you order lunch in a restaurant, the amount of calories may not be not listed on the menu. In addition, if you are like most people, you have no clue how many calories you burn on a given day.

CHAPTER TWENTY-TWO:
Levers

There are two ways to grow your business: increase revenue or decrease expenses. There is only one right way to grow your business in the long term: increase your revenue. It is as simple as that.

The way to increase your revenue is to think of your business as a machine. You have new levers, existing levers, cogs, and growth levers.

Existing levers offer the opportunity for organic growth within your company. Ask yourself where you want each existing lever to be in three years. Where should this lever be to make sure everyone reaches their full potential, taking into account industry trends, competitors, and company potential?

To increase your revenue and profitability, you need to have all your levers and cogs working like a well-oiled machine. Randy Nelson outlines the process in his book, *The Fourth Decision: The Maximized Entrepreneur.*

- Increase existing revenue streams (existing levers)
- Increase your productivity in your organization with existing revenue streams (metrics)
- Implement new organic revenue streams by developing your "growth pyramid:" vision and execution (new levers)
- Employ growth leaders who can lead revenue growth (levers)
- Manage mergers and acquisitions (inorganic growth levers)
- Decrease expenses ("cogs")

Common "levers" in most businesses are:

- The number of customers and revenue per customer
- The number of products sold and price per product
- The number of services sold and price per service

- The markets/industry segments served
- Geographic locations
- Customer retention
- Customer turnover
- Salespeople
- The method of sales delivery (direct or online)

There are different methods you can use to analyze your total company revenues. But, for the next exercise to work, the levers must add up to the total company revenue.

Once you have identified which levers generate what income, you can determine what each lever would deliver. Now you can know the key thrusts that will propel your business and start to generate increased revenue.

According to Nelson: "By identifying all of the levers in your organization and conducting a three-year projection for each, you should see where your greatest opportunities are in the future, by different levers, and where your growth is not as strong. The levers are the starting point, the pure gold in your organization. They clearly identify how you operate today When you add your intuition and decide where you should be with each lever, that is how you mine for the real diamonds for the future!"

Begin by defining your core values; for instance, what are your hire and fire rules? Then, focus on your core purpose. Why does this organization exist? Your three- to five-year key thrusts will show you where to focus your efforts. Your annual goals and plans define what you will accomplish; the quarterly goals and plans specify how you will do it; and your daily, weekly, and monthly goals outline who does what and by when. Without the foundational knowledge of your core values and purpose, your day-to-day work will never head in the right direction.

CHAPTER TWENTY-THREE:
Metrics

Randy Nelson talks about metrics, and we know how to easily measure some of them. But, how do you capture metrics for leading indicators? Turns out, it is not all that different from collecting information for lagging indicators.

To obtain your metrics, you need to—

- Collect the data;

- Input the data into a spreadsheet;

- Convert the numbers to percentages;

- Data sort the numbers and percentages;

- Analyze the trends; and

- Make decisions regarding current and future targets.

> ...revenue is vanity, margin is sanity, cash is reality.

In this model, as in life, it is wise to remember that "revenue is vanity, margin is sanity, cash is reality," according to Nelson.

From your metrics, you need to create a one-page decision sheet that includes five years of history, expenses as a percentage of revenue, with input from your income statements. On the same page is your target for this fiscal year. Then one year and three years from today.

PART SIX:
DISCUSSION QUESTIONS AND BUSINESS ASSIGNMENTS

Once a leader decides they have found
the truth, the decline begins.

QUESTION 1:

What are management's responsibilities in today's world?

Managers who excel in today's environment have particular personality characteristics such that they thrive on constant challenges and surprises. These personality types tend to be low in patience, high in preference for autonomy, and low to moderate preference for detail orientation. When they possess these personality traits, managers are often excited by new challenges and are often able to handle uncertainty without becoming overwhelmed or discouraged. Likewise, a high autonomy preference is associated with high aggression such that these personality types seek psychological rewards from "winning" and overcoming the challenges that today's rapid-paced management environment presents. Enjoying challenges and welcoming adversity is perhaps the most important skill set for a leader in today's environment.

High aggression or high autonomy leaders are often more resilient as well, which is another key criterion for a successful manager in today's environment. Resilience allows leaders to find advantage and opportunity in adversity as they adapt to challenging market dynamics, consumer behavior, government regulation, political situations, technology changes, and competitor dynamics. The best "change leaders" enjoy the process so much that when they succeed—and even if they fail—they come back again and again for the next challenge. These types of leaders don't burn out because climbing mountains is what they love to do.

QUESTION 2:

Why do some companies have long-term leadership?

There are numerous factors that account for why some companies have a lot of CEO turnover and management turnover, whereas other companies have long-tenured CEOs and management:

1. **Type of shareholder.** Often, privately held companies with low leverage are family-owned and take a much longer, often generational view on their business. Contrast this with public companies with an activist shareholder who pushes for management change. Sometimes for the short-term gain of boosting the stock price or selling off key assets (e.g., the Carl Icahn or Bill Ackman model).

2. **Intentionality of the culture in the business.** Was the business created from day one with a specific, unique culture that has been written down and taught to employees and managers? This intentional culture and values system in an organization allows the organization to quickly eject those that don't fit into the culture and thus the remaining employees tend to stay longer. Likewise, employees who are trained in this intentional culture tend to stay with the company longer, particularly if the culture is highly unique. The more unique the culture, the more tenured the management and employees will be. This is simply because when someone has worked at a business for 10 years and has mastered a very unique culture at this business, moving to a new business with a markedly different culture and value system will seem entirely foreign—somewhat like moving to a foreign country and having to learn to speak a foreign language.

3. **Ability of the shareholders and Board of Directors to empower ownership thinking** at all levels of the organization, from the CEO to the front-line managers. The more freedom leaders have, the more accountability they will bring to the organization. By maximizing autonomy for the organization's leaders, the shareholders encourage leaders to think and act like owners. Once leaders begin thinking and acting like an owner, they are fully accountable for the results of the organization. They don't blame others for failures, and they take responsibility for outcomes. Most successful leaders have a high preference for autonomy. This "empowerment by autonomy" type of shareholder interaction with management often leads to high job satisfaction for those managers. This high satisfaction then tends to promote management longevity because it satisfies a core human need for self-actualization.

QUESTION 3:

Can you learn people skills?

People skills can absolutely be learned. The art of leadership is hiring people who complement your strengths and offset your weaknesses. The right leader, with the night amount of humility, self-awareness and emotional fortitude, will realize quickly where new hires need to be made. Perhaps the leader is very low social. So, the leader hires a high social number two. Perhaps the leader is a philosopher type who does not find enjoyment in day-to-day operations. The leader hires an aggressive "get it done" type as their number two. Or perhaps the leader comes to the realization that coaching and motivation is not their strength. They might decide to hire a strong number two for exactly this role. The best leaders will apply this same process to everyone on their team to ensure that the right diversity of talent and execution ability is present, regardless of the leader's own innate people skills.

The possibilities for team configuration are endless, and they only depend on the open-mindedness of the leader to get out of their comfort zone, to bring in people that are fundamentally different than they are. In order to accomplish this, the leader must also be fully immune to the fear of competition from followers. If they fear hiring the right people to build a strong team, they will fail. If they have the right amount of humility and true self-awareness of their own personality type, strengths, and weaknesses, then anyone can learn to be a great people person.

QUESTION 4:

Why have a "boss-less" organization?

The "boss-less" organization is here to stay and will become ever more prevalent since it offers the most self-actualization and empowerment to the people in the organization. The trend toward boss-less organizations is driven by rapid technology changes that allow groups of people to work together with clear accountability for results for each team member. Progress on various tasks is readily apparent to all team members using today's collaborative technology.

> The amount of freedom you permit to your employees will determine how accountable they are for upholding their commitment to you.

This enforces the peer review effect whereby peers hold each other accountable and motivate those who may not be fully accountable on their own. Blockchain applications, a number of which are, by definition, "distributed

> The tribes that followed the leader who was the closest to reality survived. Those that didn't perished.

autonomous organizations" are a good example of this. There is no "one boss" of Ethereum, Cardano, or Solana, or any of the blockchains that are emerging as platforms for distributed autonomous applications and decentralized exchanges. Governments struggle to regulate blockchain precisely because there is often no one central authority. However, blockchains are booming. They offer more freedom and empowerment to individuals. Rigid top-down hierarchies that we see today in Google, Facebook, and Amazon face significant risk of disruption from the "distributed, autonomous, encrypted, decentralized, and tokenized" blockchains that empower individuals by allowing them to profit from data activities versus give up most of that profit to a central authority. All of this means the "boss-less" organization is going to thrive and leaders must learn to adapt.

Perhaps the most important skill for a leader in the boss-less world is vision and staying close to reality. In any group of human beings, the leader in the group is the person closest to reality. This is a survival mechanism that we humans developed many tens of thousands of years ago when we operated in small hunting tribes and had to decide who to follow. The tribes that followed the leader who was the closest to reality survived. Those that didn't perished. This implies that in a boss-less organization, different team members will become leaders, depending on who is the closest to reality in any given situation.

QUESTION 5:

What is the "Labor-Waste" elimination system under the "Scientific Management" school of thought?

Any management philosophy in today's world that attempts to treat highly diverse groups of individuals as the same and does not appreciate them as human beings in their own context is bound to fail. The best ideas and suggestions come from empowered front line team members who are the closest to the customer. Enlightened leaders will understand that the person with the best information is the leader on any given topic, and often that person is the frontline leader. Requiring standard methods at the expense of individual creativity can stifle innovation.

For some businesses, particularly those involved with physical assets, control of assets in some fashion is critical and scientific management can assist in training workers on standardized methods of control. For example, UPS has billions of dollars of machinery that moves every day and is highly dangerous if moved in the wrong direction: think airplanes, trucks and forklifts being driven in the wrong direction. People will get hurt. Contrast this with a software start-up where scientific management would kill the ethos and creativity of the company. Perhaps UPS will evolve its system over time to be more of a coaching system to individuals so they can develop their own unique strengths.

QUESTION 6:

Are you studying the future first?

A manager's success is directly related to the distance into the future that the manager can anticipate events, develop a vision, and empower their team to act in concert with that vision on a day-to-day basis. Studying the future is by far the most important role for a truly visionary leader. Studying the present is second, and studying the past should come last. The more business leaders study the past, the more likely they are to become mired in old business models, old ways of thinking and old habits.

A "re-evaluation of all values" is often necessary for a leader and their organization to survive rapid changes in technology, politics, regulation, climate, competition, levels of demand, and consumer tastes. Such a re-evaluation will certainly take into account all the facts from the past and present but, most importantly, it will be grounded in a clear view of future developments in their technology, cultural, consumer, political, and regulatory environment.

QUESTION 7:

Are you managing your people or your technology?

As organizations evolve in today's market, they are using more and more technology. However, that technology is becoming easier to use, easier to manage and far more seamless to integrate into an organization. Think about the ease of use of an iPhone versus a Blackberry. Today's cloud-based applications require little technology talent on the part of the organization that uses them. They are intentionally designed to empower the human side of the organization. As organizations shift more towards "boss-less" organizations, communication technology is critical to empower teams to hold each other accountable.

Yes, major technology decisions and in-house technology talent will always be important, particularly in the area of IT security. Likewise, technology talent will always be important for leaders to possess so that they can understand the technology trends that are impacting their business. A leader who is client-server focused, for example, will have already likely missed the transition to cloud technologies and may be entirely clueless on blockchain technologies which will disrupt the cloud.

QUESTION 8:

Should leaders fire a top-performer who doesn't adhere to the values of the organization?

Yes. It's always the right decision to fire an employee—regardless of their level of performance—if they don't fit the values and culture of an organization. For example, a high-performing employee may show disrespect for employees. In today's environment, this disrespect could very easily create far more liability for the company than any profits this "high-performing" employee produces. Someone who disrespects other people may also be prone to sexual harassment or other violations of various labor laws that could create liability for the company and drive away employees.

The current $3.5 trillion spending bill in Congress would also make directors and managers personally liable for violations of labor laws and proposes fines that could be very substantial if a manager fails to correct a persistently abusive employee situation. Fundamentally, a company's values system are only values if adherence to them is required. Values are nothing more than the behavior that is observed. Once you have an "exception to the values" practice, then the values become like Swiss cheese and stop meaning anything. A political environment develops where certain "friends of the boss" have special "privileges" in that they can routinely violate the company's values with impunity. This will not produce a healthy, well-functioning corporate environment. It will produce a highly politicized and ineffective work environment.

QUESTION 9:

How can leaders help their employees succeed so that they work harder?

The best thing a leader can do to motivate their employees is to help them succeed in their career. This means subordinating the leader's own ego and needs to the needs of the employee to receive the individualized coaching that will help the employee succeed. Every employee requires something different and, by giving this kind of individual one-on-one treatment to the employee, the leader will help the employee achieve greater career success.

The effective leader will also supplement their own leadership with leadership coaching from third parties, leadership training, and other career development tools that can help each of their employees succeed on their own individually chosen career path. The leader can also give the employee autonomy with a new project or task that can help the employee build confidence to move forward in their career. A leader who constantly takes from an employee by not appreciating the employee's need for a successful career will find both their employee's career and their own organization suffering. Managing employees requires nurturing and care over a long period of time. A leader who carelessly disregards the needs of an employee for respect and individual attention can lead to even the most loyal employees looking for a position elsewhere.

QUESTION 10:

What are some examples of transformational, transactional, and charismatic leadership?

Transformational leaders have the talent of being able to both create a long-term vision for the organization years, if not decades, into the future, while at the same time motivating team members to act in concert with that vision on a day-to-day basis. The longer the time span of the leader's vision that inspires the team to day-to-day action in concert with that vision, the more effective the leader will be. Given today's fast pace of change in environmental, social, technological, political, and regulatory environments, transformational leadership is required for any organization to be successful long-term. Some industries such as retail have been more rapidly transformed by technology than other industries and these require particularly transformational leadership.

Wal-Mart and Target have invested deeply in transformational e-commerce leadership and have seen their investments pay off with both retailers having fast-growing online businesses. Sears and Kmart took a different approach and did not invest in transformational e-commerce leadership, and they found themselves in bankruptcy.

Sometimes the company is in a short-term turnaround situation where transactional leadership is required instead of transformational leadership. For example, the cruise industry has been decimated by the Covid-19 pandemic. The successful cruise industry leaders were, by necessity, very transactionally focused on executing key financing priorities to provide sufficient liquidity for these businesses to survive the pandemic. In other cases, charismatic leadership is the most important leadership skill, particularly when the vision is clearly established, and the team requires motivation to "step up" to the task ahead of them. A charismatic leader can help the team climb a mountain that they did not think they could climb. Start-up leaders might fall into this category and use their charisma to help their team overcome the fear, uncertainty and doubt that are common in start-up situations. Start-up leaders might require charisma particularly when the vision for the new product or service is clear and the question is simply, can we build this product?

In summary, transformational leaders bring about innovation and change, and they challenge people to look at old problems in new ways. Transaction leaders clarify the role and task requirements, create structure, and provide rewards. Charismatic leaders inspire people to do more than they thought they could do.

QUESTION 11:

How can you empower followers?

Perhaps more attention is given to leadership than followership in management training and education because it's assumed that people want to strive to be leaders. Yet organizations consist mostly of team members and individual contributors, and the most effective organizations find ways to empower everyone on the team. For example, a highly effective organizational culture focuses on the value of team members by empowering followers to pursue their own critical thinking. The best cultures give everyone a chance to lead when they are the person in the room who is closest to reality. Anyone, regardless of rank, can be a leader if they are the person with the right answer for the leadership question or the right behavior of the leadership situation. A non-autocratic, non-hierarchical culture where followers are encouraged to speak up and challenge the status quo is critical for this type of "follower leadership" to develop.

In essence, an effective follower has the same traits as an effective leader: facing the brutal facts, close to reality, challenging and probing, contributing, and staying silent as necessary. In fact, being a good follower is a critical talent to learn before someone can be a good leader. One cannot command without first learning the discipline of how to obey. The prison experience is an excellent school in how to obey the hundreds of different rules we prisoners follow every day.

Learning how to obey all of the numerous and unforgiving rules of Federal Prison Camp Montgomery will make me a better commander and leader when I am "back on the street."

QUESTION 12:

What type of leadership do flat organizations require to thrive?

Leadership in today's flatter organizations is even more important than in hierarchical organizations, especially if you define leadership as a leader's self-awareness of which of their traits is a strength and which is a weakness in that organization. A flatter organization will require the leader to adapt to numerous leadership styles depending on the wider variety of team members who report to the leader. Some of these team members may require direct commands and direction, whereas others may require an entirely hands off, "check in with me once a year," approach.

The leader must have the self-awareness and emotional fortitude to manage across that entire spectrum. This diversity of management approache requires strict discipline on the part of the leader to conform their management style to the needs of the follower vs. their own egotistical needs. This is servant leadership at its best in terms of subordinating your ego to the ego needs of your team members.

QUESTION 13:

How can leaders become better communicators?

A training program to become a better communicator might include the following components:

a) Susan Scott's book *Fierce Conversations.* This book provides an extensive discussion on how the best cultures are very close to reality and provide numerous suggestions for ways managers can improve their ability to get the "elephants in the room" on the table for discussion. In a poorly functioning corporate culture, the "elephants in the room" are never discussed in meetings and are left for side conversations and gossip. A strong leader will address these matters squarely and publicly if needed to eliminate gossip and provide direction for the entire team, even if the message is one that people don't want to hear.

b) **A meeting code that the manager can use for meetings.** Some items on that code might be that everyone is given a chance to speak up. "We face the brutal facts without fear. We discuss the elephants in the room that people are afraid to talk about. If you don't participate, then why are you here? The leader in the room is the person closest to reality"...etc.

c) **Public speaking training.** Sometimes new managers may struggle with speaking before large groups. Training in this can improve presentation skills dramatically.

QUESTION 14:

Who needs to know what about strategic plans?

Does a minimum wage employee in the janitorial department at a hospital really need to understand the strategic plan for the hospital? Absolutely. Never underestimate the importance of front-line workers in helping organizations achieve their strategic plans. Management hubris often leads top-level executives to pay little or no attention to the feedback and ideas of front-line employees, particularly minimum wage employees such as the cleaning staff. This is always a mistake. A person's wage level does not determine the level of their ability to contribute to the organization.

For example, in today's COVID-19 era, if the front-line cleaning staff is not aware of the strategic plans of the hospital, the cleaning staff may not take the additional steps necessary to prevent the spread of COVID in the facility. This could then create a cascade of negative effects that can impact the strategic plan of the hospital. Perhaps the cleaning staff, unaware of the strategic plans, fails to take some action that then leads to a hospital-acquired COVID-19 infection, which then generates negative publicity for the hospital.

Another example: Currently, I am employed as janitor in the Education Department at Federal Prison Camp Montgomery, earning a minimum wage of around 30 cents per hour. As a minimum wage front-line employee, I greatly appreciate the opportunity to be included in any strategic plans and decisions of the prison Education Department. For example, the head of the department told me a few months ago that there was an important inspection coming up in November of this year and that she wanted to make sure the education building was extra clean ahead of the inspection. Knowing this strategic information, I suggested a fresh coat of paint on the interior walls of the department would go a long way to improving the overall appearance of the department. My supervisor agreed with this suggestion and proceeded to paint the interior walls of the building. In sum: frontline workers can have a direct and important impact on helping any organization achieve their strategic goals and, as such, they should be included in all communications on strategic plans.

Getting the right people on your bus is 90% of success.

QUESTION 15:

How do organizations hire the right people?

Getting the right people on your bus is 90% of success.

Human Resource Management (HRM) is the single most important strategic factor in driving organizational performance, especially in today's environment of rapid changes in technology, politics, regulation, social preferences, and consumer behaviors. The people in an organization are the most important determinant in the success or failure of that organization to continuously adapt to these rapid changes. An organization that can recruit and retain talent who can lead the organization through rapid transformation into new products, new services, and new vertical industries entirely can survive and thrive in the long run. An organization that fails to recruit and retain this talent won't make it.

QUESTION 16:

What's the top characteristic or talent leaders should have?

Self-awareness is one of the most critical talents a leader can have for a number of reasons. First, self-awareness allows the leader to determine, with a high degree of honesty, their own strengths and weaknesses. This, in turn, allows the leader to hire the right team members who complement those strengths and weaknesses. If the leader is sufficiently self-aware that they lack detail orientation, for example, they can choose to hire a very detailed number two on their team who can help them keep track of the various moving parts of the business. If the leader is self-aware of their low preference for social interaction, they can hire a team member with a high social preference to accommodate for this weakness.

Self-awareness is also critical in identifying your own feelings in various situations, and thus a self-aware individual is able to manage those feelings instead of having their feelings manage them. A simple example is a leader who is very aware of situations that make them angry, and they use this self-awareness to remove themselves quickly from those situations so that their anger does not lead them to make an emotional decision that could be damaging to their overall objectives.

QUESTION 17:

How can new managers build trust with their team?

A new manager can quickly build trust with subordinates by opening up and being vulnerable. For example, the manager could hand out all their psychological profile results to team members and invite the team members to discuss the manager's strengths and weaknesses. This would open up the discussion to everyone's strengths and weaknesses, and could go a long way to establishing trust with subordinates.

When I was in a direct leadership role, I would hand out, an entire package of my psychological test results including Meyers-Briggs, Culture Index, and 360 Degree survey results from various leadership development programs, to my team members. One of the first things I will do when I am released from prison is to attend the Center for Creative Leadership's Leadership at the Peak program. I attended this program 15 years ago and it provided valuable feedback to me from my team members and led to numerous new areas for improvement in my behavior. Attending such a program and being vulnerable by sharing that feedback with my team members will enhance the trust that I have built with the Global Growth team members.

QUESTION 18:

What's the best way to measure employee success?

Humans must have some measurement of their progress in life to remain motivated. Trying to remain motivated at any work or personal pursuit is like bowling without seeing the pins. It won't be satisfying for very long. On a psychological level, the human brain releases endorphins and dopamine when a task is accomplished. I find myself, for example, looking forward to the psychological reward of checking items off my to-do list. This is because my brain has become accustomed to the shot of neurohormones that are released when I accomplish something on that list. So, in a very real way, giving team members regular rewards and appreciation as evidence of their progress towards their goals becomes a psychologically necessary part of their brain chemistry. Perhaps some people even become addicted to these rewards.

> ... on a quantum level reality does not exist unless it's measured.

On a deeper, quantum physics level, all reality exists in the superposition and classical reality is only "created" when the wavelength of the superposition is collapsed through observation and measurement. So, quite literally, on a quantum level reality does not exist unless it's measured. If there is no measurement and no observation of a specific event then, from the classical reality perspective of others, that action does not exist. Quantum mechanics also stipulates that certain quantum particles can be "paired," while others are not paired. This pairing of particles was called "spooky action at a distance" by Einstein; however, it's not all that spooky in that quantum computers are based on the quantum pairing of photons. It's entirely possible that the unrecognized, unobserved, and unmeasured team member has far fewer photon pairings on a quantum level than the team member who is well-recognized, well-observed, and well-measured.

Management science (unlike computer science) has not yet crossed over into the field of quantum mechanics. But it's possible that, when it does, managers will realize that their contagious enthusiasm and motivational communication and appreciation for their team members is creating a pairing of quantum particles that is a much deeper linkage than the psychological linkages of classical reality.

QUESTION 19:

How can organizations help employees find pleasure in their work?

It is absolutely a leader's responsibility to help people find all three pathways to happiness in their work: pleasure, engagement, and meaning. Humans spend far too much time "working" to not find all three components of happiness in their work. My father gave my one piece of career advice: do what you love and you will never work a day in your life. He was an airline pilot and he often said that he would "fly for free." In fact, after he retired, he purchased a small airplane and did exactly that.

The Global Growth business has always been a labor of love for me, and I have never seen anything that I do related to Global Growth as work. This created stress from my failed marriage when my wife accused me of loving my business more than I loved her. In hindsight, there was likely some truth to her comment. For the three decades of building my business, I found great pleasure in learning and growing intellectually as the business grew, and great engagement and meaning in what we were able to accomplish.

As a leader, I want to bring this same joy and empowerment to everyone who works for Global Growth. The key for me in helping others find their three pathways of happiness at Global Growth is encouraging relentless personal growth The never-ending process of learning creates pleasure through increased neural connections in the cerebral cortex as well as through releases of endorphins and dopamine from accomplishing various tasks. Likewise, all of our companies deliver Global Good on their respective industries, which gives our work meaning.

QUESTION 20:

How can managers motivate employees?

Herzberg's two factor theory of motivation postulates that there are two factors in a person's motivation: those factors that motivate the person and those factors that de-motivate the person. In my experience, this theory is precisely correct, and it has the added benefit of a loving manager to hire self-motivated people so that they only have to worry about removing the demotivators. If self-motivated people are placed in an environment where they have sufficient responsibility and authority that they can drive their own achievement and personal growth, then they do not require recognition from their superiors or other motivating influences from the organization. What they require instead is that the organization remove the "areas of dissatisfaction," as Herzberg calls them: poor working conditions, company bureaucracy, micromanaging supervisors, and poor company culture.

The owners of Zimmerman's Community of Businesses appear to have adopted this approach using the Herzberg theory to motivate their team members. They removed bureaucracy. They gave people opportunities to grow on a professional basis. They encouraged people to take significant responsibility, including giving one employee the role of leading a start-up.

QUESTION 21:

What are the most common ways your career can be derailed?

1. Associating with the wrong people and letting the wrong people into your life.

2. Lack of humility to learn.

3. Becoming enamored with being the boss and forgetting you got here by being a student.

4. Failing to learn from everyone you meet.

5. Fear of learning new morals, new cultures, and new technologies.

6. Fear to expand beyond your comfort zone.

7. Inability to launch visionary new initiatives to rejuvenate your business or organization.

8. Becoming satisfied and content with the existing status quo.

9. Narrow-minded thinking about global talent, offshoring & multi-sharing.

10. Fear of losing your position.

11. Untrustworthiness; playing politics.

12. Failure to read broadly all manner of books, magazines, newsletters, newspapers, and research reports to keep your knowledge fresh.

13. Failure to demand "A players" in every seat on your bus.

14. Lack of self-awareness.

15. Inability to see one's weaknesses and inability to hire the right people to compensate for those weaknesses.

16. Failure to appreciate the environmental improvement.

17. Making your organization all about you instead of all about your team and your customers.

18. Impatience.

19. Inability to master finance and capital markets.

20. Taking credit instead of giving credit to your team.

QUESTION 22:

What is the single most important factor distinguishing a successful leader?

Your Timespan of Management

The caliber of your leadership is directly proportionate to the distance in the future you can plan your actions and act consistently in the present with those plans.

Perhaps the single most important distinguishing factor for a successful leader is how far they can extend their vision into the future while, at the same time, acting today with relentless discipline toward that vision. The length of time that you can stretch your discipline over is directly proportional to your talent as a leader. Intentional fasting is a simple example. You are the leader of 37 trillion cells in your body and even more tens of trillions of bacteria and microbes that live inside you and are critical to sustaining life. This community of hundreds of trillions of individual units has only one leader that is responsible for the life and death of the entire community. And that is you. Intermittent fasting has been shown by dozens of highly credible medical studies to turn on autopilot, which is the body's built-in repair mechanism. This, in turn, removes the "junk" that accumulates in cells from the cells to avoid cellular breakdown and malfunction. Autophagy is like changing the oil on your car. It is a necessary maintenance routine. Over years and decades, regular maintenance will have a dramatic impact on any system. The challenge with intermittent fasting is the extraordinary daily discipline it requires. So, do you have the type of management to lead your body's hundreds of trillions of individual units to a longer life decades from now with specific disciplined action today? To be a powerful leader, you will have to master extraordinary discipline and focus on a daily and hourly basis that drives towards your life vision. Act today and every day in harmony with where you want your company and life to be in 50 years. If you think and act for results and rewards today, you are not a leader. There is nothing wrong with not being a leader, as long as you recognize your place on the bus. For tens of thousands of years, we humans were hunter-gatherers, and the leader was the person who could guide the tribe in concert with the long-term survival of everyone in the tribe. They were the most disciplined and the closest to reality with their day-to-day actions to carry out a long-term goal of survival.

APPENDICES

APPENDIX A:
Taking the Bullets—My Case

Forth Circuit Opinions: Text and audio can be found here:
https://www.ca4.uscourts.gov/cal/internetcaldec072021ric.pdf
https://www.ca4.uscourts.gov/opinions/204470.P.pdf

IN THE UNITED STATES DISTRICT COURT
FOR THE WESTERN DISTRICT OF NORTH CAROLINA
Statesville Division

No. 5:19-cr-22-MOC-DSC
UNITED STATES OF AMERICA,
v.
GREG E. LINDBERG, et al.,
Defendants.

MEMORANDUM IN SUPPORT OF DEFENDANT GREG LINDBERG'S MOTION FOR JUDGMENT OF ACQUITTAL UNDER RULE 29(c) OR, ALTERNATIVELY, FOR A NEW TRIAL UNDER RULE 33

Aaron Zachary Tobin (N.C. Bar. No. 50019) CONDON TOBIN SLADEK THORNTON, PLLC
8080 Park Lane, Suite 700
Dallas, TX 75231
214-265-3800
atobin@ctstlaw.com

Paul J. Johnson (admitted *pro hac vice*)
900 Jackson Street, Suite 650
Dallas, TX 75202
214-761-0707
pjjdoc@aol.com

Rajesh R. Srinivasan (admitted pro hac vice) KATTEN MUCHIN ROSENMAN LLP
2900 K Street, NW – Suite 200
Washington, DC 20007
202-625-3500
rajesh.srinivasan@katten.com

Brandon N. McCarthy
(admitted *pro hac vice*)
Rachel M. Riley (*admitted pro hac vice*)
KATTEN MUCHIN ROSENMAN LLP
1717 Main Street, Suite 3750
Dallas, TX 75201
214-765-3600
brandon.mccarthy@katten.com
rachel.riley@katten.com

Jeffrey C. Grady (N.C. Bar. No. 32695)
KATTEN MUCHIN ROSENMAN LLP
550 S. Tryon Street, Suite 2900
Charlotte, NC 28202
704-444-2036
jeff.grady@katten.com

Counsel for Defendant Greg E. Lindberg

TABLE OF CONTENTS

TABLE OF AUTHORITIES

CASES:

OTHER AUTHORITIES:

INTRODUCTION

Under Federal Rules of Criminal Procedure 29(c) and 33, Defendant Greg E. Lindberg moves for a judgment of acquittal for the reasons stated below and renews all his prior motions for a judgment of acquittal. Tr. 1253:24-1266:23, 1269:1-20, 1272:18-19, 1277:4-10, 1508:24-1509:5; Def.

Greg E. Lindberg's Suppl. To Oral Mot. For Judgment of Acquittal, Dkt. No. 192 ("Rule 29 Suppl."). In the alternative, Mr. Lindberg moves for a new trial for the reasons stated in this memorandum and for the reasons stated in support of prior motions for a judgment of acquittal. See Tr. 1253:24-1266:23, 1269:1-20, 1272:18-19, 1277:4-10, 1508:24-1509:5; Rule 29 Suppl.[1]

LEGAL STANDARD

A "court on the defendant's motion must enter a judgment of acquittal of any offense for which the evidence is insufficient to sustain a conviction." Fed. R. Crim. P. 29(a). "The test for deciding a motion for a judgment of acquittal is whether there is substantial evidence (direct or circumstantial) which, taken in the light most favorable to the prosecution, would warrant a jury finding that the defendant was guilty beyond a reasonable doubt." *United States v. MacCloskey*, 682 F.2d 468, 473 (4th Cir. 1982). Notably, "[s]ubstantial evidence" does not mean merely "a scintilla" of evidence. *United States v. Taylor,* 800 F.3d 701, 711 (6th Cir. 2015) (quoting *United States v. Martin*, 375 F.2d 956, 957 (6th Cir. 1967)). Rather, "substantial evidence is evidence that a reasonable finder of fact could accept as adequate and sufficient to support a conclusion of a defendant's guilt beyond a reasonable doubt." *United States v. Burgos*, 94 F.3d 849, 862 (4th Cir. 1996).

---

[1] As the defendants informed the Court in a February 19, 2020, filing, the government began producing hundreds of thousands of pages of discovery that it deemed could be potentially relevant to the case just days before trial. Dkt. No. 161. The government continued producing documents until February 18, 2020, the date of jury voir dire and arguments on the motions in limine. Given the volume of discovery, Mr. Lindberg has been unable to review all these documents. Mr. Lindberg thus reserves the right to bring a motion under 28 U.S.C. § 2255 or the Federal Rules of Criminal Procedure if continued review of the documents reveals *Brady* or other material whose earlier disclosures were required.

If the Court denies a motion for judgment of acquittal, it may nonetheless "vacate any judgment and grant a new trial if the interest of justice so requires." Fed. R. Crim. P. 33. Various circumstances satisfy this standard. "When the evidence weighs so heavily against the verdict that it would be unjust to enter judgment, the court should grant a new trial." *United States v. Arrington*, 757 F.2d 1484, 1485 (4th Cir. 1985). A court may also order a new trial where "a defendant was unduly harmed or his trial made unfair by the erroneous admission or exclusion of evidence." *United States v. Fuentes*, No. 13-cr-0125, 2015 WL 144409, at *3 (E.D. Wash. Jan. 12, 2015) (citing *United States v. Johnson*, 337 F.2d 180, 203 (4th Cir. 1964)), *aff'd sub nom. United States v. Alarcon*, 682 F. App'x 556 (9th Cir. 2017) (non-precedential); see also *United States v. Lis*, 120 F.3d 28, 29 (4th Cir. 1997) (ordering a new trial based on the erroneous exclusion of evidence); *United States v. Stapleton*, 730 F. Supp. 1375, 1380 (W.D. Va. 1990) (ordering a new trial when the admission of evidence was "improper" and created "unfair[ ] prejudice[ ]"). Improper jury instructions also justify a new trial. See *McDonnell v. United States*, 136 S. Ct. 2355, 2375 (2016).

In deciding whether to order a new trial, "the court's authority is much broader than when it is deciding a motion to acquit on the ground of insufficient evidence." *Arrington*, 757 F.2d at 1485. For example, "the district court is not constrained by the requirement that it view the evidence in the light most favorable to the government," and it "may evaluate the credibility of the witnesses." *Id.*

ARGUMENT

I. **A Properly Instructed, Reasonable Jury Could Not Have Found the Existence of an "Official Act," an Essential Element of the Offenses.**

The Supreme Court's decision in *McDonnell v. United States*, 136 S. Ct. 2355 (2016), points up three deficiencies in the verdicts rendered by the jury—all related to the required element of an "official act." As explained below, these deficiencies require the Court to set aside the verdicts in their entirety and, ultimately, enter a judgment of acquittal on both counts brought against Mr. Lindberg.

First, the Court's instruction to the jury on "official act" had the effect of relieving the government of proving this critical element beyond a reasonable doubt. In *McDonnell,* the Supreme Court held that "[i]t is up to the jury, under the facts of the case, to determine whether the public official agreed to perform an 'official act' at the time of the alleged *quid pro quo.*" 136 S. Ct. at 2371. And the Supreme Court has held elsewhere that "the jury's constitutional responsibility is not merely to determine the facts, but to apply the law to those facts and draw the ultimate conclusion of guilt or innocence." *United States v. Gaudin*, 515 U.S. 506, 514 (1995). Here, however, after informing the jury that the government's theory of official act was premised on "the removal and replacement of the senior deputy commissioner in charge of overseeing the regulatory review of Defendant Lindberg's insurance companies," the Court applied the law to the facts for the jury:

You're hereby instructed that the removal or replacement of a senior deputy commissioner by the commissioner would constitute an official act.

Tr. 1781:2-7. As explained below, this instruction had the effect of taking the element of an official act away from the jury. At a minimum, then, the Court must order a new trial on Count One, which charged conspiracy to commit honest-services wire fraud.

Second, the Court is required to enter a judgment of acquittal on Count One because, even viewing the evidence in the light most favorable to the government, no reasonable jury could have concluded that the removal and replacement of the senior deputy commissioner constituted an official act. As the Supreme Court clarified in *McDonnell,* the jury was required to find, among other things, that the defendants intended to influence "a formal exercise of governmental power that is similar in nature to a lawsuit, administrative determination, or hearing." 136 S. Ct. at 2370. Here, however, there was undisputed evidence that the Commissioner reassigned matters through informal conversation. Tr. 593:6-594:2; *id.* at 1216:13-24; *id.* at 95:3-14. And North Carolina law clarifies that any formal exercise of the Commissioner's authority had to be "made in writing and signed by the Commissioner or by his authority." N.C. Gen. Stat. § 58-2-45. Critically, the evidence undermined the basis upon which the Court saved the indictment at the motion-to-dismiss stage. At that time, the Court referenced the Commissioner's statutory authority to "appoint" and "employ" new deputies, N.C. Gen. Stat. § 58-2-25, analogizing it to the congressional hiring decision at issue in *United States v. Fattah*, 914 F.3d 112 (3d Cir. 2019). See Mot. to Dismiss Order at 8, Dkt. No. 120. At trial, however, it became apparent that the removal and replacement of a senior deputy commissioner did not involve the same level of formality as the hiring of a new employee at the Department. Thus, as explained in further detail below, because the act that the government sought to prove at trial is neither formal nor similar to a "lawsuit, hearing, or administrative determination," *McDonnell*, 136 S. Ct. at 2368, the Court must enter a judgment of acquittal on the Count One—conspiracy to commit honest-services wire fraud.

Finally, the requirement of an official act applies with the same force to the second count of the indictment—federal-program bribery under 18 U.S.C. § 666. That outcome is dictated by the logic of *McDonnell*. There, the Supreme Court was able to avoid three constitutional infirmities—implicating the First Amendment, vagueness, and federalism—only because it read into honest-services wire fraud the "official act" element of the federal anti-bribery statute, 18 U.S.C. § 201. *Id.* at 2372-73. As explained below, because § 666 would otherwise implicate the same constitutional infirmities, the Court must read § 666 to also require proof of an official act. Yet, over Mr. Lindberg's objection, the Court refused to instruct the jury that it must find an official act to convict under § 666. At a minimum, then, a new trial is required on Count Two. And for the reasons explained above and below, because no reasonable jury could have concluded that the removal and replacement of the senior deputy commissioner was an official act, the Court must also enter a judgment of acquittal on this count.

A. The Instruction on "Official Act" Deprived Mr. Lindberg of His Right to Have a Jury Determine this Critical Element of the Charged Offenses.

The Fifth Amendment guarantees that no one will be deprived of liberty without "due process of law," and the Sixth Amendment guarantees that, "[i]n all criminal prosecutions, the accused shall enjoy the right to a speedy and public trial, by an impartial jury." U.S. Const. amends. V, VI. These guarantees include "the right to have a jury determine, beyond a reasonable doubt, [the defendant's] guilt of every element of the crime with which he is charged." *Gaudin*, 515 U.S. at 522-23.

Thus, although the Court is responsible for instructing the jury "on the law applicable to the issues raised at trial," the "next two steps are strictly for the jury: (1) determining the facts as to each element of the crime, and (2) applying the law as instructed by the judge to those facts." *United States v. Johnson*, 71 F.3d 139, 142 (4th Cir. 1995). Here, the Court's instruction failed both steps.[2] Moreover, as explained further below, because these errors were structural—that is, "they 'defy analysis by "harmless-error" standards'"—the verdicts are *per se* invalid. *United States v. Ramirez- Castillo*, 748 F.3d 205, 214-16 (4th Cir. 2014) (quoting *Arizona v. Fulminante*, 499 U.S. 279, 309 (1991)); *see also Johnson*, 71 F.3d at 144-45 (holding that, where an instruction relieved the jury of its obligation to find an essential element of the offense, the error was structural and harmless-error analysis did not apply). At a minimum, then, this Court must order a new trial.

> 1. **The Court's Instruction Did Not Require the Jury to Find All of the Facts Necessary to Find an Official Act.**

As an initial matter, the Court's instruction relieved the jury of its obligation to find all of the facts necessary to determine whether the defendants intended to influence an "official act." According to the Court, the jury was simply required to determine whether the defendants intended to secure "the removal and replacement of the senior deputy commissioner in charge of overseeing the regulatory review of Defendant Lindberg's insurance companies." Tr. 1781:2-4. The Court made clear that, once the jury resolved that issue, its inquiry was at an end:

---

[2] Mr. Lindberg preserved this objection at the charge conference, Tr. 1579:13-1580:3, 1583:2-12, 1584:20-25, and through a supplemental filing objecting to the Court's proposed instruction, *see* Defs.' Response in Support of Gov't's Mem. Regarding the Jury's Right to Decide Official-Act Element, Dkt. No. 190. In addition, Mr. Lindberg's proposed instructions preserving the issue of an official act for the jury. *See* Defs.' Joint Proposed Jury Instructions 88-90 (Proposed Instruction No. 74); *see also* Resp. to Gov't's Preliminary Objection to Defs. Proposed Jury Instr., Dkt. No. 159. Mr. Lindberg also preserved objections to the other parts of the instruction for both honest-services wire fraud and

§ 666(a)(2) that excluded the defendants' proposed instructions. Tr. 1579:13-1580:3, 1584:20-25; *also*

Resp. to Gov't's Preliminary Objection to Defs. Proposed Jury Instr. 10-11.

"You're hereby instructed that the removal or replacement of a senior deputy commissioner by the commissioner would constitute an official act." *Id.* at 1781:4-7; *see also id.* at 1465:12-16 ("The thing I'm not going to allow is that—it's not going to do you any good to get up there and argue this was not an official act when I'm going to tell the jury during the charge it is an official act."); *id.* at 1466:5-8 (explaining that "if somebody argues to the jury that this is not an official act, then I'll have to step in and say the Court's going to rule that it is an official act.").

This was error. *McDonnell* makes clear that a jury must resolve much more than whether the defendant intended to influence the government action that is said to constitute the official act. As such, a jury must be instructed that, before finding an official act, it is obliged to—

- identify a "'question, matter, cause, suit, proceeding or controversy' [] involv[ing] a formal exercise of governmental power that is similar in nature to a lawsuit before a court, a determination before an agency, or a hearing before a committee";

- decide that "the pertinent 'question, matter, cause, suit, proceeding or controversy'" is "something specific and focused that is 'pending' or 'may by law be brought before any public official'"; and

- find that the public official "made a decision or took an action—or agreed to do so—

on the identified 'question, matter, cause, suit, proceeding, or controversy.'" *McDonnell*, 136 S. Ct. at 2371-72, 74-75; *accord United States v. Van Buren*, 940 F.3d 1192, 1204 (11th Cir. 2019). Equally important, the Supreme Court clarified that it is "up to the jury, under the facts of the case, to determine whether the public official agreed to perform an 'official act' at the time of the alleged *quid pro quo*." *McDonnell*, 136 S. Ct. at 2371.

Thus, under *McDonnell*, the issue whether the Senior Deputy Commissioner was removed and replaced was just one component of the jury's fact finding. The jury also had to find that the removal and replacement of the Senior Deputy Commissioner amounted to an "official act."

And yet, here, the Court instructed the jury that it need not resolve the three issues that the Supreme Court held were essential to the charge at issue in *McDonnell*. Specifically, after reciting the law generally, the Court said that, "*[i]n this case*," the relevant "question or matter is the removal and replacement of the senior deputy commissioner," and "[y]ou're hereby instructed that the removal or replacement of a senior deputy commissioner by the commissioner *would constitute an official act.*" Tr. 1781:1-7 (emphasis added). The instruction therefore relieved the jury of its obligation to find critical facts that, the Supreme Court has held, are "up to the jury" to decide. *McDonnell*, 136 S. Ct. at 2371.

At least two cases illustrate the error in the Court's instruction. In *Medley v. Runnels*, after a defendant allegedly used a flare gun during the commission of a crime, he was charged with a violation of a California statute that included an enhancement for using a "firearm." 506 F.3d 857, 864 (9th Cir. 2007) (en banc). A State court had allowed the jury to determine whether the defendant used the flare gun, but it instructed the jury that a flare gun was a firearm within the meaning of the statute under which he was prosecuted. In a federal habeas action, an en banc panel of the Ninth Circuit held that this instruction violated the defendant's "clearly established" Fifth and Sixth Amendment rights: "By instructing the jury that a flare gun is a firearm, the court did not permit the jury to make the factual determination as to whether the object used by [the defendant] was designed to be used as a weapon and expels a projectile through a barrel by the force of an explosion." *Id.* at 864, 867.

As a second example, in *United States v. DeFries*, two former union officials were charged with, among other things, violations of the Racketeer Influenced and Corrupt Organizations Act. 129 F.3d 1293, 1296-97 (D.C. Cir. 1997) (per curiam). On the enterprise element, the district court had explained that the indictment alleged that the enterprise was a specific union and its successor union. It then instructed the jury "'that, for purposes of this element of counts one and two, you should regard the two unions as a single enterprise.'" *Id.* at 1310 (emphasis omitted). The District of Columbia Circuit reversed: "The district court's RICO instruction did not obligate the government to prove the existence of an enterprise. Instead the instructions on the enterprise element concluded with the admonition that the jury 'should regard the two unions as a single enterprise.'" *Id.* at 1311; *see also id.* ("Rather than permitting the jury to determine whether an enterprise existed, and, if it did, which unions it included, the instruction removed those questions from the jury's consideration.").

A similar infirmity plagues the instructions at issue here. The Court allowed the jury to determine whether the defendants intended to influence the removal and replacement of the senior deputy commissioner, but on the critical issue of whether that action constituted an official act, the Court concluded with an admonition: "You're hereby instructed that the removal or replacement of a senior deputy commissioner by the commissioner would constitute an official act." Tr. 1781:4-7 (emphasis added). That was error.3

Because the jury was not instructed to find every fact necessary on the element of an official act, the Court must set aside the jury's verdict on this ground alone. The Court's decision to treat "official act" as beyond the province of the jury violated bedrock principles of constitutional law.

2. The Court's Instruction Relieved the Jury of Its Obligation to Apply the Law to the Facts.

The Court's instruction also deprived the jury of its duty to apply the law to the facts as it found them. As the Supreme Court recognized in *United States v. Gaudin*, "the jury's constitutional responsibility is not merely to determine the facts, but to apply the law to those facts and draw the ultimate conclusion of guilt or innocence." 515 U.S. 506, 514 (1995). "Thus, although a judge may direct a verdict for the defendant if the evidence is legally insufficient to establish guilt, he may not direct a verdict for the [government]"—even a partial verdict—"no matter how overwhelming the evidence." *Sullivan v. Louisiana*, 508 U.S. 275, 277 (1993); *see also DeFries*, 129 F.3d at 1311-12 ("The court may never direct a verdict for the government on an element of a criminal offense, 'no matter how overwhelming the evidence.'" (quoting *Sullivan*, 508 U.S. at 277)). And yet, that is exactly what the Court did here.

---

[3] The Court's instruction also assumes that the removal and replacement of a senior deputy commissioner is a fixed process that cannot change over time or vary among insurance departments. This, in turn, shows that the Court was engaged in fact-finding reserved for the jury. For example, an insurance department might assign its deputies to review insurers with the same formality that a federal agency assigns administrative law judges to adjudicate administrative disputes, whereas another department might assign deputies through informal conversation (as was the case here). By instructing the jury that the removal or replacement of a senior deputy commissioner would constitute an official act in every instance, the Court was determining a factual issue that only the jury could resolve. *See, e.g., United States v. Uchimura*, 125 F.3d 1282, 1285 (9th Cir. 1997) (explaining that, on the mixed question of materiality, the answer "in each case is necessarily different").

On the ultimate question of whether the contemplated action amounted to an "official act," the Court resolved that question for the jury: "You're hereby instructed that the removal or replacement of a senior deputy commissioner by the commissioner would constitute an official act." Tr. 1781:4-7. And the Court was clear that it erroneously viewed this inquiry as the province of the Court: "So what it is down to is the Court making a determination, the Court believes, legally as to whether something is an official act under the statute." *Id.* at 1451:2-4.

Once again, two cases illustrate the error in this aspect of the Court's instruction. In *Gaudin*, for example, the district court instructed the jury that, to convict the defendant of making false statements, the government was required to prove that the defendant made the statement in question. *See* 515 U.S. at 508. But, the district court continued, "You are instructed that the statements charged in the indictment are material statements." *Id.* (internal quotation mark omitted). Writing for a unanimous court, Justice Scalia explained that this instruction amounted to reversible error, because the Constitution guarantees the "right of criminal defendants to demand that the jury decide guilt or innocence on every issue, which includes application of the law to the facts." *Id.* at 513; *see also, e.g., United States v. DiRico*, 78 F.3d 732, 736 (1st Cir. 1996) (explaining that the Constitution "requires the jury to apply the legal definition of materiality to the particular facts of a given case").

As a second example, in *United States v. Ramirez-Castillo*, the Fourth Circuit recognized that "the jury's constitutional responsibility is not merely to determine the facts, but to apply the law to those facts and *draw the ultimate conclusion of guilt or innocence.*" 748 F.3d 205, 214 (4th Cir. 2014) (quoting *Gaudin*, 515 U.S. at 514 (internal quotation mark omitted). In that case, the defendant was charged with two counts of possession of a prohibited object while in prison in violation of 18 U.S.C. § 1791. The district court gave the jury a special verdict form that asked it to determine whether the government's exhibits were prohibited objects within the meaning of the statute, but it never asked the jury to resolve the ultimate question of guilt. *Id.* at 208-09, 213-14. The Fourth Circuit vacated the defendant's conviction, explaining that "the district court erred when it treated the jury as a mere fact finder with respect to the elements the court considered to be in dispute, and thereby prevented the jury from making the ultimate, indispensable conclusion of whether [the defendant] was guilty." *Id.* at 214.

A similar error occurred here. The Court decided for itself the elements of "official act" that it considered to be in dispute, and thereby prevented the jury from determining whether the contemplated action amounted to an official act. Tr. 1781:4-7.

Notably, even the government raised concerns about the Court's instruction. In a highly unusual exchange in which the government pleaded with the Court to reconsider its instruction, the prosecutor explained: "My only concern is that the way that the Supreme Court has come down, *McDonnell*—with *McDonnell* and the courts post-*McDonnell* is with respect to a jury instruction and leaving it up to the jury." Tr. 1453:20-23; id. at 1456:15-19 (responding to the Court that official act is a "jury question"). And the government submitted a supplemental memorandum highlighting its concern with the Court's proposed instruction. *See* Dkt. No. 186.

In response to the government's plea for an amended instruction, the Court offered two rationales. Neither is correct.

First, the Court stated that "the Supreme Court [wa]s not saying [in *McDonnell*] that [an official act is] a jury question." Tr. 1454:9-10. But that view runs contrary to the Supreme Court's admonition in *McDonnell*: "It is up to the jury, under the facts of the case, to determine whether the public official agreed to perform an 'official act' at the time of the alleged quid pro quo." 136 S. Ct. at 2371. And it also contradicts the procedural posture of that case. After finding the district court's instruction deficient, the Supreme Court remanded to the Fourth Circuit for a determination whether the evidence was sufficient to sustain the conviction against Governor McDonnell. *Id.* at 2375.

But even if the Fourth Circuit held that the evidence was sufficient under the new standard for an "official act," the Supreme Court recognized that Governor McDonnell still would have been entitled to "a new trial" precisely because only a jury can apply the facts to the correct legal standard and render guilt. *Id.*

As a second rationale for its instruction here, the Court stated that "it cannot be that a jury in the same state can find an act to be unofficial and another jury find it to be official when it's the same act." Tr. 1454:21-23. But *Gaudin* and *Sullivan* hold otherwise: "[A]lthough a judge may direct a verdict for the defendant if the evidence is legally insufficient to establish guilt, he may not direct a verdict for the [government], no matter how overwhelming the evidence." *Sullivan*, 508 U.S. at 277; *see also Gaudin*, 515 U.S. at 513 (holding that, where a defendant invokes his right to trial by jury, only the jury may apply "the law to the facts" and decide guilt). Indeed, under the Constitution, two juries could—and sometimes do—*hear the exact same evidence* and render *contradictory verdicts*. But that is the bargain the framers struck when they refused to "entrust plenary powers over the life and liberty of the citizen to one judge or to a group of judges." *Duncan v. Louisiana*, 391 U.S. 145, 156 (1968).

To be sure, the public and elected officials need some level of certainty so that they can comport their conduct to what the law requires. *See* Tr. 1452:21-23 (lamenting that the law needs to provide elected officials with certainty otherwise the public would not know what the law forbids). But that certainty is not secured by the right to a trial by jury. It is secured instead by the Due Process Clause and its mandate that "a penal statute define the criminal offense with sufficient definiteness that ordinary people can understand what conduct is prohibited and in a manner that does not encourage arbitrary and discriminatory enforcement." *Kolender v. Lawson*, 461 U.S. 352, 357 (1983). A court can enforce that definiteness in a case where the indictment fails to allege a violation of the offense, or where the government fails to submit evidence sufficient to sustain a conviction beyond a reasonable doubt. But once the court determines that the facts alleged and proved could constitute an offense, it is up to the jury to decide guilt. Otherwise, the court's ruling would have the effect of directing a verdict for the government—something it can never do. *Sullivan*, 508 U.S. at 277.

3. **The Court's Error is Structural, But Even if It Were Not, the Government Cannot Sustain Its Burden of Demonstrating that the Error Was Harmless Beyond a Reasonable Doubt.**

The Fourth Circuit has held that where, as here, an instruction relieves the government of its burden to prove an element beyond a reasonable doubt, that error is structural and not susceptible to harmless error analysis. In these situations, the court has an obligation to aside the verdict.

In *United States v. Johnson*, for example, the defendant was charged with, among other things, one count of armed robbery of a credit union in violation of 18 U.S.C. § 2113. 71 F.3d 139, 141 (4th Cir. 1995). On this count, the district court instructed the jury: "'You are told that the [Arlington Schools Federal Credit Union] is a credit union within the terms of [the charged] statute.'" *Id.* The Fourth Circuit held that this instructed violated the defendant's constitutional right to have a jury determine the facts of each element and apply the law to those facts. *Id.* at 142-43. The court of appeals then turned to the question of remedy. Relying on *Sullivan v. Louisiana*, 508 U.S. 275 (1993), the Fourth Circuit held that, where the jury was relieved of an element, "the entire premise of harmless error review" is "absent": "'There being no jury verdict of guilty-beyond-a-reasonable-doubt, the question whether the *same* verdict of guilty-beyond-a-reasonable-doubt would have been rendered absent the constitutional error is utterly meaningless. There is no *object*, so to speak, upon which harmless-error scrutiny can operate.'" *Johnson*, 71 F.3d at 143-44 (quoting *Sullivan*, 508 U.S. at 280).

The Fourth Circuit reached a similar result in *United States v. Ramirez-Castillo*, 748 F.3d 205 (4th Cir. 2014). There, as discussed above, the Fourth Circuit held that the district court violated the defendant's constitutional rights by giving the jury a special verdict form that asked whether the government's exhibits amounted to prohibited objects under 18 U.S.C. § 1791, but never asked the jury to render a verdict of guilty. *Id.* at 213-14. According to the Fourth Circuit, because "the district court in effect directed a guilty verdict for the Government," the error was "structural" and a harmless- error analysis did not apply. *Id.* at 216.[4]

The same outcome is compelled here. As explained above, the Court's instruction had the effect of directing a partial verdict for the government on the element of an official act. It both deprived the jury of its obligation to resolve every fact necessary to find an official act and prevented the jury from exercising its duty to apply the law to the facts. As a result, the remedy is automatic: the Court must, at minimum, order a new trial.

In opposition, the government might argue that this Court should nonetheless apply a harmless-error analysis. But that will get the government nowhere. Even if the Court's error were susceptible to such an analysis, the government cannot establish that the Court's instructional error was harmless beyond a reasonable doubt. *See, e.g., Neder v. United States*, 527 U.S. 1, 15-16 (1999) (holding that, under a traditional harmless-error analysis, the government bears the burden of showing that the error was harmless beyond a reasonable doubt).[5]

---

[4] *See also DeFries,* 129 F.3d at 1312 n.13 ("The district court's failure to allow the jury to decide the enterprise element was, *per se,* a reversible error."); *DiRico,* 78 F.3d at 737 ("Here, because the jury did not determine whether the government had proved, beyond a reasonable doubt, the existence of an essential factual element of the crime of false subscription (*i.e.,* materiality), there was 'no jury verdict within the meaning of the Sixth Amendment;' and harmless error analysis is inapplicable."); *United States v. Kerley,* 838 F.2d 932, 937 (7th Cir. 1988) ("Nevertheless, not only does the harmless-error doctrine not apply when the error consists in directing a verdict against a criminal defendant; it also does not apply when the judge directs a partial verdict against the defendant by telling the jury that one element of the crime—such as guilty knowledge in this case—has been proved beyond a reasonable doubt, so the jury needn't worry its collective head over that one." (citation omitted)).

[5] In *Neder,* the Supreme Court held that where a court does not direct an outcome on an element, but instead neglects to instruct the jury on the existence of that element, the error is subject to harmless-error analysis. 527 U.S. at 8-9; *see also Van Buren,* 940 F.3d at 1204 (holding that the failure of the court to properly instruct the jury on the element of official act, like a failure to instruct the jury on the existence of an element, is subject to harmless-error analysis, and holding that the improper instruction was not harmless). In contrast, in *Ramirez-Castillo* and *Johnson* (as here), the district court's instruction relieved the jury of its obligation to find an element of the offense. As a result, there is no inconsistency between *Neder,* on the one hand, and *Ramirez-Castillo* and *Johnson,* on the other. *Ramirez-Castillo,* 748 F.3d at 215-16 (mentioning *Neder* but deeming it inapplicable because the error before it was structural); *Johnson,* 71 F.3d at 143-44 (decided before *Neder* but invoking the same distinction at issue in *Ramirez-Castillo).*

Here, the Court's instruction had the effect of instructing the jury to disregard evidence that the "replacement and removal of the senior deputy commissioner" did not amount to an official act, because it was not "a formal exercise of governmental power that is similar in nature to a lawsuit, administrative determination, or hearing," *McDonnell*, 136 S. Ct. at 2370; see Tr. 1781:4-7 ("You're hereby instructed that the removal or replacement of a senior deputy commissioner by the commissioner would constitute an official act."). Thus, even though formal actions of the Commissioner are not effective unless they are "made in writing and signed by the Commissioner or by his authority," N.C. Gen. Stat. § 58-2-45, the jury was told to ignore undisputed evidence that the Commissioner can reassign a senior deputy commissioner through an informal conversation, Tr. 593:6-594:2 (testimony of Commissioner Causey agreeing that it took a simple conversation to reassign a deputy insurance commissioner from one matter to the next); *id.* at 1215:23-1216:24 (testimony of former Department employee Scott Wicker that his reassignment resulted from a simple conversation); *id.* at 95:3-14 (testimony of Senior Deputy Commissioner Obusek explaining that the reassignment of matters did not require any formal process, approval, or writing).

Compounding the effect of that error, the Court ruled that it would not allow the defendants to put on additional evidence about the informality of the Department's reassignment process. *Id.* at 1450:6-1456:25; *see also id.* at 1457:6-1465:6 (offer of proof of a witness testifying that a reassignment could occur based on a conversation or e-mail). Thus, the Court excluded what would have amounted to Mr. Lindberg's principal defense to the charges—that he did not intend to influence an official act.

See id. at 1451:21-22 (explaining that the Court's ruling "will drastically reduce our day"—and that the defense would have "one witness only").

Finally, the Court warned counsel that if they argued "to the jury that this is not an official act, then [the Court will] have to step in and say the Court's going to rule that it is an official act." *Id.* at 1466:3-8; *see also id.* at 1465:12-16 ("The thing I'm not going to allow is that – it's not going to do you any good to get up there and argue this was not an official act when I'm going to tell the jury during the charge it is an official act."). In this regard, the Court was clear that it was treating official act as a matter for the Court to resolve: "So what it is down to is the Court making a determination, the Court believes, legally as to whether something is an official act under the statute." *Id.* at 1451:2-4; *cf. Van Buren*, 940 F.3d at 1204 (noting that the district court's improper instruction was not harmless because it deprived the defendant of any "effective way to highlight the government's failure to identify an appropriate 'question,'" and the defendant "very well could have successfully made that argument").

The upshot is that, even if harmless-error analysis applies, the government cannot satisfy its burden under that standard. At a minimum, then, the Court must order a new trial on Count One.

> ### B. A Judgment of Acquittal Is Required on the Count of Conspiracy to Commit Honest-Services Wire Fraud Because No Reasonable Jury Could Have Found that Task Reassignment Is an Official Act.

But Mr. Lindberg is entitled to more than a new trial; he is entitled to a judgment of acquittal on the count of conspiracy to commit honest-services wire fraud. That's because, even accepting the evidence in the light most favorable to the government, no reasonable jury could have concluded that the removal and replacement of the senior deputy commissioner constituted an official act.

Here, Mr. Lindberg is reviving a prior argument, but under changed circumstances. Although the Court denied Mr. Lindberg's motion to dismiss the indictment, which was also premised on the lack of an official act, the Court did so by invoking the Commissioner's statutory authority to "appoint" and "employ" new deputies, N.C. Gen. Stat. § 58-2-25, which the Court analogized to the congressional hiring decision at issue in *Fattah*, 914 F.3d at 155-59. Mot. to Dismiss Order at 8, Dkt. No. 120. But the evidence at trial fell short of that standard. Indeed, as previously mentioned, the jury heard undisputed evidence that the Commissioner carried out the removal and replacement of existing employees through informal conversation. Tr. 593:6-594:2; *id.* at 1216:13-24; *id.* at 95:3-14; *cf.* N.C. Gen. Stat. § 58-2-45 (explaining that a formal exercise of the Commission's authority had to be "made in writing and signed by the Commissioner or by his authority").

As a result, this Court is now presented with a fundamentally different question—whether a reasonable jury could have found, based on substantial evidence, that an informal (and strictly internal) assignment process is "a formal exercise of governmental power" akin to a "lawsuit, hearing, or administrative determination." *McDonnell*, 136 S. Ct. at 2368. Because what the government offered does not satisfy that standard, this Court must enter a judgment of acquittal.

In *McDonnell*, the Supreme Court substantially narrowed the scope of federal bribery laws. There, the Court imported the definition of "official act" from 18 U.S.C. § 201 as a limitation on the scope of honest-services wire fraud under 18 U.S.C. § 1346. *McDonnell*, 136 S. Ct. at 2365. That step, the Court explained, saved honest-services wire fraud from three potential constitutional infirmities— implicating First Amendment, vagueness, and federalism concerns. *Id.* at 2372-73, 2375.

The Supreme Court then interpreted the definition of official act to impose three requirements—the government must: (i) identify a formal "question, matter, cause, suit, proceeding or controversy" that is "similar in nature to a lawsuit before a court, a determination before an agency, or a hearing before a committee," (ii) prove that the relevant "question, matter, cause, suit, proceeding, or controversy" was one that "may at any time be pending, or which may by law be brought before any public official," and (iii) show a decision or action *on* that question, matter, cause, suit, proceeding, or controversy. *Id.* at 2367, 2369, 2372. Under this definition, not every action taken by a government official is an "official act." As the Supreme Court explained in *United States v. Sun-Diamond Growers*, some "actions [taken by government officials]—while they are assuredly 'official acts' in some sense— are not 'official acts' within the meaning of" the federal anti-bribery statute. 526 U.S. 398, 407 (1999).

Here, what the government ultimately proved up at trial—the mere reassignment of a task from one employee to another—fell far short of the statutory definition of an "official act." Most notably, the government failed to prove that such a reassignment "involve[d] a *formal* exercise of governmental power that is similar in nature to a lawsuit before a court, a determination before an agency, or a hearing before a committee." *McDonnell,* 136 S. Ct. at 2372 (emphasis added). Mr. Causey testified that switching assignments within the Department of Insurance requires only an informal conversation. Tr. 593:6-594:2. Scott Wicker, a former employee of the Department, testified that he was reassigned away from Global Bankers Insurance Group based on a simple conversation. *Id.* at 1216:13-24. And Jackie Obusek, the senior deputy commissioner at the center of this case, testified that her assignments were within Mr. Causey's discretion and that assignment changes did not require any formal process, approval, or writing. *Id.* at 95:3-14. In fact, before any of the alleged unlawful conduct at issue here, Mr. Causey changed Ms. Obusek's role in regulating Global Bankers Insurance Group, and he made that change through a simple conversation with Ms. Obusek. *Id.* at 98:25-99:6. None of this shows a formal exercise of government power akin to a lawsuit, agency determination, or committee hearing.

Notably, when the Insurance Commissioner takes formal action—action that can affect an "insurer, insurance agent, insurance broker or other person" subject to the Insurance Code—the Department is required to issue an order "in writing and signed by the Commissioner or his authority."

N.C. Gen. Stat. § 58-2-45. This State-law requirement only serves to reinforce that the act the government proved up here—the informal reassignment of tasks from one employee to another— does not qualify as a formal exercise of government power within the meaning of *McDonnell*.

Beyond that, it would seem odd to describe the informal reassignment of a task from one employee to another—a chore strictly internal to the Department of Insurance—as a "decision or action on" a "matter" that is "*pending,* or which may by law be *brought before* any public official, in such official's official capacity." 18 U.S.C. § 201(a)(3) (emphasis added). Pending, as an adjective, denotes some level of formality. Merriam-Webster Dictionary, *Pending,* https://www.merriam-webster.com/ dictionary/pending ("the case is still *pending*"); *accord* Cambridge Dictionary, *Pending,* https://dictionary.cambridge.org/us/dictionary/english/pending ("the appeal is still pending"). And a matter that "may by law be *brought before*" a public official suggests a formal request for a decision that the public typically requests of a government official. *See McDonnell,* 136 S. Ct. at 2367, 2369 (emphasis added). Thus, a matter or decision is pending—or might be of the type that is brought by law before a public official—if it bestows some benefit upon or take some right away from private citizens, requires private citizens to do something, prohibits private citizens from doing something, or changes the law that governs private citizens' conduct. Deciding that one government employee is going to take on a task once assigned to another employee does not rise to that level. For example, no one would describe a judge's contemplation of whether to reassign cases among his law clerks as a "matter" that "may be brought by law before" the judge, but on which his decision is still "pending." A contrary approach offers no limiting principle. There are any number of actions by government officials that are taken in some form of official capacity. For example, a chief judge might reallocate courtroom deputies, or an agency head might modify intake procedures for government benefits. But the Supreme Court has been clear that not all government action rises to the level of an official act within the meaning of the federal anti-bribery statutes. *McDonnell,* 136 S. Ct. at 2370; *accord Sun-Diamond Growers,* 526 U.S. at 407.

As a secondary basis for finding an "official act" here, the Court noted that, under *McDonnell*, "[a] decision or action on a qualifying step" would constitute an official act. See Tr. 1580:6-7. But to constitute a "qualifying step," a decision or action must be a step in a larger decision or action that would, in turn, constitute an "official act." *McDonnell*, 136 S. Ct. at 2370. Thus, in *McDonnell*, the Supreme Court explained that "a decision or action to initiate a research study—or a decision or action on a qualifying step, such as narrowing down the list of potential research topics—would qualify as an 'official act.'" *Id.* Here, in contrast, there is no evidence that the removal and replacement of the senior deputy commissioner was part of some larger "official act" that Mr. Lindberg sought to influence—and the government has never sought to prove otherwise. There was no evidence, for example, that Mr. Lindberg sought to bring about a particular outcome on a review of his companies. Just the opposite, Debbie Walker, a Department of Insurance employee whom Mr. Lindberg suggested as a regulator for his companies, testified that there was no "side deal" with Mr. Lindberg or his company, that neither Mr. Lindberg nor his company ever approached her "about doing something inappropriate," and that there was no "type of guaranteed financial benefit" that would come from her "looking over these files" instead of Ms. Obusek. Tr. 1306:13-16, 1306:24-1307:4, 1308:4-8.

Finally, in addressing the meaning of "official act" throughout this case, the Court has expressed concern that if a reassignment of tasks among agency employees is not an official act, then the door will be opened to a corrupt government. But this concern is overridden by three considerations. First, the Supreme Court has made clear that not all acts by a public official are "official acts" that justify a criminal conviction under the federal anti-bribery statutes. *Id.* at 2369-70; *Sun- Diamond Growers*, 526 U.S. at 407. A broad reading of the federal anti-bribery statutes would ignore this critical point and risk the constitutional infirmities that the Supreme Court sought to avoid in *McDonnell*. 136 S. Ct. at 2372-73, 2375. Second (and relatedly), the federal anti-bribery statutes are not meant to "set[ ] standards of good government for local and state officials." *Id.* at 2373 (quoting *McNally v. United States*, 483 U.S. 350, 360 (1987)) (internal quotation marks omitted). Thus, even if the conduct at issue is not proscribed by a federal statute, the State of North Carolina—as the sovereign most affected by the alleged conduct— certainly has the authority to regulate interactions between the public and its elected officials. *See id.* (noting that a State's authority "includes 'the prerogative to regulate the permissible scope of interactions between state officials and their constituents.'"); *see also Sorich v. United States*, 129 S. Ct. 1308, 1310 (2009) (Scalia, J., dissenting from denial of cert.) (noting the serious federalism concerns posed by allowing the federal government to "define the fiduciary duties that a town alderman or school board trustee owes to his constituents"). And third, the Court's concern overlooks other federal statutes that could apply in this scenario. For example, 18 U.S.C. § 600 punishes anyone who "promises any employment, position, compensation, contract, appointment, or other benefit … made possible … in part by any Act of Congress, or any special consideration in obtaining any such benefit, to any person as consideration, favor, or reward for any political activity." This statute appears broad enough to punish officials of federally funded State agencies who offer a position in exchange for a campaign contribution. And liability also would attach to aider and abettors of this offense. *See* 18 U.S.C. § 2.

This Court may view the conduct at issue here negatively. But as the Second Circuit warned, "viewing something negatively is not the same as finding that the elements of a crime have been met." *United States v. Silver*, 864 F.3d 102, 121 (2d Cir. 2017). Because no reasonable jury could have concluded that reassignment of tasks among employees at the Department of Insurance constituted an official act, the Court must enter a judgment of acquittal on Count One of the indictment.

    C. **Because the Element of "Business, Transaction, or Series of Transactions" in 18 U.S.C. § 666 Must be Read to Have the Same Meaning As "Official Act" to Avoid the Constitutional Infirmities Identified in** *McDonnell*, **the Court Must Also Set Aside the Verdict on the Second Count.**

The second count of the indictment is based on an alleged violation of the federal-program- bribery statute, 18 U.S.C. § 666(a)(2), which punishes one who intends to influence a State agent "in connection with any business, transaction, or series of transactions of such organization, government, or agency." This statutory language, like the balance of the federal anti-bribery statutes (specifically, 18 U.S.C. §§ 201 and 1346), must be read as limited to "official acts." Because the Court refused to instruct the jury that this element required an official act, see Tr. 1782:14-1786:2, Mr. Lindberg is, at minimum, entitled to a new trial on this count. And beyond that, because no reasonable jury could have found that the removal and replacement of the senior deputy commission constituted an official act, Mr. Lindberg is entitled to a judgment of acquittal on this count as well.[6]

1. Section 666 Must Be Read to Include an "Official Act" Requirement in Cases Involving Public Officials.

Over the years, the Supreme Court has narrowed the scope of the federal anti-bribery statutes to avoid serious constitutional and practical concerns. The latest attempt was, of course, in *McDonnell*. There, with the government's consent, the Supreme Court interpreted honest-services wire fraud and Hobbs Act extortion, 18 U.S.C. §§ 1346, 1951(a), to incorporate the "official act" requirement from 18 U.S.C. § 201(a)(3). The Court did so because, otherwise, honest-services fraud raised a trident of constitutional infirmity—involving the First Amendment, vagueness, and federalism. *McDonnell*, 136 S. Ct. at 2372-73, 2375.

As the Supreme Court recognized in *McDonnell*, an overly broad view of the federal anti-bribery statutes "would likely chill [public] officials' interactions with the people they serve and thus damage their ability effectively to perform their duties." 136 S. Ct. at 2372 (quoting Br. for Former Fed. Officials as *Amici Curiae* 6) (internal quotation mark omitted). That's because "conscientious public officials" perform services for their constituents. *Id.* Indeed, "[t]he basic compact underlying representative government *assumes* that public officials will hear from their constituents and act appropriately on their concerns—whether it is the union official worried about a plant closing or the homeowners who wonder why it took five days to restore power

---

[6] Mr. Lindberg preserved his objection to the Court's instruction omitting an "official act" requirement from the charge on § 666 at the charge conference, Tr. 1584:20-25, and through his proposed jury instructions, Dkt. No. 163-1, and his trial brief, Dkt. No. 164.

to their neighborhood after a storm." *Id.* For these reasons, the Court rejected the government's reading of "official act"—under which virtually any action taken by a public official would qualify—because it would "cast a pall of potential prosecution over these relationships if the union had given a campaign contribution in the past or the homeowners invited the official to join them on their annual outing to the ballgame." *Id.*

Separately, an overly broad view of the *quo* necessary to sustain a federal bribery conviction would raise significant vagueness concerns. "As generally stated, the void-for-vagueness doctrine requires that a penal statute define the criminal offense with sufficient definiteness that ordinary people can understand what conduct is prohibited and in a manner that does not encourage arbitrary and discriminatory enforcement." *Kolender*, 461 U.S. at 357. Where a statute fails to provide such definiteness, it could permit "a standardless sweep [that] allows policemen, prosecutors, and juries to pursue their personal predilections." *Id.* at 357-58 (quoting *Smith v. Goguen*, 415 U.S. 566, 575 (1974)) (internal quotation marks omitted). And that risk is heightened in the political sphere, because there is real concern that prosecutors might use overly broad statutes to punish political rivals or seek headlines in "pursuit of local officials, state legislators, and corporate CEOs who engage in any manner of unappealing or ethically questionable conduct." *Sorich*, 129 S. Ct. at 1310 (Scalia, J., dissenting from denial of cert.). For that reason, *McDonnell* rejected the government's reading of official act, under which "public officials could be subject to prosecution, without fair notice, for the most prosaic interactions." 136 S. Ct. at 2373.

Finally, an overly broad view of the federal anti-bribery statutes would "raise[ ] significant federalism concerns." *Id.* at 2373. In *McDonnell*, for example, the Court expressed serious doubt about the federal government's authority to establish ethical practices for State and local governments. *See id.* (explaining that the States have "the prerogative to regulate the permissible scope of interactions between state officials and their constituents."). Because "a more limited interpretation of 'official act'" was available, the Court "decline[d] to 'construe the statute in a manner that leaves its outer boundaries ambiguous and involves the Federal Government in setting standards' of 'good government for local and state officials.'" *Id.* (quoting *McNally*, 483 U.S. at 360).

In addition to these constitutional concerns, the Supreme Court highlighted some of the practical concerns associated with an overly broad reading of the *quo* that a government official might be said to provide in exchange for a *quid* under the federal anti-bribery statutes—drawing on its prior decision in *Sun-Diamond Growers*. *Id.* at 2370. In that case, the government had argued that the defendant, a trade association, could be convicted of providing the Secretary of Agriculture with a gratuity under 18 U.S.C. § 201(c)(1)(A) based on the prospect that the defendant might be affected by some future "official act," however ill-defined, that might be taken by the Secretary. *Sun-Diamond Growers*, 526 U.S. at 405-06. In rejecting this argument, the Court explained that a sweeping definition of "official act" would have made it a crime for a sports team to give the President a replica jersey, for the principal of a high school to present the Secretary of Education with a school baseball cap, or for a group of farmers to provide the Secretary of Agriculture with a complimentary lunch after he delivered a speech to them on agricultural policy. *Id.* at 406-07. That's because "the Secretary of Agriculture always has before him or in prospect matters that affect farmers, just as the President always has before him or in prospect matters that affect college and professional sports, and the Secretary of Education matters that affect high schools." *Id.* at 407. For these reasons, the Court explained that "the existence of such pending matters was not enough to find that any action related to them constituted an 'official act.'" *McDonnell*, 136 S. Ct. at 2370 (citing *Sun-Diamond Growers*, 526 U.S. at 407). Instead, the Court continued, "[i]t was possible to avoid the 'absurdities' of convicting individuals on corruption charges for engaging in such conduct … *'through the definition of that term"*— that is, "by adopting a more limited definition of 'official acts.'" *Id.* (quoting *Sun-Diamond Growers*, 526 U.S. at 408). The point here is that, in both *McDonnell* and *Sun-Diamond Growers*, the Court explained that it was imperative to give the term "official act" a narrow definition, otherwise all manner of government acts—from attending a ceremony to giving a speech—could trigger criminal liability under the federal anti-bribery statutes.

The same constitutional and practical concerns are implicated in a prosecution under § 666. Indeed, because the Commonwealth of Virginia is a recipient of federal funding, the government could have charged Governor McDonnell with a violation of that statute. He was unquestionably an "agent ... of a State" that received more than $10,000 in federal funding, and according to the government, he "agree[d] to accept" money and gifts "intending to be influenced or rewarded in connection with [some] business of such [State]." 18 U.S.C. § 666(a)(1)(B). Thus, if, as the Court initially ruled here, *McDonnell* places no limits on the *quo* necessary to sustain a conviction for federal-program bribery under § 666, then the government could have convicted Governor McDonnell under that statute based on the same constitutionally problematic theory that the Supreme Court rejected in *McDonnell* for honest-services fraud prosecutions.

For all of these reasons, § 666 must be read to include § 201's requirement of an official act. And the official act requirement incorporates easily into § 666's element of "any business, transaction, or series of transactions" and provides that vague phrase with much-needed clarity in prosecutions involving public officials. 18 U.S.C. § 666(a)(1)(B). Indeed, the Fourth Circuit's decision in *United States v. Jennings,* 160 F.3d 1006 (4th Cir. 1998), provides support for this conclusion. There, the court affirmed the defendant's conviction under § 666 because "a reasonable juror could have concluded that there was a course of conduct involving" payments of bribes "in exchange for a pattern of *official actions* favorable to [the defendant's] companies." *Id.* at 1018 (emphasis added). And although the Fourth Circuit was not presented directly with the question whether § 666 requires an official act, the court repeatedly read that phrase into the elements of the offense, invoking "official act" or "official action" *thirty-five times. See generally id.* An official act is thus a natural way to describe the type of business or transaction that would qualify as a *quo* under § 666.

Section 666's statutory pedigree likewise supports reading into it the official act requirement from § 201. *McDonnell* has already read § 201's definition of "official act" into § 1346, and the Supreme Court has recognized that §§ 666(a)(2) and 1346 define "similar crimes." *Skilling v. United States*, 561

U.S. 358, 412 (2010). If anything, it is even more natural to read § 201's definition of "official act" into § 666 than it was for *McDonnell* to read the same into § 1346. As the Fourth Circuit explained in *Jennings*, § 666 is a direct outgrowth of § 201. It was enacted to resolve a circuit split over whether § 201 applied to State and local officials. *See Jennings*, 160 F.3d at 1012-13 ("Before § 666 was enacted in 1984, a circuit split raised doubt as to whether state and local officials could be considered 'public officials' under the general statute, 18 U.S.C. § 201."). Section 666(a)(2) thus "make[s] clear that federal law prohibits 'significant acts of ... bribery involving Federal monies that are disbursed to private organizations or State and local governments pursuant to a Federal program.'" *Id.* at 1013 (quoting S. Rep. No. 98-225, at 369 (1984), *reprinted in* 1984 U.S.C.C.A.N. 3182, 3510). In short, because § 666 is a direct outgrowth of § 201, and because it was meant to proscribe only significant acts of bribery, it makes sense that the "official act" requirement applies to § 666 in cases involving public officials.

A contrary construction—reading § 666 differently than §§ 201 and 1346—is nonsensical. If *McDonnell* does not apply equally to §§ 201, 666, and 1346, then federal law would regulate *State* officials more strictly than *federal* officials. The federalism concerns that animated *McDonnell* require the opposite—that the federal government has *less* authority to enact broadly written statutes that curtail the relationship between State officials and their constituents. *McDonnell*, 136 S. Ct. at 2373.

To be sure, a handful of courts have opined that *McDonnell*'s "official act" requirement does not apply to § 666, but their reasoning is not persuasive, and none is binding upon this Court. In *United States v. Suhl*, for example, the Eighth Circuit suggested that *McDonnell* would not apply to § 666 because that provision "does not include the term 'official act.'" 885 F.3d 1106, 1112 (8th Cir. 2018). The court never resolved this issue, however, because it went on to hold that, even if *McDonnell*'s definition of official act applies to federal-program bribery, the indictment alleged an official act— specifically, a requested "increase [in] Medicaid reimbursements" to the defendant's companies. *Id.* at 1112-13. And even if the Eighth Circuit's statement constituted a holding—and thereby declined to apply *McDonnell* to § 666—its rationale is wholly unpersuasive. Like § 666, § 1346 "does not include the term 'official act,'" *id.* at 1112, but the Supreme Court agreed to read that requirement into § 1346 to avoid the serious constitutional and practical issues discussed above. *McDonnell*, 136 S. Ct. at 2372- 73, 2375.

Similarly, in *United States v. Ng Lap Seng*, the Second Circuit implied that § 666 does not embrace an "official act" requirement because § 666's language "is more expansive than [§] 201," and "[n]owhere does [§ 666] mention 'official acts." 934 F.3d 110, 133 (2d Cir. 2019) (quoting *United States v. Boyland*, 862 F.3d 279, 291 (2d Cir. 2017)), *petition for cert. filed*, No. 19-1145 (U.S. Mar. 16, 2020). As in *Suhl*, this discussion was not necessary to the Second Circuit's decision in *Ng Lap Seng*, because the district court gave an "official act" instruction under § 666, *id.* at 138-39, and the Second Circuit found the evidence sufficient to support the conviction, *see id.* at 140. And like in *Suhl*, the Second Circuit's rationale for refusing to apply *McDonnell* to § 666 is unpersuasive. The fact that § 666's language is "more expansive" than § 201's militates in favor of applying *McDonnell*, not jettisoning it. Otherwise, § 666's expansive reach risks *heightened* constitutional and practical concerns of the nature otherwise tamped down by *McDonnell*'s application. And the fact that § 666 makes no mention of an "official act" is no impediment either, because the same could have been said about honest-services wire fraud and Hobbs Act extortion.

The Second Circuit ignored these issues and instead claimed that § 666 was different, because § 666 invoked Congress's "power to keep a watchful eye on [its] expenditures." *Id.* at 138 (quoting *Sabri v. United States*, 541 U.S. 600, 608 (2004)).

But while Congress's spending-clause authority might empower it to impose some strings on the recipients of congressional appropriations, the Supreme Court has insisted upon an "unmistakably clear" textual statement before it will infer that Congress intended to "alter the 'usual constitutional balance between the States and the Federal government.'" *Gregory v. Ashcroft*, 501 U.S. 452, 460-61 (1991) (quoting *Will v. Mich. Dep't of State Police*, 491 U.S. 58, 65 (1989)). And nothing in § 666 suggests—let alone unmistakably proclaims—that Congress meant to disregard basic principles of federalism or criminalize "prosaic interactions" between State and local officials and their constituents. *McDonnell*, 136 S. Ct. at 2373.

> 2.   **Mr. Lindberg Is Entitled to a Judgment of Acquittal on Count Two Based on the Absence of Sufficient Evidence to Establish an Official Act or, At a Minimum, a New Trial.**

That § 666 must be read to include an official act requirement is obvious. The only issue that remains is remedy.

For the reasons explained above, no reasonable jury could have concluded that the removal and replacement of the senior deputy commissioner constituted an official act. *See* Section I.B. As a result, the Court must enter a judgment of acquittal on Count Two.

At a minimum, though, because the Court failed to instruct the jury on the requirement of an official act before it could convict on Count Two, Mr. Lindberg is entitled to a new trial. Unlike the instructional error discussed above, which involved a directed verdict on the official act requirement of Count One, the Court's omission of this element from Count Two is subject to harmless-error analysis. *See Neder*, 527 U.S. at 8-9; *see also supra* note 5. Yet, for reasons similar to those explained above, the omission of this element is far from harmless. First, the error was not harmless beyond a reasonable doubt because, as in *McDonnell*, the jury "may have convicted [Mr. Lindberg] for conduct that is not unlawful." 136 S. Ct. at 2375. And as discussed above, there was compelling evidence to show that the reassignment of tasks between employees is not an official act—significant enough evidence that acquittal is required. Moreover, the Court's erroneous conception of an official act— that it was a "legal[ ]" issue for the Court to resolve, Tr. 1451:2-4—meant that it excluded additional evidence about the informality of the Department's reassignment process. *Id.* at 1450:6-1456:25; *see also id.* at 1464:19-1465:6. This evidence would have made it even less likely that the jury would have found an official act in this case. Taken together, these points show that the government cannot establish that the omission of an "official act" instruction from Count Two was harmless beyond a reasonable doubt. *See Van Buren*, 940 F.3d at 1204 (holding that the failure to properly instruct the jury on "official act" was not harmless).

D. Even if § 666(a)(2) Has No Official Act Requirement, A New Trial Is Required Because the Court's Erroneous Official Act Instruction Infected this Count.

The Court's erroneous directive on Count One—that "the removal or replacement of a senior deputy commissioner . . . would constitute an official act," Tr. 1781:4-7—infected more than just the verdict on Count One. In the Court's instructions, the jury was told that § 666 required less than an official act; it required proof only of a "business, transaction, or series of transactions," which the instructions suggested was anything other than "setting up a meeting, hosting an event, talking to another official, sending a subordinate to a meeting, or simply expressing support for a constituent." Tr. 1783:6-7, 1784:13-18. A reasonable jury, having been instructed that the removal or replacement of a senior deputy commissioner was an official act, would have automatically assumed that the same removal or replacement constituted a business or transaction within the meaning of § 666. In effect, then, the Court's instruction also partially directed the verdict on Count Two. So even if the Court disagrees that § 666 requires proof of an official act, a new trial is still warranted.[7]

---

[7] Mr. Lindberg renews and preserves his arguments that § 666(a)(2) and the honest-services wire fraud statutes are unconstitutional, as discussed in his first oral motion for judgment of acquittal, Tr. 1262:9-1266:21, and his written supplement to that motion, Rule 29 Suppl. at 21-23, Dkt. No. 192, and as renewed in his second oral motion for judgment of acquittal, Tr. 1508:24-1509:5.

II. Mr. Lindberg is Entitled to a Judgment of Acquittal or a New Trial on Entrapment.

Mr. Lindberg renews the entrapment argument made at the close of the government's evidence and the close of the defense's evidence, based on the reasoning explained in Mr. Lindberg's Supplement to his Oral Motion for Judgment of Acquittal. Tr. 1258:22-1260:21; Rule 29 Suppl. at 17- 21, Dkt. No. 192. "An entrapment defense has two elements: government inducement and the defendant's lack of predisposition to commit the crime." *United States v. Sligh*, 142 F.3d 761, 762 (4th Cir. 1998). Inducement involves "governmental overreaching and conduct sufficiently excessive to implant a criminal design in the mind of an otherwise innocent party." *Id.* at 763. "[T]he defendant has the initial burden to 'produce more than a scintilla of evidence that the government induced him to commit the charged offense,' before the burden shifts to the government to prove beyond a reasonable doubt that the defendant was predisposed to commit the crime." *Id.* (quoting *United States v. Daniel*, 3 F.3d 775, 778 (4th Cir. 1993)). Government inducement of the crime includes inducement by "federal, state or local law enforcement officials or their agents." *United States v. Perl*, 584 F.2d 1316, 1321 n.3 (4th Cir. 1978). Once inducement is shown, the government must prove that the defendant's predisposition existed before he was approached by government agents. *Sligh*, 142 F.3d at 762. "Even if the defendant denies one or more elements of the crime," as Mr. Lindberg did in this case, "he is entitled to an entrapment instruction whenever there is sufficient evidence from which a reasonable jury could find entrapment." *Mathews v. United States*, 485 U.S. 58, 62 (1988).

As discussed in his supplement to his first oral motion for acquittal, Mr. Lindberg met his initial burden of showing evidence of inducement, and the government failed to meet its burden of proving Mr. Lindberg's criminal predisposition beyond a reasonable doubt. Rule 29 Suppl. 17-21. The defense's evidence only bolstered Mr. Lindberg's claim of entrapment. Acquittal, or at minimum a new trial, is warranted.

A. Mr. Causey Induced Mr. Lindberg and the Other Defendants to Commit Bribery.

Mr. Lindberg has met his burden of showing more than scintilla of evidence of inducement. The first inducement occurred on March 5, 2018: After a conversation with Mr. Lindberg about regulatory issues, Mr. Causey asked "what's in it for me?" and suggested that he wanted support that would be "[u]nder the radar screen." Gov't Ex. 113C at 9.[8] This evidence alone was enough to show inducement. *See Sligh*, 142 F.3d at 766 (noting that an entrapment instruction was warranted where, like here, a government agent "invited a bribe more explicitly by asking ... in essence, 'What's in it for me?'"). And this Court has acknowledged that Mr. Causey's "question can amount to entrapment and thus may entitle a defendant to an entrapment jury instruction at trial." Mot. to Dismiss Order at 14, Dkt. No. 120.

Mr. Causey's testimony further demonstrates that this question was an inducement. Mr. Causey admitted that he was asked to insert this question "at the direction of the FBI agents" into the "business conversation" that he was having with Mr. Lindberg:

> Q. Okay. And so the FBI told you that at some point during this business conversation that you were having, that they instructed you to interject this phrase in here, "What's in it for me?"
>
> A. Something to that effect.

Tr. 538:7-21. Mr. Causey also agreed that such a question would not have been part of a "typical conversation with somebody [he] regulate[d]," Tr. 539:22-23, and that it was the only time he had asked such a question to someone whom he regulates:

> A. No, it's not a typical conversation. This is not a typical situation.
>
> Q. Okay. How many other—if it's not typical, then have you ever done it before?
>
> A. No, I've never done it before.

---

[8] This motion uses quotations from transcriptions of any recordings. As the Court has noted, the recordings themselves are what constitutes evidence.

Q. Have you ever done it since?

A. I've never done it since.

Tr. 540:3-9.

Although this evidence would have been sufficient to demonstrate inducement, trial evidence provided other examples. For instance, in a conversation with defendant John Gray, Mr. Causey remarked on Mr. Lindberg's donations to other politicians and suggested that he was worth as much those politicians:

You know they gave him another twenty-three thousand for his campaign, gave two hundred thousand to the guy running for governor. Gave Dan Forest a million and a half in one pop, and I'm thinking, you know hell I'm the insurance commissioner. I should be as high on his [Mr. Lindberg's] uh radar list as—as Dan Forest or any—or any of these other guys in other states and ... he's putting millions of dollars out there in— in total ...

Gov't Ex. 119 at 4. Mr. Causey later expressed disappointment to Mr. Gray that, despite having begun a discussion with Mr. Lindberg months ago regarding independent expenditure committees, he had not "seen anything that's concrete." Gov't Ex. 120B at 3-4.

Mr. Causey also remarked to Mr. Lindberg, regarding a regulatory issue that he had worked related to Mr. Lindberg's companies, that he had failed to see any benefit from helping Mr. Lindberg:

You had folks here workin on it, you know they all got bonuses, this that and the other, well I'm a regulator, but as a candidate, as uh, uh commissioner or candidate or whatever. I didn't personally see any benefit from it ...

Gov't Ex. 121 at 11.

And in a July 25, 2018, meeting, Mr. Causey asked for money from Mr. Lindberg that he could "control," Gov't. Ex. 127A at 4, such as money in his personal checking account:

[Mike Causey:] How 'bout, how 'bout some, a deposit in one of my accounts that I can do what I want to with? [OV]

[John Gray:] Your campaign accounts?

[Mike Causey:] Non-campaign account. I'm talking about just a, a non-campaign account.

> *[John Gray:] Wha-, what account is that?*
>
> *[Greg Lindberg:] I don't know if we can do that.*
>
> *[John Gray:] Wha, wha, what account would it be?*
>
> *[Mike Causey:] I mean, I've got two or three.*
>
> *[John Gray:] You mean like your personal checking account?*
>
> *[Mike Causey:] Some, yeah.*

Gov't Ex. 127A at 5. At trial, Mr. Causey testified that he talked to the FBI before this meeting about the investigation:

> *Q. Mr. Causey, when you're at that meeting with Greg Lindberg on July the 25th, this is—was there a discussion with you and the FBI regarding that you needed to come in there and try to close this whole investigation out on this particular occasion?*
>
> *A. I don't—I don't recall that.*
>
> *Q. You don't recall that.*
>
> *A. What's your question? You're asking if I had a discussion?*
>
> *Q. With the FBI about how this thing has gone on for so long and you've asked for money so many times and that you need to finally bring it to a head on this particular occasion. Was there a discussion between you and the FBI?*
>
> *A. I don't know that it was anything like that. I know we had—had some discussion of it, but I didn't understand it to be, well, this is the final chance or anything like that.*

Tr. 595:6-14. This testimony tends to show that Mr. Causey and the FBI were discussing ways to bring the investigation to a close.

Finally, evidence that Mr. Causey had changed Ms. Obusek's role regarding the regulation of Mr. Lindberg's companies in February 2018 further supports a finding of inducement. Tr. 98:25-99:4 (*"Q. And then in February of 2018, Mr. Causey actually moved you off of GBIG accounts due to complaints that you were discussing concerns on GBIG with other state regulators, correct? A. That is correct."*); *id.* at 110:19-111:12. Yet Mr. Causey continued to invite Mr. Lindberg to offer a quid in exchange for a reassignment of tasks away from Ms. Obusek.

These examples from the government's case-in-chief do not represent the full extent of Mr. Causey's inducement, but they are enough to show that Mr. Causey's conduct went beyond mere solicitation.

The defense's evidence only bolstered the showing of inducement. That evidence suggests that Mr. Causey misled the FBI to persuade them to open an investigation into Mr. Lindberg. During trial, Mr. Causey testified that he had talked to his campaign fundraiser, Joyce Kohn, about a donation of $110,000 that Mr. Lindberg had supposedly given to the North Carolina Republican Party, and he testified that he told the FBI about this donation. Tr. 453:1-454:14. FBI Special Agent Michael Scherger testified that this alleged $110,000 offer "was a part of the predication for the reason we opened the case." Tr. 1504:16-17. So did FBI Special Agent Jacqueline Granozio. Tr. 1103:12-14 ("That was one of the reasons that this investigation was opened."). Yet the evidence at trial showed that Mr. Causey was never offered or given $110,000 by the NC GOP on Mr. Lindberg's behalf and that Mr. Causey had never spoken to Ms. Kohn about it. *See* Tr. 1484:3-10 (testimony of Joyce Kohn); *id.* at 1107:18-21 (testimony of Agent Granozio "*Q. Isn't it true, ma'am, that there is no wire, no check, no record from the GOP, no record from Mike Causey's campaign, to substantiate receipt, much less return of $110,000? A. Not that I'm aware of.*"); *id.* at 1374:1-4 (testimony of Agent Scherger: "*Q. And isn't it true there's no wire, no check, no record of this $110,000? A. That is true, there is no wire or check of that money given to Mr. Causey at that time.*"). Taken together, this testimony makes it more likely that Mr. Causey's repeated attempts to talk to Mr. Lindberg about campaign contributions were, in fact, inducements.

Thus, the evidence more than surpassed the "scintilla" necessary to show that Mr. Causey's actions constituted inducement. The government itself implicitly acknowledged that this evidence was sufficient to show inducement, since it proposed a jury instruction to the Court on entrapment. And the fact that the Court ultimately instructed the jury on entrapment shows that Mr. Lindberg met his burden, since "[a] defendant is not entitled to an entrapment instruction unless he can meet this initial burden of producing some evidence of government inducement." *Sligh*, 142 F.3d at 762-63.

B. The Government Has Not Sustained Its Burden of Proving Mr. Lindberg's Predisposition Beyond Any Reasonable Doubt.

Because the evidence adequately demonstrated inducement, the burden shifted to the government to offer evidence of predisposition. For the reasons discussed in Mr. Lindberg's supplement to his first oral motion for acquittal, the government failed to offer sufficient evidence to show, beyond a reasonable doubt, that Mr. Lindberg was predisposed to committing the charged bribery offenses. Rule 29 Suppl. at 20-21.

First, the government cannot argue that Mr. Lindberg's attempted donations to Mr. Causey or other politicians showed a criminal predisposition. The government's evidence must show a "predisposition to commit an *illegal* act." *Jacobson v. United States*, 503 U.S. 540, 550 (1992) (emphasis added). The First Amendment gives Mr. Lindberg the right to donate to causes and candidates that he supports, and the government has offered no evidence that these prior donations were criminal. The government has not shown that any of Mr. Lindberg's attempted contributions to Mr. Causey were illegal before Mr. Causey's first inducement on March 5. Thus, these attempted contributions cannot be used to show criminal predisposition. They merely show that Mr. Lindberg was exercising his First Amendment rights, as every constituent is allowed to do.

Second, for similar reasons, the government also cannot rely on the fact that Mr. Lindberg responded to Mr. Causey's first inducement of "what's in it for me?" with the idea of funding an independent expenditure committee. An offer of a campaign contribution becomes a bribe only if it is made in exchange for an explicit promise to perform an official act. *McCormick v. United States*, 500 U.S. 257, 273 (1991). When this conversation occurred, Mr. Causey had made no explicit promise to perform the official act charged in the indictment: the removal of Ms. Obusek. Gov't Ex. 113C at 7-9. Thus, Mr. Lindberg's response shows only a willingness to contribute to politicians, which is not a criminal act.

At most, viewing the evidence in the light most favorable to the government, Mr. Lindberg raised the idea with a "generalized hope or expectation of ultimate benefit," which does "not constitute a bribe." *Jennings*, 160 F.3d at 1013; *see McCutcheon v. Fed. Election Comm'n*, 572 U.S. 185, 192 (2014) (noting that ingratiation and access are not corruption).

The government also cannot rely on evidence that the idea continued to be discussed in the ensuing months as evidence of criminal predisposition. "[P]redisposition is tested at a time 'prior to the Government acts intended to create predisposition.'" *United States v. Skarie*, 971 F.2d 317, 321 (9th Cir. 1992) (quoting *Jacobson*, 503 U.S. at 553). So the government has the burden of proving that Mr. Lindberg was predisposed to committing the crime *before* Mr. Causey induced him to do so. Predisposition thus cannot be proven through the conversations about independent expenditure committees that occurred after March 5, 2018.

Finally, Mr. Causey's repeated inducements over a series of many months are strong evidence of a lack of predisposition. As the Ninth Circuit observed in *United States v. Skarie*:

Where evidence of "predisposition" comes only after the government has devoted considerable time and effort to persuading the defendant, "[r]ational jurors could not say beyond a reasonable doubt that petitioner possessed the requisite predisposition prior to the Government's investigation and that it existed independent of the Government's many and varied approaches to petitioner."

971 F.2d 317, 321 (9th Cir. 1992) (quoting *Jacobson*, 503 U.S. at 553) (internal quotation marks omitted). Here, the evidence shows that a government agent needed to spend over half a year filled with numerous meetings and phone calls before the government felt comfortable charging Mr. Lindberg with a crime. Tr. 1177:2-1178:19. A person with criminal predisposition would not need so many opportunities and repeated inducements to commit the crime.

Because the government has failed to sustain its burden, acquittal is required on both counts. In the alternative, the Court should order a new trial given the significant lack of evidence of predisposition. *See Arrington*, 757 F.2d at 1485 ("When the evidence weighs so heavily against the verdict that it would be unjust to enter judgment, the court should grant a new trial.").

III. The Government Failed to Offer Sufficient Evidence that the Department of Insurance Received Benefits Under a Federal Program, as Required By § 666(a)(2).

To obtain a conviction for federal-program bribery, the government must prove that the organization in question "receives, in any one year period, benefits in excess of $10,000 under a Federal program." 18 U.S.C. § 666(b). This requirement is often referred to as the "jurisdictional element" of § 666. *United States v. McLean*, 802 F.3d 1228, 1235 (11th Cir. 2015). Like other elements of the crime, it must be decided by the jury. *See United States v. Taylor*, 754 F.3d 217, 224 (4th Cir. 2014) (affirming a jury finding of the jurisdictional element of an effect on interstate commerce in a Hobbs Act prosecution), *aff'd*, 136 S. Ct. 2074 (2016); see also 136 S. Ct. at 2088 (Thomas, J., dissenting) (noting that an effect on interstate commerce, like other elements, "must be proved to a jury"); *see also Apprendi v. New Jersey*, 530 U.S. 466, 477 (2000) (holding that a criminal defendant is entitled to "a jury determination that [he] is guilty of every element of the crime with which he is charged, beyond a reasonable doubt" (alteration in original) (quoting *Gaudin*, 515 U.S. at 510)); *McLean*, 802 F.3d at 1247 ("[B]ased on our circuit precedent, if we were to address this issue, we would determine that the decision to classify assistance as a federal benefit was properly submitted to the jury.").[9]

"The government has the burden of producing adequate evidence for" the jury to determine whether any federal funds rise to the level of a benefit in excess of what is required by the statute. *United States v. Bravo-Fernandez*, 913 F.3d 244, 247 (1st Cir. 2019); *see also United States v. Doran*, 854 F.3d 1312, 1322 (11th Cir. 2017)

---

[9] Some courts have disagreed that this element is a jury question. *E.g., United States v. Insaidoo*, 765 F. App'x 522, 524 (2d Cir. 2019) (non-precedential) (finding the jurisdictional element to be a legal question), *cert. denied*, 140 S. Ct. 552 (2019); *United States v. Peery*, 977 F.2d 1230, 1233 (8th Cir. 1992) (same). These decisions cannot be correct. For over a century, the Supreme Court has repeatedly made clear that a jury must find "every fact necessary to constitute the crime charged" beyond a reasonable doubt. *Davis v. United States*, 160 U.S. 469, 493 (1895); *In re Winship*, 397 U.S. 358, 363 (1970); *Apprendi*, 530 U.S. at 477; *Hurst v. Florida*, 136 S. Ct. 616, 621 (2016).

(Pryor, J., concurring in the judgment) ("We 'scrutinize the actual evidence' the government presented as to whether federal funds rise to the level of 'benefit.'"); *McClean*, 802 F.3d at 1230 ("To protect against the infringement on the inherent powers of the states by federalizing traditional state offenses, the government is required to prove beyond a reasonable doubt each element of a criminal offense.").

A receipt of federal funds does not automatically equal a receipt of "benefits" for purposes of § 666. *See Fischer v. United States*, 529 U.S. 667, 681 (2000) ("Any receipt of federal funds can, at some level of generality, be characterized as a benefit. The statute does not employ this broad, almost limitless use of the term."). Rather, this element requires examination of "the conditions under which the organization receives the federal payments." *Fischer*, 529 U.S. at 681; *see also United States v. Pinson*, 860 F.3d 152, 167 (4th Cir. 2017). And critically, for funds to qualify as "benefits," the government must prove beyond a reasonable doubt the receipt of federal funds "in connection with programs defined by a sufficiently comprehensive 'structure, operation, and purpose.'" *McClean*, 802 F.3d at 1243 (quoting *United States v. Edgar*, 304 F.3d 1320, 1327 (11th Cir. 2002)); *see Fischer*, 529 U.S. at 681. The Supreme Court's decision in *Fischer* illuminates this element. In *Fischer*, the Court held that hospitals receive "benefits" within the meaning of the statute based on their *"role and regulated status* ... as health care providers under the Medicare program." *Fischer*, 529 U.S. at 669 (emphasis added). The Court explained that Medicare imposes on hospitals intricate and comprehensive "statutory and regulatory requirements," which serve to assure the government that "participating providers possess the capacity to fulfill their statutory obligation" of providing adequate medical care. *Id.* at 672. For example, participating providers "must satisfy a series of qualification and accreditation requirements," *id.* at 680, and "[p]eer review organizations monitor providers' compliance with these and other obligations," *id.* at 672. The Court drew a distinction between these heavily regulated entities and contractors, which do not receive "benefits" because the government does not "regulate or assist

[them] for long-term objectives or for significant purposes beyond performance of an immediate transaction." *Id.* at 681.

Applying *Fischer*, federal courts of appeals, including the Fourth Circuit, have vacated convictions under § 666 where the receipt of federal funds did not qualify as "benefits." *See, e.g., Pinson*, 860 F.3d at 167-68; *Bravo-Fernandez*, 913 F.3d at 249 (holding that the parties' stipulation that federal funds were received was insufficient to establish "benefits" under the statute, and that the jury could not "exercise[e] common sense and rely[ ] on general knowledge" to reasonably infer that "the federal funds constituted 'benefits'").

The Eleventh Circuit's application of *Fischer* in *McClean* is particularly instructive. In *McClean*, the defendant served on the board of the Margate Community Redevelopment Agency ("MCRA"), which "is a component of the City [of Margate] with a purpose to promote the physical and economic development of the City." 802 F.3d at 1232. The Court found that the MCRA received federal funds during the relevant time period, but that "the government's evidence failed to establish a connection" between those funds and "any identifiable federal program so that its 'structure, operation, and purpose' could be reviewed to permit a determination that the funds qualified as a federal benefit under the jurisdictional element of § 666(b)." *Id.* at 1243. Fatally "absent from the government's proof was any evidence identifying the relationship between the program authorizing a disbursement of federal funds and the ultimate use of those funds at the local level." *Id.* at 1244.

This case law clarifies that the proof of "benefits" under § 666 is not a formality. To the contrary, the careful application of the federal-benefits element is critical to "safeguard[ ] the accused's constitutional rights, ensure[ ] the government does not overreach by prosecuting actions that do not comport with the statutory language, and guarantee[ ] that federal crimes remain distinct from state crimes." *Id.* at 1230-31. This makes sense, since not "all recipient fraud" is covered by § 666. *Fischer*, 529 U.S. at 681. So the meaning of "benefits" in the statute cannot be interpreted to be "limitless" because "[d]oing so would turn almost every act of fraud or bribery into a federal offense, upsetting the proper federal balance." *Id.*

Applying the foregoing principles here, the government's evidence fails in two ways.

First, as in *McClean,* the evidence at trial did not show that the federal funds that the North Carolina Department of Insurance received were "part of any program with a sufficiently comprehensive structure, operation, or purpose to meet the requirement under § 666(b) as a federal benefit." *Doran,* 854 F.3d at 1316. The government's sole evidence of the federal-benefits element was the testimony of Laresia Everett, the Department's Controller. Ms. Everett explained at a high level that the Department received federal grants in 2017 and 2018 through the State Health Insurance Assistance Program (SHIP). Tr. 874:17-25. She testified generally that SHIP grants aim to assist States with informing seniors about Medicare. *Id.* at 880:4-10. And she testified as to the dollar amounts of the grants received. *E.g., id.* at 872:17, 872:24, 875:3, 876:89, 876:17. But this high-level testimony did not adequately explain the federal program's structure, operation, or purpose.

Judge Jill Pryor, concurring in *United States v. Doran,* 854 F.3d 1312 (11th Cir. 2017), found similarly general testimony to be insufficient. There, the testimony was the following:

> *[Y]ou look at the federal programs that Florida State receives, the National Institute of Health, you know, they are designed—and this is technical, so it's something that I'm not really exactly experienced in, but—the technical side of the National Institute of Health is for disease control, for new drugs. And then, for instance, the National Science Foundation, we get a lot of money from them to advance more of the psychology, the biological sciences, where they are looking at the new discoveries and new technologies to, in other words, help the common good for the public.*

Id. at 1323 (Jill Pryor, J., concurring in judgment). Despite the mention of federal entities, Judge Pryor noted that "[s]uch generalized descriptions cannot suffice to demonstrate the existence of a federal program 'defined by a sufficiently comprehensive structure, operation, and purpose to merit characterization of [its] fund[ing] as benefits.'" *Id.* (quoting *McLean,* 802 F.3d at 1237). Mr. Everett's testimony was no more detailed. Therefore, it was not sufficient evidence to show that the funds received by the North Carolina Department of Insurance were part of a federal program with a "sufficiently comprehensive structure, operation, and purpose." *Id.*[10]

Second, the government did not provide evidence that the federal government retained a meaningful role in supervising how the grant monies are applied, including maintaining an intricate regulatory scheme to control the expenditure of federal funds. *Fischer* and the Fourth Circuit's decision in *United States v. Pinson,* 860 F.3d 152 (4th Cir. 2017), make clear that entities receive a "benefit" for purpose of § 666 when they are the subject of "substantial Government regulation" that helps them achieve "long-term objectives" or policy goals "beyond performance of an immediate transaction." *Id.* at 167 (quoting *Fischer,* 529 U.S. at 680) (internal quotation marks omitted). But here, Ms. Everett testified that the State—and not the federal government—defines the contours and requirements of its SHIP program. Tr. 880:7-881:11. The federal government exercises oversight over the program only through certain reporting requirements as to expenditures and administrative issues, but does not maintain substantive oversight or requirements for the SHIP program. *Id.; see also id.* at 883:18-884:3, 885:1-9. Thus, the funds at issue here are more closely aligned with the example of the contractor in *Fischer,* as opposed to the hospitals.

Finally, it makes no difference to this analysis that the Department of Insurance is a governmental entity. Although *Fischer* concerned federal funds received by non- governmental entities, the statute does not differentiate between private and governmental entities with regard to the "benefits" element. Thus, the same proof that is required for non-governmental entities should be required for governmental entities.

---

[10] In Doran, the majority reversed the defendant's conviction because, in its view, the government had failed to prove that the relevant local organization received any federal benefits. 854 F.3d at 1316. Judge Pryor concurred separately because she disagreed on the organization relevant to the Court's analysis, but she agreed that the government had not proven the receipt of a federal benefit as to this organization. Id. (Jill Pryor, J., concurring).

These two defects each require the entry of a judgment of acquittal on Count Two or, at a minimum, a new trial, since the evidence was far below the sufficiency needed to establish this element.

IV. A Variety of Evidentiary Rulings Justify a New Trial.

Significant and incorrect evidentiary rulings affected the fairness of this trial. To begin with, the Court excluded evidence that the jury needed for assessing Mr. Lindberg's guilt. In addition to the exclusion of official-act evidence discussed above, the Court excluded two other critical categories of evidence. The first category consists of evidence that bore directly on the bias, credibility, and motive to testify of the government's key witness: Commissioner Causey. The second category consists of proposed testimony by the defendants' expert witness, Chris Gober. Because both categories bear materially on the offenses in this case, their exclusion prejudiced Mr. Lindberg's defense. *See Lis*, 120 F.3d at 31. The exclusion of either category justifies a new trial.

The Court also admitted evidence related to a suggestion that Mr. Causey hire defendant John Palermo to the Department of Insurance. This evidence should have been excluded as prejudicial and irrelevant. Because the erroneous admission of this evidence also unfairly prejudiced Mr. Lindberg's defense, a new trial is warranted for this reason as well.

A. The Court Should Have Admitted Evidence of Prior Deposition Testimony of Mr. Causey So That the Jury Could Properly Assess Mr. Causey's Bias and Motivation to Entrap Mr. Lindberg.

For the reasons discussed in Mr. Lindberg's Memorandum Regarding Mr. Causey's Motivation to Testify, Dkt. No. 187, a new trial is warranted because Mr. Lindberg was not allowed to introduce key evidence bearing on Mr. Causey's motivation to cooperate with the government, and he was not allowed to cross-examine Mr. Causey on past untruthful statements—even though Mr. Causey was the most important government witness.

First, defense counsel should have been allowed to introduce extrinsic evidence of prior deposition testimony of Mr. Causey and fully explore the testimony through cross-examination. *See* Tr. 342:5-354:14, 358:2-373:8; Mem. Re. Causey's Motivation to Testify, Dkt. No. 187. The deposition occurred in a lawsuit filed by an entity regulated by the Department of Insurance. In the deposition, Mr. Causey was questioned about whether he engaged in an illegal "pay to play" scheme by accepting a campaign contribution from a supporter and then punishing a business competitor of that supporter. After Mr. Causey's attorney, Daniel Johnson, objected to that line of questioning, this followed:

> *MR. BIBBS: Well, Mr. Johnson, when the FBI asks him these questions, I'm just getting him ready for it.*

> *Q Because it appears, Mr. Commissioner, that you have committed a federal offense, and your lawyer needs to inform you of that, that this appears to be a pattern and a practice, by you, to take campaign money to punish a competitor to campaign supporters of yours' business. That is illegal.*

> *MR. JOHNSON: Object to your ridiculous testimony.*

> *MR. BIBBS: Well, you can call it ridiculous if you want to. You let him explain that to a federal grand jury.*

Ex. A at p. 157:12-25. About a month or less later, Mr. Causey first approached federal authorities about Mr. Lindberg and later agreed to work with the FBI to investigate him. Tr. 434:14-441:25.

This evidence should have been admissible because it bore on Mr. Causey's bias. Evidence of bias is admissible as long as it is relevant. *United States v. Lindemann*, 85 F.3d 1232, 1243 (7th Cir. 1996) ("The admissibility of evidence regarding a witness's bias, diminished capacity, and contradictions in his testimony is not specifically addressed by the Rules, and thus admissibility is limited only by the relevance standard of Rule 402."). Particularly where a witness "may have some [ ] substantial reason to cooperate with the government, the defendant should be permitted wide latitude in the search for the witness'[s] bias." *Hoover v. Maryland*, 714 F.2d 301, 305 (4th Cir. 1983) (quoting *United States v. Tracey*, 675 F.2d 433, 437 (1st Cir.1982)). Since "bias is not a collateral issue," exploration of bias is not limited to cross examination; it is "permissible for evidence on this issue to be extrinsic in form." *Lindemann*, 85 F.3d at 1243.

Counsel may also explore bias through cross-examination. Indeed, "prohibiting a criminal defendant from cross-examining a witness on relevant evidence of bias and motive may violate the Confrontation Clause, if the jury is precluded from hearing evidence from which it could appropriately draw adverse inferences on the witness's credibility." *United States v. Turner*, 198 F.3d 425, 429 (4th Cir. 1999). "Where [the cross-examination] involves the government's most crucial witness, the constitutional concerns are especially heightened." *United States v. A & S Council Oil Co.*, 947 F.2d 1128, 1133 (4th Cir. 1991). The Federal Rules of Evidence echo these concerns by authorizing "cross- examination of witnesses on matters affecting their 'credibility.'" *United States v. Smith*, 451 F.3d 209, 221 (4th Cir. 2006); *see* Fed. R. Evid. 607.

This deposition transcript should have been admissible because it revealed a substantial reason for Mr. Causey to cooperate with the government. The testimony showed that the attorney deposing Mr. Causey suggested that he would be investigated by federal authorities for illegal activity. Soon after this deposition, Mr. Causey approached federal law enforcement about Mr. Lindberg and then agreed to serve as an agent of the FBI in investigating Mr. Lindberg. Based on this timeline, a reasonable jury could have inferred that Mr. Causey's cooperation with the FBI was an attempt to avoid investigation into his own activities.

In particular, this inference could have affected how the jury assessed Mr. Causey's testimony with regard to entrapment. Knowing that Mr. Causey had a motivation to cooperate with the government, the jury may have been more likely to find that Mr. Causey's recorded conversations with the defendants and his testimony about those conversations were efforts to entrap Mr. Lindberg. Thus, the Court should have allowed the jury to see the deposition transcript and permitted Mr. Lindberg's counsel to cross-examine Mr. Causey more fully about this deposition transcript.

This conclusion does not change even if federal law enforcement never considered or instituted an investigation of Mr. Causey. *But see* Tr. 361:5-10 (analysis by this Court suggesting otherwise). When it comes to bias, the question is not whether the government was objectively likely to investigate Mr. Causey. Rather, the question is what "the *witness* understands he or she will receive" by cooperating with the government, "for it is *this* understanding which is.of probative value on the issue of bias." *Hoover*, 714 F.2d 301, 305 (4th Cir. 1983) (second emphasis added). So regardless of whether the federal government would have actually instituted an investigation, Mr. Causey's subjective belief that he was in danger of an investigation would have been relevant to his bias. Counsel should have been allowed to explore that subjective belief, and the jury should have been allowed to see the deposition testimony that could have created that subjective belief.

Because entrapment was one of Mr. Lindberg's key defenses, this exclusion was particularly prejudicial and cannot be considered harmless. Nor was the prejudice cured by the fact that the Court allowed Mr. Lindberg to cross-examine Mr. Causey about some aspects of the deposition. After Mr. Causey reviewed the deposition transcript, Mr. Lindberg's counsel was allowed to ask whether "the counsel conducting that deposition question[ed] the legality of [Mr. Causey's] unrelated campaign finance contributions." Tr. 438:17-20. In response, Mr. Causey testified that the deposing lawyer was trying to show that Mr. Causey "had received money from competitors of Cannon Surety" and that these contributions were "a reason for [Mr. Causey's] going after examining Cannon Surety." Tr. 438:23-439:3. But the cross-examination did not reveal the key fact: that the deposing lawyer warned Mr. Causey that he could be investigated by the FBI. And since the Court told counsel to "[m]ove on" after Mr. Causey gave this answer, *id.* at 439:4, counsel was deprived of the opportunity to explore this topic through further questioning.

> **B. The Court Should Have Permitted Cross-Examination About Mr. Causey's Prior Untruthful Statements Because Those Statements Bore on His Credibility.**

The Court also should have allowed counsel to cross-examine Mr. Causey about his lies related to his activities in a farmer's market. As explained by Mr. Gray's counsel during argument on motions in limine, the evidence would have shown that Mr. Causey lied to operators of a farmer's market about whether he grew the blueberries that he was selling. February 18, 2020 Tr. 8:4-9:19.[11] Under Federal Rule of Evidence 608, "the court may, on cross-examination, allow" specific instances of a witness's conduct "to be inquired into if they are probative of the character for truthfulness or untruthfulness of … the witness."

Here, cross-examination would have been probative of Mr. Causey's character for untruthfulness: A jury could conclude that a person who was willing to lie about something as trivial as the growing of blueberries would embellish the truth in other instances. Admittedly, the Court has discretion to disallow such cross-examination. But it should have authorized cross-examination here because Mr. Causey was the key government witness. This cross-examination—when paired with Mr. Causey's motive to cooperate with the government—would have given the jury a substantial reason to distrust Mr. Causey's testimony and may have dissuaded it from finding Mr. Lindberg guilty.

C. Expert Testimony Should Have Been Allowed Because It Was Essential to the Jury's Understanding of the *Quid Pro Quo* Alleged in This Case.

For the reasons stated in the defendants' motion in limine regarding proposed expert testimony, Dkt. No. 133-1, February 18, 2020 Tr. 16:19-20:25, the exclusion of the expert testimony of Christopher Gober on campaign finance was erroneous and prejudicial to Mr. Lindberg.

Federal Rule of Evidence 702 governs the admission of this testimony. It states:

A witness who is qualified as an expert by knowledge, skill, experience, training, or education may testify in the form of an opinion or otherwise if:

(a) the expert's scientific, technical, or other specialized knowledge will help the trier of fact to understand the evidence or to determine a fact in issue;

(b) the testimony is based on sufficient facts or data;

(c) the testimony is the product of reliable principles and methods; and

(d) the expert has reliably applied the principles and methods to the facts of the case.

---

[11] A final certified copy of the transcript on argument on the motions in limine was not available to counsel at the time of filing. Citations to the motion in limine arguments are to the rough transcript.

This rule requires a court to "ensur[e] that an expert's testimony both rests on a reliable foundation and is relevant to the task at hand." *Belville v. Ford Motor Co.,* 919 F.3d 224, 232 (4th Cir. 2019) (quoting *Daubert v. Merrell Dow Pharms., Inc.,* 509 U.S. 579, 597(1993)) (internal quotation marks omitted).

In its ruling to exclude Mr. Gober's proposed testimony, the Court did not question whether the testimony would be reliable. Nor did the Court rule that the defendants had not complied with expert-notice requirements. Rather, the Court precluded the proposed testimony based on relevance. February 18, 2020 Tr. 16:19-18:5, 19:21-20:10.

But Mr. Gober's proposed testimony was directly relevant to a key issue in the case: whether the defendant gave "anything of value" as part of a *quid pro quo* with Mr. Causey. The government's theory of bribery in this case did not target direct payments from any defendant to Mr. Causey. Rather, the government argued that the defendants gave "[a]thing of value" to Mr. Causey through contributions made to an independent expenditure committee (IECs) and through a contribution made from the North Carolina Republican Party to Mr. Causey, purportedly with funds that Mr. Lindberg had contributed to the Republican Party. The jury was tasked with deciding whether these transfers were things of value that were part of a *quid pro quo. See Jennings,* 160 F.3d at 1019.

A jury or other factfinder is not required to find that any transfer of anything to anyone is a *quid pro quo.* For example, the Second Circuit has held in a *quid-pro-quo* analysis under tax law that an expected benefit or subjective desire for something to occur does not always constitute a thing of value. *See Scheidelman v. Comm'r,* 682 F.3d 189, 200 (2d Cir. 2012) ("A donee's agreement to accept a gift does not transfer anything of value to the donor, even though the donor may desire to have his gift accepted, and may expect to derive benefit elsewhere (such as by deductibility of the gift on her income taxes)."). Thus, the jury was not required to accept the government's theory that the transfers alleged by the government constituted "[a]thing of value" given by any defendant.

To properly assess the government's theory, the jury needed to understand the structure of IECs and donations to the North Carolina Republican Party, and the campaign finance law that governs them. Mr. Gober would have provided that information. For example, Mr. Gober would have testified about the rules that govern how these entities receive and spend money on behalf of candidates and whether they are permitted to contribute to candidates. He would have testified about the rules governing how these entities spend money. And he could have clarified who controlled these entities' funds and who had the authority to transfer funds. *See* Defs.' Notice of Intent to Use Expert Witness at Trial, Dkt. No. 133-2.

A reasonable jury that had this information may have decided that the transfer of funds to an IEC, which cannot coordinate spending with or consult a candidate, was at most an expected benefit and not something of value. *N. Carolina Right to Life, Inc. v. Leake*, 525 F.3d 274, 278 (4th Cir. 2008) (quoting N.C. Gen. Stat. § 163–278.6(9a) (2007)). A reasonable jury may have concluded the same about Mr. Lindberg's contribution to the North Carolina Republican Party. Mr. Gober's testimony could have clarified whether the defendants or the Republican Party controlled the funds once Mr. Lindberg transferred money to the party. If the jury concluded that the North Carolina Republican Party had full control over the funds, it may have concluded that the Party's transfer of funds to Mr. Causey could not constitute "anything of value" given by Mr. Lindberg.

Although the government may argue that the transfer of funds by Robin Hayes, the then- chairman of the North Carolina Republican Party, to Mr. Causey should be attributed to the codefendants, this argument should be rejected. The government did not introduce sufficient evidence to show that Robin Hayes was part of the charged conspiracy. Rule 29 Suppl. 14, Dkt. No. 192. Thus, to convict Mr. Lindberg, the jury needed to conclude that Mr. Lindberg's initial contribution to the North Carolina Republican Party was part of a transfer of something of value to Mr. Causey. And if the jury found, based on Mr. Gober's testimony, that the Party had full control over the money after receiving it, the jury may have rejected this pivotal conclusion.

Without Mr. Gober's testimony, Mr. Lindberg was unable to fully present one of his main defenses: that neither he nor any coconspirator gave "anything of value" to Mr. Causey. Thus, the Court should grant a new trial that allows this evidence to be admitted.

D. The Admission of Evidence of the Suggestion to Hire John Palermo Warrants a New Trial.

During trial, the government introduced recorded conversations between Mr. Causey and the defendants in which they discussed whether Mr. Causey could hire defendant John Palermo to the Department of Insurance. For the reasons stated in support of Mr. Lindberg's motion in limine, Dkt. 141-1, this evidence should have been excluded.

Evidence is inadmissible if it is not relevant. Fed. R. Evid. 401, 402. Evidence is relevant "only if 'it has any tendency to make a fact more or less probable than it would be without the evidence' and 'the fact is of consequence in determining the action.'" *United States v. Zayyad*, 741 F.3d 452, 459 (4th Cir. 2014) (quoting Fed. R. Evid. 401). Thus, evidence is not relevant if it does "not connect to" an "element of the charged offenses." *Id.* at 460.

Evidence of Mr. Palermo's suggested hiring was both irrelevant and unfairly prejudicial, confusing, and misleading.

First, the evidence related to the suggestion that Mr. Causey hire Mr. Palermo was not relevant because it did not connect to any element of the charges. Although the Court found this evidence "inextricably tied to the conspiracy," February 18, 2020 Tr. 24:20, this analysis was incorrect. The suggested hiring of Mr. Palermo was not part of the "scheme or artifice" to deprive the public of honest services, which was the object of the conspiracy charged in the indictment. In honest-services wire fraud, "scheme or artifice" means a *quid pro quo* involving an official act. *McDonnell* v, 136 S. Ct. at 2365. The official act charged in this indictment was the removal of Senior Deputy Commissioner Obusek. But trial evidence showed that Mr. Causey never considered hiring Mr. Palermo into Ms. Obusek's position and ultimately declined to hire Mr. Palermo. Tr. 168:4-14, 177:2-16, 698:6-701:25. Thus, Mr. Palermo's suggested hiring could not have been part of the charged "scheme or artifice." For similar reasons, Mr. Palermo's hiring was not relevant to the "business, transaction, or series of transactions" element of § 666(a)(2). The alleged transaction was the transfer of Senior Deputy Commissioner Obusek. Indictment ¶ 86, Dkt. No. 3. Mr. Palermo's suggested hiring had nothing to do with that action. It was thus irrelevant to both offenses.

The dates of the wire transfers relied on by the government also prove that Mr. Palermo's hiring was not part of the alleged scheme or artifice. An essential element of wire fraud is that the defendants "used or caused the use of wire communications in furtherance of" their "scheme to defraud." *United States v. Burfoot*, 899 F.3d 326, 335 (4th Cir. 2018); see 18 U.S.C. § 1343. The wire transfers relied on by the government in furtherance of the scheme occurred on various dates from June 11, 2018, to July 26, 2018. Indictment ¶ 84. But the idea of hiring Mr. Palermo was abandoned on March 27, 2018—months before the wire transfers. Tr.750:18-751:11. Based on this timeline, Mr. Palermo's hiring necessarily could not have been part of the charged wire-fraud scheme, since those later wire transfers could not have "further[ed]" an already-rejected idea.

Even if this evidence were relevant, it should have been excluded under Federal Rule of Evidence 403. Under Rule 403, the "court may exclude relevant evidence if its probative value is substantially outweighed by a danger of . . . unfair prejudice, confusing the issues, [or] misleading the jury." Evidence is unfairly prejudicial if it "lure[s] the factfinder into declaring guilt on a ground different from proof specific to the offense charged" or if it "suggest[s] decision on an improper basis." *Old Chief v. United States*, 519 U.S. 172, 180 (1997); Fed. R. Evid. 403, Advisory Committee's Note. For example, a jury cannot be asked to "generaliz[e] a defendant's earlier bad act into bad character and tak[e] that as raising the odds that he did the later bad act now charged." *Old Chief*, 519 U.S. at 180. Evidence confuses the issues or misleads the jury if it "cause[s] a diversion" from the ultimate issue that it must decide. *Huskey v. Ethicon, Inc.*, 848 F.3d 151, 162 (4th Cir. 2017).

Evidence of Mr. Palermo's suggested hiring wrongly diverted the jury's attention from the relevant official act or transaction—the alleged transfer or removal of Senior Deputy Commissioner Obusek. This evidence also could have only served to imply that Mr. Lindberg tried to influence a separate official act or transaction. The use of this evidence is improper. Given the lack of relevance and the strong prejudicial effect of this evidence, a new trial is warranted.

V. Various Jury Instructions—Beyond the Erroneous "Official Act" Instruction—Justify a New Trial.

In addition to the erroneous "official act" instruction discussed above, multiple other erroneous jury instructions require a new trial. Mr. Lindberg objected, as appropriate, to the Court's jury instruction during the jury-charge conference. Mr. Lindberg renews each objection to the Court's instructions or its failure to give an instruction, including the particular instructions discussed below.[12]

A. The Definition of "Corruptly" Failed to Include a Requirement of Conscious Wrongdoing, a Bad or Evil Motive, or Acting Intentionally with an Unlawful Purpose.

For the reasons discussed at length in Mr. Lindberg's trial brief, Dkt. No. 164 at 4-5, 6, his response to the government's objections to jury instructions, Dkt. No. 159 at 7-8, and at the jury- charge conference, Tr. 1567:2-1569:14, Mr. Lindberg believes that the Court incorrectly defined the word "corruptly" in its instruction on 18 U.S.C. § 666(a)(2) and incorrectly omitted the requirement that the defendant act "corruptly" in its instruction on honest-services wire fraud.

---

[12] Because Mr. Lindberg objected to jury instructions that he believed were erroneous during the jury-charge conference, no further action, including discussion in this motion, is needed for these objections to be preserved for appellate review. Fed. R. Crim. P. 30(d); Tr. 1510:19-1609:25. Objections that were made at the conference but not discussed in this motion are still preserved for appeal.

First, the defendants' proposed definition of "corruptly" should have been given. This proposed definition read: "An act is 'corruptly' done if it is done intentionally with an unlawful purpose. This involves conscious wrongdoing or, as it is sometimes expressed, a bad or evil state of mind. If a defendant acts with the belief that his purpose was lawful, he does not act 'corruptly.'" Defs.' Joint Proposed Jury Instr. at 72, 83 (Instruction Nos. 59, 69), Dkt. No. 163-1. Instead, the Court defined "corruptly" as follows:

An act is done "corruptly" if it is done with the intent to engage in some specific *quid pro quo*, that is, to receive a specific benefit in return for the payment, or to induce a specific act. A payment is made with corrupt intent only if it was made or promised with the intent to corrupt the particular official. Not every payment made to influence or reward an official is intended to corrupt him. One has the intent to corrupt an official only if he makes a payment or a promise with the intent to engage in a specific *quid pro quo* with that official. The defendant must have intended for the official to engage in some specific act, or omission, or course of action or inaction in return for the payment charged in the bill of indictment.

Tr. 1785:15-1786:2. This instruction fairly tracked the definition of "corruptly" offered by the Fourth Circuit in United States v. Jennings, 160 F.3d 1006, 1019 (4th Cir. 1998).

But intervening Supreme Court precedent and other appellate decisions on similar bribery statutes undercut the Court's definition and support the defendants'. In *Arthur Andersen LLP v. United States*, 544 U.S. 696 (2005), the Supreme Court interpreted the word "corruptly" in a federal obstruction statute and observed that "corruptly" is associated with "wrongful, immoral, depraved, or evil" conduct. *Id.* at 705. Therefore, it held that the phrase "knowingly ... corruptly persuad[e]" limited criminal liability to those who were "conscious of wrongdoing." *Id.* at 706. Other cases have defined "corrupt" intent in a similar way to *Arthur Andersen*. For example, the Fourth Circuit has approved a similar definition of "corrupt" intent in the context of § 201, of which § 666 is an outgrowth. *See United States v. Quinn*, 359 F.3d 666, 674 (4th Cir. 2004) (approving a district court's instruction that corrupt intent involves "conscious wrongdoing or, as it is sometimes expressed, a bad or evil state of mind"). The Ninth Circuit has affirmed a jury finding of "corrupt" intent in a § 201 prosecution because the evidence showed that the defendant "was aware of the illegality of the transaction" at issue. *United States v. Hsieh Hui Mei Chen*, 754 F.2d 817, 822 (9th Cir. 1985). And the Fifth Circuit pattern instructions define "corruptly" in § 201 as follows: "An act is 'corruptly' done if it is done intentionally with an unlawful purpose." Pattern Crim. Jury Instr. 5th Cir. 2.09A (2019). "Corruptly" should have a similar definition in the context of § 666(a)(2), given the relationship between § 201 and § 666.

Moreover, the defendants' proposed definition of "corruptly" is supported by cases interpreting "corruptly" in other bribery statutes. *E.g., United States v. Kay*, 513 F.3d 432, 446 (5th Cir. 2007) (stating that "corrupt" in the Foreign Corrupt Practices Act requires "bad purpose or evil motive of accomplishing either an unlawful end or result").

Unlike the Court's definition based on *Jennings*, the defendants' proposed definition of "corruptly" follows the rule that courts "must 'give effect ... to every clause and word'" in a statute. *Setser v. United States*, 566 U.S. 231, 239 (2012) (quoting *United States v. Menasche*, 348 U.S. 528, 538-39 (1955)). In contrast, the Court's definition mimics the statutory language that requires a defendant to "give[ ], offer[ ], or agree[ ] to give anything of value to any person, with intent to influence or reward" a State agent. 18 U.S.C. § 666(a)(2). Thus, the Court's definition effectively reads the word "corruptly" out of the statute or renders it superfluous. The defendants' proposed definition does not.

This definition of "corruptly" also makes sense in light of the harm that bribery statutes seek to prevent: the violation of a public official's duty to serve the public. *See, e.g., United States v. Jacobs*, 431 F.2d 754, 759 (2d Cir. 1970) ("The evil sought to be prevented by the deterrent effect of 18 U.S.C. § 201(b) is the aftermath suffered by the public when an official is corrupted and thereby perfidiously fails to perform his public service and duty."). Liability under federal bribery law should be limited to those who act with an evil motive to subvert the political process. It should not extend to people who lack an evil or bad motive. Nor should it extend to people who do not know that they are procuring a breach of an official's duties or otherwise violating the law. A bribery statute that punished such people would raise constitutional issues by criminalizing innocent, First Amendment-protected interactions between constituents who donate to politicians based on the politicians' promised actions. Second, the Court incorrectly failed to include an instruction on "corruptly" for honest- services wire fraud. Honest-services wire fraud should be defined with reference to § 201. *See McDonnell v., 136 S. Ct.* at 2365. Since § 201 requires corrupt intent, so should this offense.

B. The Instruction on Material Concealment of Fact Was Erroneous.

The Court's instruction on a material misrepresentation or material concealment of fact stated that the "Government may be able to prove this element if you find that the bribe was concealed from the public." For the reasons explained in Mr. Lindberg's objections to the jury instructions, Tr. 1613:21-13, 1628:10-22, Dkt. No. 191 at 1-2, this instruction was incorrect for this case. The Court cited three cases to support its instruction. The first two cases involved public servants or public- servant coconspirators whose positions gave them fiduciary duties to the public: *United States v. Foxworth*, 334 F. App'x 363, 365-66 (2d Cir. 2009) (non-precedential), and *United States v. Harvey*, 532 F.3d 326, 334 (4th Cir. 2008); *see also United States v. Foxworth*, No. 06-cr-81, 2006 WL 3462657, at *1 (D. Conn. Nov. 16, 2006). *Harvey* also involved a situation where the defendant was explicitly required to disclose the payments made to him. *Id.* at 332. So did the third case, which involved private parties who disregarded an explicit rule requiring them to disclose offers of gratuities. *United States v. Rybicki,* 354 F.3d 124, 127 (2d Cir. 2003) (en banc). If this were a situation in which Mr. Lindberg or a coconspirator were under an explicit obligation or fiduciary duty to disclose a payment to the public or some other entity, the Court's instruction may have been appropriate. But the government failed to establish a rule or fiduciary duty that required Mr. Lindberg to disclose the contributions.

C. The Court Failed to Instruct the Jury Fully on the Requirements for a Quid Pro Quo, Single or Multiple Conspiracies, the Good-Faith Defense, the Definitions of Benefits and the Value of a Transaction Under § 666, and Entrapment.

The Court also omitted several crucial instructions. First, for both offenses, the Court's instruction on *"quid pro quo"* left out the requirement that a public official must make an *explicit promise* to perform an official act in exchange for a campaign contribution. Defs.' Proposed Jury Instructions 22, 73, 85 (Instruction Nos. 15, 60, 71), Dkt. No. 163-1; Tr. 1569:15-22. This requirement comes from *McCormick v. United States*, 500 U.S. 257, 273 (1991), which made clear that campaign contributions can form the basis of a bribery charge only when a public official explicitly promises action in exchange for the contribution. Without this requirement, federal bribery law risks running afoul of free-speech rights. *Id.* at 272-73. For the same reasons, the Court also erred by failing to instruct the jury that § 666(a)(2) also requires proof of a *quid pro quo*, and not merely the "intent to engage in some specific *quid pro quo*." Without this requirement, innocent constituents could be held liable for campaign contributions that do not deprive the public of any honest-services.

Second, the Court should have instructed the jury that, for § 666(a)(2), "the government must prove beyond any reasonable doubt that the transfer of Senior Deputy Commissioner Obusek off a regulatory assignment was valued at $5,000 or more, not that the alleged bribe offer was $5,000 or more." Defs.' Proposed Jury Instructions 84 (Instruction No. 70); Tr. 1591:9-1592:12. This requested instruction finds support in *United States v. Tillmon*, — F.3d —, 2019 WL 921534 (4th Cir. Feb. 26, 2019), which states that "this element requires proof of the value of whatever was exchanged for the bribe." *Id.* at *11-12. The defendants' proposed instruction would have informed the jury that the amount of the bribe is not dispositive evidence of the value of the transaction. Although *Tillmon* observes that the amount of a bribe offer is one valid method of valuing the transaction, *id.* at *11, the defendants' proposed instruction would have assured the jury that it was free to use other methods to value the transaction.

Third, the Court should have instructed the jury about single and multiple conspiracies. Defs.' Proposed Jury Instructions 61 (Instruction No. 49); Tr. 1554:11-1562:1. The conspiracy charged in this case was a *quid pro quo* to remove a Senior Deputy Commissioner. But the evidence at trial also focused on a proposed hiring of another co-defendant, John Palermo, by the Department of Insurance. Because this instruction was omitted, the jury may have wrongfully convicted Mr. Lindberg of this separate alleged conspiracy. *See supra* Section IV.D.

Fourth, the Court should have instructed on the good-faith defense for both offenses. Defs.' Proposed Jury Instructions 92-93 (Instruction No. 75); Tr. 1550:7-1551:23; Dkt. No. 159 at 9. The validity of the good-faith defense is well established in the wire-fraud context, *e.g., United States v. Ammons*, 464 F.2d 414, 417 (8th Cir. 1972) (holding in context of mail fraud that "[g]ood faith constitutes a complete defense to one charged with an offense of which fraudulent intent is an essential element"), and it has been approved in charges brought under § 666, *see United States v. Baroni*, 909 F.3d 550, 582-83 (3d Cir. 2018) (writing approvingly of instruction as to good-faith in context of § 666(a)(1)(A)), *cert. granted sub nom. Kelly v. United States*, 139 S. Ct. 2777 (2019). As explained in Mr. Lindberg's jury-objection response brief, good faith is inconsistent with corrupt intent and an intent to defraud, Dkt. No. 159 at 9.

Fifth, the Court should have provided the jury with a definition of "benefits" under § 666. Dkt. No. 189 at 4; Tr. 1595:9-1597:9. As discussed in Section III of this brief, this issue is a jury question, and the government did not sufficiently prove that the Department of Insurance received "benefits in excess of $10,000 under a Federal program." At minimum, this issue was genuinely disputed and should have been submitted to the jury. An instruction on this element would have guided the jury in its deliberation.

Finally, the Court should have given the defendants' proposed instruction on entrapment, which is adapted from the model Ninth Circuit instruction. Defs.' Proposed Jury Instructions 94-95 (Instruction No. 76); Tr. 1603:24-1605:22. This instruction offers the jury more guidance than the instruction delivered by the Court. The importance of additional guidance was made clear during jury deliberations, when the jury sent the Court a note asking for help distinguishing between inducement and solicitation. Tr. 1816:8-11.

VI. The Government Failed to Introduce Substantial Evidence of Criminal Intent.

Honest-services wire fraud requires proof of an intent to defraud, and § 666(a)(2) requires proof of corrupt intent. Tr. 1776:4-5, 1784:1. A defendant has an intent to defraud if he acts "knowingly and with the intention or the purpose to deceive or cheat." Tr. 1776:22-24. This intent is "accompanied ordinarily by a desire or a purpose to bring about some gain or benefit to oneself or some other person or by a desire or purpose to cause some loss to some person." Tr. 1776:24-1777:2. As discussed above, corrupt intent should require proof of conscious wrongdoing, a bad or evil motive, and an intentional act with an unlawful purpose. *Supra* Section V.A. But if it does not, then it requires at least "intent to corrupt the particular official" and "intent to engage in some specific *quid pro quo*, that is, to receive a specific benefit in return for the payment." Tr. 1785:15-20.

Regardless of the definition, the government failed to introduce substantial evidence of Mr. Lindberg's criminal intent. Evidence throughout trial showed Mr. Lindberg's intent to follow the law and act properly. *See, e.g.,* Gov't Ex. 127A at 19 (statement by Lindberg that the "bottom line" was that he would do what was "in the bounds of North Carolina election law"); Gov't Ex. 127A at 18 (statement by Lindberg that he did not "know election law well enough" but that it was "compliant" to give "money to NCGOP" and for the NC GOP to "give money to" Causey); Gov't Ex. 118 at 9 (statement by Lindberg urging, with regard to setting up independent expenditure committee, that they "do this the right way"); Lindberg Ex. 91F (Lindberg noting, on request by Causey for transfer to personal checking account, "I don't think that complies"); Gov't Ex. 128A at 4 (statement by John Gray: "We're not wanting anything outside the rule of law and the rules of … of your department and want you're comfortable with."); Lindberg Ex. 59B (statement by John Gray that Causey would "have to pay [his] way" on a proposed trip to Washington, D.C., on Lindberg's plane because of "Board of elections requirements"). Thus, as discussed in Mr. Lindberg's prior motions, the evidence does not support a showing of corrupt intent under the proper definition of that term. Rule 29 Suppl. 15. Moreover, in light of this evidence, the government's evidence at trial was not sufficiently "substantial" to support a finding of corrupt intent under the Court's definition or a finding of an intent to defraud. Acquittal, or at least a new trial, is thus required.

VII. **The Government Failed to Present Sufficient Evidence of Proper Venue, a Quid Pro Quo, False or Fraudulent Pretenses, or Intent to Influence a Future Official Action.**

At the close of the government's evidence, Mr. Lindberg moved for judgment of acquittal based on, among other things, insufficiency of evidence of proper venue, a *quid pro quo*, corrupt intent, false or fraudulent pretenses, and intent to influence a future official action. Mr. Lindberg renewed each of these arguments at the close of the defense's evidence in a second oral motion, which was denied. Tr. 1508:24-1509:5. Mr. Lindberg now renews his motion for judgment of acquittal based on these and all other arguments stated in his oral motion at the close of the government's evidence and in his memorandum supplementing his first oral Rule 29 motion. *See* Tr. 1253:20-1266:21, 1268:20- 1269:20; *see also* Rule 29 Suppl., Dkt. No. 192. If the Court disagrees that Mr. Lindberg is owed acquittal based on these arguments, it should nonetheless find that the government's failure of evidence supports a new trial.

VIII. **The Combined Prejudice of These Errors Requires a New Trial.**

Mr. Lindberg is entitled to acquittal based on the arguments set forth above. In the alternative, he is owed a new trial based on each error identified above. Each of the errors discussed above, at minimum, independently justifies a new trial.

But if the Court disagrees, it should still order a new trial based on the cumulative prejudice from these errors. "Pursuant to the cumulative error doctrine, '[t]he cumulative effect of two or more individually harmless errors has the potential to prejudice a defendant to the same extent as a single reversible error.'" *United States v. Basham*, 561 F.3d 302, 330 (4th Cir. 2009) (quoting *United States v. Rivera*, 900 F.2d 1462, 1469 (10th Cir. 1990)). If the Court agrees that it erred in more than one of the crucial rulings discussed above, the Court should find that the combined effect of the errors "violated the trial's fundamental fairness" and order a new trial. *Id.* (quoting *United States v. Bell*, 367 F.3d 452, 471 (5th Cir. 2004)) (internal quotation mark omitted).

CONCLUSION

For the foregoing reasons, the Court should enter a judgment of acquittal on both counts brought against Mr. Lindberg or, in the alternative, order a new trial.

Dated: April 2, 2020

Paul J. Johnson (admitted *pro hac vice*)
900 Jackson Street, Suite 650
Dallas, TX 75202
214-761-0707
pjjdoc@aol.com

Aaron Zachary Tobin (N.C. Bar. No. 50019) CONDON TOBIN SLADEK THORNTON, PLLC
8080 Park Lane, Suite 700
Dallas, TX 75231
214-265-3800
atobin@ctstlaw.com

Jeffrey C. Grady (N.C. Bar. No. 32695) KATTEN MUCHIN ROSENMAN LLP
550 S. Tryon Street, Suite 2900
Charlotte, NC 28202
704-444-2036
jeff.grady@katten.com

Respectfully submitted,

Rajesh R. Srinivasan (admitted pro hac vice) KATTEN MUCHIN ROSENMAN LLP
2900 K Street, NW – Suite 200
Washington, DC 20007
202-625-3500
rajesh.srinivasan@katten.com

Brandon N. McCarthy
(admitted *pro hac vice*)
Rachel M. Riley (admitted *pro hac vice*)
KATTEN MUCHIN ROSENMAN LLP
1717 Main Street, Suite 3750
Dallas, TX 75201
214-765-3600
brandon.mccarthy@katten.com
rachel.riley@katten.com

Counsel for Defendant Greg E. Lindberg

CERTIFICATE OF SERVICE

I hereby certify that on April 2, 2020, I electronically filed the foregoing memorandum and accompanying exhibit with the Clerk of Court using the CM/ECF system, which will send notification to counsel of record.

Dated: April 2, 2020

Respectfully submitted,

/s/ Rajesh R. Srinivasan

Rajesh R. Srinivasan
Admitted Pro Hac Vice
KATTEN MUCHIN ROSENMAN LLP
2900 K Street NW, North Tower, Suite 200 Washington, DC 20007
202-625-3761, rajesh.srinivasan@katten.com

Counsel for Defendant Greg E. Lindberg

APPENDIX B:
Helping Those Who Can't Afford to Fight

The full text here of the article published on June 2nd, 2020:

"Greg Lindberg Donates $1 Million To ACLU To Help People Who Can't Afford to Fight Injustice"

DURHAM, N.C., June 2, 2020 /PRNewswire/ — Greg Lindberg announced today a $1 million pledge to the ACLU's Criminal Law Reform Project (CLRP). This program focuses its work on the "front end" of the criminal legal system—from policing to sentencing—seeking to end excessively harsh criminal justice policies that result in mass incarceration, over-criminalization, racial injustice, and stand in the way of a fair and equal society.

"People have taken to the streets to air their frustration with a system that is stacked against them," Mr. Lindberg said. "This contribution is meant to help people who don't have the resources to fight injustice."

Mr. Lindberg commented, "I have been disturbed by the consequences of prosecutorial abuses and unjust incarceration of nonviolent offenders for some time. Recent events have exacerbated these concerns. Most people can't afford to fight and they get rolled over by prosecutors and their bag of tricks. 'Justice for all' is sadly a mirage in much of today's America."

The donation will support the objectives of the Criminal Law Reform Project to ensure that someday 'justice for all' are not mere empty words—and that the United States justice system truly operates without regard to income, race, or political persuasion, said Mr. Lindberg.

"The 'Justice' system is broken and your freedom is at risk. Major reforms are needed. Even for someone with an ability to hire the best counsel, fighting the U.S. or State Government can wipe people out—emotionally, financially, physically, spiritually. Most unfortunately emerge not 'rehabilitated' but ruined and defeated. They can't get a job, start a business, or even open a bank account. And for what end? Families, lives, and futures are destroyed," Mr. Lindberg continued.

Mr. Lindberg said he hopes the donation will help expose abusive prosecutors and law enforcement officers, including local, state and federal government agents, who prey on law-abiding citizens, sometimes for their own personal gain.

Mr. Lindberg continued, "We call ourselves a free society but the truth is the United States has the highest prison and jail population (2,121,600 in adult facilities in 2016), and the highest incarceration rate in the world (655 per 100,000 population in 2016)." According to the World Prison Population List (11th edition) there were around 10.35 million people in penal institutions worldwide in 2015. The US had 2,173,800 prisoners in adult facilities in 2015. That means the US held 21.0% of the world's prisoners in 2015, even though the US represented only around 4.4 percent of the world's population in 2015.

In The New Yorker article "The Caging of America" (2012), Adam Gopnik wrote: "Over all, there are now more people under 'correctional supervision' in America—more than six million—than were in the Gulag Archipelago under Stalin at its height."

With the emergence of COVID-19 in prison populations, both Federal and State prisons have concluded that nonviolent offenders are better off rehabilitating in home detention programs. "If these nonviolent offenders are safe for society now, why weren't they safe before? The truth is, they were always safe for society and it took a pandemic for the government to appreciate that," Mr. Lindberg stated.

As the ACLU Founder Roger Baldwin said, "So long as we have enough people in this country willing to fight for their rights, we'll be called a democracy."

APPENDIX C:
Global Growth and Global Good

About Global Growth

Global Growth is a global private investment firm with investments in healthcare technology, financial services, collectibles, alternative assets, and communications. Our companies operate in more than 20 countries and employ more than 7,500 people worldwide. We were founded by Greg Lindberg (www.greglindberg.com) on a simple yet contrarian idea: companies that make the world a better place are more likely to thrive. Since our founding, our investment team has focused on sustainable, long-term investment strategies that reflect our business principles. We believe in generating meaningful returns for our stakeholders, delivering innovative, customer-centric solutions, and helping our business leaders positively impact their communities.

www.globalgrowth.com

The full text here of the article published in the Post-Gazette on June 18th, 2020:

"Global Growth and Global Good: Greg Lindberg's Journey from Donor To Social Benefactor"

People who build great wealth tend to develop and share the same methods and habits. I first saw evidence of this when I read Napoleon Hill's famous book *Think and Grow Rich*. I'd put off reading it for a long time, because I was more interested in improving the world than building wealth. I didn't realize at the time how much wealth can be used to facilitate a better society.

Once I read Hill's book, I discovered that he was writing about routes to financial success, but also about a life rich in happiness and service.

According to Hill, he simply wanted to finance getting himself and his brother through law school, so he approached legendary steel magnate Andrew Carnegie for a job. Carnegie offered Hill an opportunity instead. He introduced him to rich and famous friends who shared their successful philosophies and habits. This research became Hill's bestseller book and secured his legendary career.

When I first met Tony Robbins, he was living in a two-bedroom apartment in Venice Beach, California. He was going around meeting highly successful people. Tony knew something successful journalists learn, that people of great achievement love to give advice. In Hollywood terms, it's called "giving back."

Successful people seek wisdom, mentors, and like-minded people all their lives. It's one of their most important good habits. People help them, and they help others.

Author Thomas C. Corley spent five years learning about the daily habits of 177 self-made millionaires and dubbed their best practices "rich habits." He chronicled his findings in the books *Rich Habits: The Daily Success Habits of Wealthy Individuals* and *Change Your Habits, Change Your Life*.

One curious thing Corley discovered was why many wealthy people turn to charity. It's not a case of building good public relations, like the old John D. Rockefeller story of handing out shiny new dimes to poor kids as reporters snapped photos. The millionaires Corley studied contribute to charities to network with other like-minded people. According to Corley, "This is why so many wealthy people volunteer for charitable organizations, civic groups, or trade groups. It helps them expand their network of other success-minded people."

There's also another reason. Many self-made millionaires grew up struggling and thus understand human needs from personal experience. Corley discovered that 41% of the self-made millionaires in his Rich Habits Study (which resulted in his book) came from poverty.

Greg Lindberg had a family legacy like that. Today, his Global Growth conglomerate encompasses dozens of companies, with 8000 employees worldwide. He built his fortune from a $5,000 investment while in college. He was the first Lindberg to graduate from college. From a working-class family with occupations like plumber and auto-mechanic, Greg learned that hard work and discipline is rewarded with success. He was also aware he came from meager beginnings. When he perused a ledger book that his grandfather kept, he saw that at one time granddad was making only 8 cents an hour.

That's enough to make anyone sensitive to the struggles and needs of the less fortunate.

Lindberg was civic minded as his fortune grew. At one point, making him so well-known his charity work became big news.

While working his way through the justice system, Greg had a front-row seat to the challenges that low-income people and non-English speakers face when trying to navigate it. He provided start-up funding for Interrogating Justice, a nonprofit that provides information to justice-impacted people about their rights and the resources available to help them exercise them. In its first year thanks to Greg's funding, they were able to help more than 100,000 justice-impacted individuals.

Lindberg's charitable involvement has continued to date. In January of 2020, he pledged a $50,000 donation to the Special Olympics of North Carolina (SONC) as a year-round Healthy Communities partner focused on nutrition. This involvement included state-level events such as the Winter Games, Summer Games, Equestrian Tournament and Fall Tournament, promoting nutrition education among SONC athletes.

Lindberg's partnership with SONC allows for employee engagement opportunities among Global Growth employees within the scope of these health-related efforts. As a Healthy Communities partner, Lindberg's support impacts SONC athletes year-round.

He also holds deep concerns for health and nutrition. In July of 2020, his companies provided the first 100,000 meals in a commitment to provide 1 million meals to areas affected by the global pandemic. The meals go to nonprofits in the U.S., Europe, India, the Philippines, Costa Rica, and the Ukraine with a focus on programs that provide the most nutritious meals at a reasonable cost.

In announcing the donation, Bridgett Hurley, the company's Chief Development Officer, said: "Our companies operate in more than 20 countries, and our giving program will do the same." With strong connections to local communities where the company operates, Global Growth's giving is targeted for optimal impact.

This new program was not some new idea prompted by worldwide troubles. Global Growth has invested in eye care surgery for underserved populations and in research for treatment of Parkinson's disease, and has been providing medical services to tens of thousands of people in developing countries since 2015. The pandemic suspended providing these services to the degree possible in the past, so the free meals offered the opportunity to make a meaningful impact. The company has a plan to expand the program during 2021.

Lindberg once again turned to charity. He pledged $1 million to the ACLU's Criminal Law Reform Project (CLRP) which focuses on the "front end" of the criminal legal system to end excessively harsh criminal justice policies that stand in the way of a fair and equal society.

"I have been disturbed by the consequences of prosecutorial abuses and unjust incarceration of nonviolent offenders for some time," Lindberg says. "Recent events have exacerbated these concerns. Most people can't afford to fight, and they get rolled over by prosecutors and their bag of tricks. 'Justice for all' is sadly a mirage in much of today's America."

With his donation, Lindberg sought to support the objectives of the CLRP to ensure that someday "justice for all" is not a meaningless phrase. He believes the United States justice system must truly operate without regard to income, race, or persuasion.

With the United States having the highest incarceration rate in the world, that kind of ambition seems very lofty, but for someone who built a worldwide company of 8000 employees from a $5000 investment in a part-time business while in college, great things are possible.

Lindberg quoted ACLU Founder Roger Baldwin, who said, "So long as we have enough people in this country willing to fight for their rights, we'll be called a democracy."

In all of his global endeavors—business and charitable—Greg Lindberg has followed the advice of Teddy Roosevelt by being one who is "actually in the arena, whose face is marred by dust and sweat and blood." He has created greater advantage in every adversity he and his companies have faced. Finding greater advantage in every adversity reflects core elements of Global Growth's organizational culture. And charitable examples like this benefit us all.

APPENDIX D:
Intermittent Fasting Resources

INTERMITTENT FASTING REFERENCES

Intermittent Fasting: What is it, and how does it work?
Intermittent fasting: What is it, and how does it work? Johns Hopkins Medicine. (n.d.).
Retrieved November 15, 2021, from https://www.hopkinsmedicine.org/health/
wellness-and-prevention/intermittent-fasting-what-is-it-and-how-does-it-work.

Excerpt:
"Research shows that the intermittent fasting periods do more than burn fat. Mattson
explains, 'When changes occur with this metabolic switch, it affects the body and brain.'

One of Mattson's studies published in the New England Journal of Medicine
revealed data about a range of health benefits associated with the practice.
These include a longer life, a leaner body and a sharper mind.

'Many things happen during intermittent fasting that can protect organs against
chronic diseases like type 2 diabetes, heart disease, age-related neurodegenerative
disorders, even inflammatory bowel disease and many cancers,' he says.

Here are some intermittent fasting benefits research has revealed so far:

- **Thinking and memory.** Studies discovered that intermittent fasting boosts
  working memory in animals and verbal memory in adult humans.

- **Heart health.** Intermittent fasting improved blood pressure and resting
  heart rates as well as other heart-related measurements.

- **Physical performance.** Young men who fasted for 16 hours showed fat
  loss while maintaining muscle mass. Mice who were fed on alternate days
  showed better endurance in running.

- **Diabetes and obesity.** In animal studies, intermittent fasting prevented
  obesity. And in six brief studies, obese adult humans lost weight through
  intermittent fasting.

- **Tissue health.** In animals, intermittent fasting reduced tissue damage in
  surgery and improved results."

The Intermittent Fasting Podcast

https://ifpodcast.com/

The Intermittent Fasting Podcast serves to demystify the intermittent fasting (IF) lifestyle: a pattern of eating in which you regulate the hours you eat each day, rather than the amount of food you eat. Intermittent fasting instigates effortless weight loss, health and vitality. The Intermittent Fasting Podcast was started by two self-published authors: Melanie Avalon (*The What When Wine Diet: Paleo and Intermittent Fasting for Health and Weight Loss*) and Gin Stephens (*Delay, Don't Deny: Living an Intermittent Fasting Lifestyle*). Melanie and Gin both actively practice intermittent fasting lifestyles, personally choosing to eat one meal per day for dinner. With intermittent fasting, they have experienced effortless and substantial weight loss, as well as many health and other "life" benefits. They also answer listener questions through their podcast and website.

Effects of Intermittent Fasting on Health, Aging, and Disease

Rafael de Cabo, Ph.D., and Mark P. Mattson, Ph.D. (2019). *Effects of Intermittent Fasting on Health, Aging, and Disease.* (381:2541-2551). 10.1056/NEJMra1905136.

Abstract:

Evidence is accumulating that eating in a 6-hour period and fasting for 18 hours can trigger a metabolic switch from glucose-based to ketone-based energy, with increased stress resistance, increased longevity, and a decreased incidence of diseases, including cancer and obesity.

Cardiometabolic Benefits of Intermittent Fasting

Krista A. Varady, Sofia Cienfuegos, Mark Ezpeleta, and Kelsey Gabel. (2021). *Cardiometabolic Benefits of Intermittent Fasting.* (Annual Review of Nutrition 41:1). pp 333-361. https://doi.org/10.1146/annurev-nutr-052020-041327.

Abstract:

This review aims to summarize the effects of intermittent fasting on markers of cardiometabolic health in humans. All forms of fasting reviewed here—alternate-day fasting (ADF), the 5:2 diet, and time-restricted eating (TRE)—produced mild to moderate weight loss (1–8% from baseline) and consistent reductions in energy intake (10–30% from baseline). These regimens may benefit cardiometabolic health by decreasing blood pressure, insulin resistance, and oxidative stress. Low-density lipoprotein cholesterol and triglyceride levels are also lowered, but findings are variable. Other health benefits, such as improved appetite regulation and favorable changes in the diversity of the gut microbiome, have also been demonstrated, but evidence for these effects is limited. Intermittent fasting is generally safe and does not result in energy level disturbances or increased disordered eating behaviors. In summary, intermittent fasting is a safe diet therapy that can produce clinically significant weight loss (>5%) and improve several markers of metabolic health in individuals with obesity.

Glucose Tolerance and Skeletal Muscle Gene Expression in Response to Alternate Day Fasting.

Leonie K. Heilbronn, Anthony E. Civitarese, Iwona Bogacka, Steven R. Smith, Matthew Hulver, Eric Ravussin. (2012). *Glucose Tolerance and Skeletal Muscle Gene Expression in Response to Alternate Day Fasting.* (Volume 13, Issue 3). Pp 574-581. https://doi.org/10.1038/oby.2005.61.

- Related: Carpenter, S. (2012, September). That gut feeling. Monitor on Psychology, 43(8). http://www.apa.org/monitor/2012/09/gut-feeling

  Excerpt: Your gut holds 90% of your serotonin.

Abstract:

Objective: Alternate day fasting may extend lifespan in rodents and is feasible for short periods in nonobese humans. The aim of this study was to examine the effects of 3 weeks of alternate day fasting on glucose tolerance and skeletal muscle expression of genes involved in fatty acid transport/oxidation, mitochondrial biogenesis, and stress response.

Research Methods and Procedures: Glucose and insulin responses to a standard meal were tested in nonobese subjects (eight men and eight women; BMI, 20 to 30 kg/m2) at baseline and after 22 days of alternate day fasting (36 hour fast). Muscle biopsies were obtained from a subset of subjects (n = 11) at baseline and on day 21 (12-hour fast).

Results: Glucose response to a meal was slightly impaired in women after 3 weeks of treatment (p < 0.01), but insulin response was unchanged. However, men had no change in glucose response and a significant reduction in insulin response (p < 0.03). There were no significant changes in the expression of genes involved in mitochondrial biogenesis or fatty acid transport/oxidation, although a trend toward increased CPT1 expression was observed (p < 0.08). SIRT1 mRNA expression was increased after alternate day fasting (p = 0.01).

Discussion: Alternate day fasting may adversely affect glucose tolerance in nonobese women but not in nonobese men. The gene expression results indicate that fatty acid oxidation and mitochondrial biogenesis are unaffected by alternate day fasting. However, the increased expression in SIRT1 suggests that alternate day fasting may improve stress resistance, a commonly observed feature of calorie-restricted rodents.

Metabolic reactions activated during 58-hr fasting are revealed by non-targeted metabolomic analysis of human blood.

Teruya, T., Chaleckis, R., Takada, J. et al. (2019). *Metabolic reactions activated during 58-hr fasting are revealed by non-targeted metabolomic analysis of human blood.* (Sci Rep 9). pp 854. https://doi.org/10.1038/s41598-018-36674-9

Abstract:

During human fasting, metabolic markers, including butyrates, carnitines, and branched-chain amino acids, are upregulated for energy substitution through gluconeogenesis and use of stored lipids. We performed non-targeted, accurate semiquantitative metabolomic analysis of human whole blood, plasma, and red blood cells during 34–58 hr fasting of four volunteers. During this period, 44 of ~130 metabolites increased 1.5~60-fold. Consistently fourteen were previously reported. However, we identified another 30 elevated metabolites, implicating hitherto unrecognized metabolic mechanisms induced by fasting. Metabolites in pentose phosphate pathway are abundant, probably due to demand for antioxidants, NADPH, gluconeogenesis and anabolic metabolism. Global increases of TCA cycle-related compounds reflect enhanced mitochondrial activity in tissues during fasting. Enhanced purine/pyrimidine metabolites support RNA/protein synthesis and transcriptional reprogramming, which is promoted also by some fasting-related metabolites, possibly via epigenetic modulations. Thus diverse, pronounced metabolite increases result from greatly activated catabolism and anabolism stimulated by fasting. Anti-oxidation may be a principal response to fasting.

Intermittent metabolic switching, neuroplasticity and brain health.

Mattson MP, Moehl K, Ghena N, Schmaedick M, Cheng A. (2018). *Intermittent metabolic switching, neuroplasticity and brain health.* Nat Rev Neurosci. doi: 10.1038/nrn.2017.156. Epub 2018 Jan 11. Erratum in: Nat Rev Neurosci. 2020 Aug;21(8):445. PMID: 29321682; PMCID: PMC5913738.

Abstract:

During evolution, individuals whose brains and bodies functioned well in a fasted state were successful in acquiring food, enabling their survival and reproduction. With fasting and extended exercise, liver glycogen stores are depleted, and ketones are produced from adipose-cell-derived fatty acids. This metabolic switch in cellular fuel source is accompanied by cellular and molecular adaptations of neural networks in the brain that enhance their functionality and bolster their resistance to stress, injury and disease. Here, we consider how intermittent metabolic switching, repeating cycles of a metabolic challenge that induces ketosis (fasting and/or exercise) followed by a recovery period (eating, resting and sleeping), may optimize brain function and resilience throughout the lifespan, with a focus on the neuronal circuits involved in cognition and mood. Such metabolic switching impacts multiple signaling pathways that promote neuroplasticity and resistance of the brain to injury and disease.

APPENDIX E:
Philosophers' Biographies

Descartes

René Descartes (1596–1650) was a French philosopher and mathematician. He is regarded as a foundational thinker in the development of Western ideas of reason and science. His philosophy was built on the idea of radical doubt, an understanding that nothing perceived or sensed is necessarily true. The only thing that can be true is doubting, or thinking, which is the essence of his famous phrase, "I think, therefore I am" (or, in Latin, "Cogito ergo sum").

Plato

Plato (c. 428 BCE–c. 348 BCE) was an ancient Greek philosopher who wrote some of the most influential works in Western thought. A student of Socrates, Plato was so impressed by his teacher's method of debate that he wrote all his works in the Socratic method of question-and-answer. Devastated after Socrates' trial and death, Plato traveled for 12 years through Europe and Egypt studying mathematics, geometry, geology, astronomy and religion. During this period, Plato wrote his most famous works, including The Republic, which contains "The Allegory of the Cave." On his return to Athens, Plato established the Academy—the first organized school in Western civilization.

Socrates

Socrates (469–399 BCE) is the founding figure of Western philosophy. His style of teaching—immortalized as the "Socratic Method"—involved asking question after question until his students arrived at their own understanding. He wrote nothing himself, so the only record we have of his teachings comprises the writings of his followers, most notably Plato. After several acts of civil disobedience, Socrates was charged with failing to honor the Athenian gods and corrupting the young and was sentenced to death. Although colleagues begged him to escape, he chose to stay, spending his last days among friends before accepting the cup of hemlock from his executioner and drinking it.

Nietzsche

Friedrich Nietzsche (1844–1900) lived on the tightrope between brilliance and madness. Largely ignored while he was alive, his insights about Western religion, music, morality and philosophy have affected generations of thinkers, psychologists, poets, novelists and playwrights. As one of his biographers wrote, "For Nietzsche, thinking was an act of extreme emotional intensity. He thought the way others feel." Nietzsche wrote his masterpieces while suffering from bad health and terrible pain. In 1889, he collapsed, never to regain his mental health. He spent the last 11 years of his life deranged and eventually in silence. He died at age 66 in the care of his sister.

Hegel

Georg Hegel (1770–1831) was a German philosopher and is considered to be the leading thinker of his era. His philosophies include the idea that progress is messy and nonlinear; ideas we disagree with hold kernels of truth we should examine; and growth requires the clash of different views, represented by the Dialectic: an accepted thesis, challenged by an opposing antithesis, resolving in a synthesis. At 48, he was appointed professor of philosophy at the University of Berlin.

Jim Collins

Jim Collins (b. 1958) is teacher and writer dedicated to studying what makes great companies tick. He has written and co-authored eight books that have sold more than 10 million copies worldwide. His book, Good to Great, was a study of the success of unassuming, determined leaders who keep their focus on clear, simple goals—much like Jim himself.

Napoleon Hill

Napoleon Hill (1883–1970) was an American self-help author. He was the first author to write about the connection between success and the powers of the mind, and his life's work has become the cornerstone of modern motivation. Hill was born into poverty in the Appalachian town of Pound, in Southwest Virginia. At age 13, he began working as a mountain reporter on his father's newspaper. He saved his earnings to enter law school, but had to withdraw due to a lack of money. He worked as a reporter until an assignment in 1908 changed the course of his life. While interviewing the powerful industrialist Andrew Carnegie, Carnegie challenged Hill to interview wealthy, successful men and see if he could discover the formula of their success. Published in 1937, Think and Grow Rich was an instant success and made Hill one of America's most beloved motivational authors. It is still among the 10 best-selling self-help books and has never been out of print.

APPENDIX F: **Letters**

May 13, 2021

To Whom it may Concern: My name is William Green I have taken to classes From mr. Lindberg Goal setting, and Entrepreneurail he has the most positive mindset I have ever seen To be an inmate he shares that with everyone he talks too. He has taken his adversity to help others inmates an everyone here respect him for that I am very pround to have met him and to call him a Friend I pray that you consider mr. Lindberg for a reduction in his sentence His perseverence, Humblenes is what makes Mr Lindberg a good person His work is better for the outside World to be able to make a better inpact on others like me in seven months that I have Known him

yours Truely

inmate 53463-079
William Green

6-14-21

MR. LINDBERG IS DOING AN EXCELLENT JOB TEACHING OTHERS VALUABLE LESSONS IN BUSINESS STRUCTURE, MARKET AWARENESS, AND DEFINING GOALS.

HIS IS USING HIS TIME TO BETTER HIMSELF AND TO TEACH THOSE THAT CAN BENEFIT FROM KNOWLEDGE THAT WILL KEEP THEM FROM RE-OFFENDING.

S. WEBSTER

5/13/21

To whom it may concern,

I have known Greg Lindberg for the last 4-5 months at FPC Montgomery. He is a great guy with lots of information to share. He is very helpful and a very good teacher. I have taken many of his classes at FPC Montgomery and learned a significant amount. He is an excellent teacher and has the life experiences to share his knowledge with me and other inmates. His teaching has had a direct impact on my life and my visions for my future in a very positive manner.

Sincerely

Shelindev Aggarwal

To whom it may concern

My name is Dwayne Rainey. I'm currently a inmate in Montgomery Federal Prison Camp. During my incarceration I enrolled in a class called Goal setting. Goal setting was taught by Greg Lindberg. The course was very informative. Greg advised us to come up with a list of our short and long term goals in our personal and financial aspects of our lives. Up on my release these tools that I aquired will assit me in achieving my goals of starting a mental health agency, being a advocate for prison reform and being a productive citizen.

Everyone wanted to take Greg's class because we heard about his wealth. Who wouldn't want to be wealthy? Greg is a down to earth person and would take out time to answer any question you had for him. Greg gave us a testimony of his personal life, marriage, case and his business. Greg will tell anyone he matriculated at a Ivy League university but his experience in prison he learned the most. I believe Greg had a opinion about prison but once he settled in and realized that it's a lot of talented people in prison who have made a lot of irrational decision in life. I believe Greg's focus in life is to inspire and to help people. It also doesn't matter of your ethnic heritage or if your a convicted felon.

Dwayne Rainey

5-18-21

To: Whom it may concern
RE: Greg Lindberg

Hi, my name is Jumaane Brisby. I would like to start off by saying that Greg is a very Motivating and positive energy force. The reason that I'm saying this is because I see him involved in the Community IE: If one has a question he answers it to the best of his ability, If he doesn't know the answer he will do the research and get it for ya. He's teaching a business class here and I'm learning a lot more here in his class than the course that I took in college by far. He's very thorough and encourages his students for feedback. Greg also works as an orderly in the education department. He is responsible for keeping it clean. He has to take out the trash, clean up the restroom's and toilet included. Both staff and inmates. When he does it he does it with a smile. He's a pillar in the community. Even though I've known him for a short period of time I believe that he deserves a second chance as evidenced by his interaction in this community. The world awaits his return. Hopefully, you will digest this letter and set this positive energy force named Greg Lindberg free.

Sincerly, Jumaane Brisby

To whom this may Concern:

My name is Calvin Maurice Buchanan and I'm writing this letter on the behalf of Mr. Greg Lindberg. Mr. Lindberg and I have been knowing each other for several months now but feels like years from all the things that he and I have learned from each other from his Money Managing, Entrepreneur Ship, and Business Planing Classes. On a Personal level, Mr. Lindberg always spoke on learning from your mistakes, bettering your Conditions, and negative Criminal thinking patterns. I've learned so much from Mr. Lindberg and speaking on his behalf is truly an honor because he has helped me with so much that I honestly don't think he knows how much I appreciate all that he has done for me as well for my family. Your Honor, I know that Mr. Lindberg has learned a lesson from all of this that he's been through and if given a chance to prove that I put my life on it that he would show you that he is a man that has truly learned from his Actions. Thank You for your time, and God Bless you.

Signed,
Calvin Maurice Buchanan #53794-074

TO WHOM IT MAY CONCERN:

I am writing you this letter today in reference to Greg Lindberg, who is a fellow inmate here at FPC Montgomery. I first met Greg in the "JOB SEARCH" class. Greg was the teacher of the class & within a caple minutes of listening to his lecture, I knew that I was IN FOR A GREAT HOUR OF Knowledge, Encouragement, & Hope. Greg helped me realize that I should embrace my time here at "THE SCHOOL OF HARD KNOCKS," & learn as much as I can. Through his teachings in the class, I HAVE LEARNED THAT I NEED TO LET GO OF THE SHAME OF MY OFFENSE. He taught us the difference between guilt & shame. Guilt: "I MADE A MISTAKE." & Shame: "I AM A MISTAKE." AFTER THE JOB SEARCH CLASS, I HAVE A RE-NEWED Vision OF Hope as I apply for employment POST RELEASE. I was also privileged to attend Greg's "Entreponuer" CLASS. As a sucesful Businessman, Greg's knowledge in this arena is unmatched. Greg's preparation, presentation, & Real world experience make this class his BEST offering yet. Most importantly though is Greg's ability to connect with an audience. Greg's ability to plant seeds of success into inmates minds is truly inspirational, as inmates leave his class with the knowledge & conviction that they can be successful bussiness people post release. I am truly grateful for the opportunity to attend Greg's classes — it has been the highlight of my time here. If you have any further questions for me regarding Greg's classes, please feel free to contact me here at FPC Montgomery.

KIND REGARDS,

Richard McDonald

To whom it may concern, My name is

Eric Henderson. I'm an inmate at Maxwell Prison Camp. I transfered to this camp to continue my progression, on being rehabilitated upon my return to society. Over the course of five months. MR Buchanan and I. Have had countless conversations on what our plans were, once being released. We Brainstormed day and night with no Real concrete plan. what we discoverd, we both had visions on how success looks. But Know real tangible way of achieveing our goals. So one day MR.Buchanan, told me about a class called (Entrepreneurship). He said, "I'm going to sign up and that I should do the same." I explained to mr. Buchanan, That I have another class to attend. But as soon as that class is completed. I will sign up, He agreed. That following night, mr Buchanan attened they Entrepreneurship course. After class mr Buchanan came Back to our unit with rejuvination in his eyes. He talked all night obaut MR lindberg, and how he gave him a new prospective on life its self. And how his failed way of thinking will send him back in prison. I was so elated! I went to bed early, just so I can sign-up for this life changing class. Unfortunatly, mr. lindberg entrepreneurship class was full. I never gotten the pleasure, to heare mr. lindberg teach. However to witness mr. buchanan be inspired by, mr lindberg in one day. I want to be attached to this phenomenon. I'm currently awaiting mr lindberg next course, mr lindberg may not know this, but he has indirectly inspired me to became a free thinker and a better man.

#45749424

To whom it may concern:

My name is John Oliver. I met Greg in passing in our housing unit. I got to know Greg in a class he is teaching called Entrepreneur I. Out of the 16 classes I have taken it the 10 months I have been here his was the first that was a real class with useful info. I was well thought out and was tailored to us as individuals. He came prepared and when we would run across something he didn't know he could come back the next class having found out the info for us. Having used his phone mins to have someone on the outside find the info. This means alot cause our access to new or current info is difficult or impossible most times. I'm glad to of meet him and learned from him. For the first time since being here I feel I have benefited from being here.

Sincerly
John Oliver 52733-074

May 19 2021

TO: Who make Concern

My name is Dr Gilberto Sanchez inmate at FPC Montgomery my Registration number is 17224-002.

I want to take a moment of your time and tell you how thankful I am For Mr. Greg Lindberg.

In a very short Period of time, Mr Lindberg has shared some of his knowledge on how to open and Manage a Company.

I have been Very Impressed with amount of Valuable Information and his humble attitude in the way that he deliver it. I believe Very Comfortable that this Knowledge will benefit me after my release.

I easy can tell, that Mr Lindberg Is a man of GOD, High honor and Sincere.

thank You — Greg

Kyle Sandler #17620-002
FPC Montgomery
1001 Willow Street
Montgomery, AL 36112

May 24, 2021

To Whom It May Concern,

My name is Kyle Sandler and I am a Federal Inmate at FPC Montgomery where Greg Lindberg is serving his federal sentence. He and I live in the same housing unit and in the same wing.We also both work in the education department and we both teach a wide variety of classes to other inmates ranging from leadership skills, re-entry programming and adult continuing education classes.

I am writing this letter today because I feel compelled to let you know that Mr. Lindberg has used his vast knowledge in business, and social causes to enrich the lives of several men incarcerated here. Not only is Mr. Lindberg a teacher, he regularly tutors inmates 1:1 based on the classes he teaches. He also mentors several men who are looking to start businesses when they get out on a pathway from inmate to entrepreneurship.

Many of us know Greg's background. We also know that he is a highly sought after speaker who loves to share his knowledge in order to help people. Here at FPC Montgomery he shares this knowledge daily.

In closing I have been incarcerated with a wide range of high profile inmates including Jeff Skilling and Nevin Shapiro. Unlike them, Mr. Lindberg leads by example, is a natural teacher and an inspiration to us all.

Thank you for your time,

Kyle G. Sandler

5-14-21

To Whom iT May ConCern i Willie Colon am WriTing This leTTer On BeHalF OF Greg lindBerg i have Taken all OF The Classes ThaT Mr. lindBerg Has TaughT i Feel like i have learned More From his Classes Than Any OTher Class ThaT i have Taken in here. he Teaches his STudenTs Tools Needed To noT only become a Success in business, buT also how To be a SuccessFul CiTizen. Since i have Taken his Classes, i have grown as a Person because OF his example While he's been aT F.P.C. MonTgomery His Willingness To go above and beyond To Share WiTh The inmaTes in his Class is an inSpiration to noT only Me, buT OThers aswell. Since Taking his Classes, iT has Made Me See liFe Through diFFrenT Eyes Which now Fuels Me To do beTTer in My liFe Once released and lowers My recidivism Thinking OF My Old Ways i am a PuerTo Rican american who is From MiaMi, Fl and have Always Seen Success Through illegal Means. buT Mr. lindberg gives me hoPe ThaT I Can Truly be a Success Through legal Means. I am Truly appreciaTive For The HelP hoPe and SuPPorT i have received From Mr. lindberg Teaching While i am APPreciaTive OF his Teaching i Feel ThaT he would beTTer Serve in The Free World HelPing individuals Succeed beFore They geT inTo The Federal Prison SySTem Thank you For allowing Me To express My SenTiments regarding a Friend Greg lindberg

Sincerly, Willie Colon

To Whom It May Concern,

Throughout my time at the FPC Montgomery, I took entrepreneurship taught by Greg Lindberg and have learned alot in his class. He has taught me how Entrepreneurship is a Mindset and not a career choice and has uplifted me in many ways being in prison telling me to never give up and this just temporary defeat. Greg is providing us the necessary tools to not only succeed once we complete our sentence but to also not become repeat offenders. We are the masters of own own fate and if we change the way we think, we can change the way we behave. I learned that from Greg Lindberg and that we must see these challenges as opportunities instead of problems. He is a great leader in this community and deserves a second chance.

Thank You,
Charles Burnett
Fed ID # 25789 - 075

10/12/21: (Letter from Kason Harry)

My little sister was shot and killed on her 25th birthday, 9 years ago. That same year my twin brother was charged with murder and even though he didn't pull the trigger he was sentenced to 31 years, leaving behind his four kids. Months later we found out that the mother of his children who I love like a sister was addicted to drugs which resulted in D.S.S coming and taking my nieces and nephew. My mother was awarded custody after a long fought year but because my oldest niece was not my brother's biological child she was placed in foster care. That hurt like hell and still does. Through adversity I found my "other self," as Napoleon Hill puts it.

I set out to be the best rapper in my area and I did so. I set out to be the best at whatever I did.   I succeeded on multiple accounts but I also failed just as many times.

I'm in here for dealing drugs and although I won't ever result back to that occupation, it has taught me a lot about business. I've failed plenty of times which impact taught me how to do better business. I learned that it's not about how much money one makes but how much one can save and invest.

Two months before I got incarcerated on this drug charge I was wrongfully incarcerated on charges of attempted murder and several other charges. I was facing 25 years to life, but by the grace of God I single handedly proved my innocence and was exonerated of all charges. (Google: Kason Harry.)

Coming to prison has helped me find my purpose in life. I discovered my love for all things surrounding writing and my gift of creativity. I've written a movie script, books, treatments for reality shows, etc. I've also discovered my passion for knowledge.

You're an inspiration to me. $5,000, fourteen years later annual revenue 24 million... amazing! I just want to thank you for being so kind as to share your knowledge with me. You're not only helping me but you're helping me to be able to one day provide for my family and help so many along the way.

Your book resonates with me because I've overcame adversity and I shall overcome this adversity. Continue being humble, helpful, and great.

May 21, 2021

To whom It May Concern:

I have very strong convictions regarding letters of reference. A letter of reference should paint a clear and accurate picture of a person as opposed to simply being a favor for a friend. It is with these strong convictions that I find comfort in sharing my opinions of Greg Lindberg.

Over a 30 year career in business, both domestic and international, I have developed an astute sense of business acumen and communication skills in a leader. At present, I am taking an entrepreneurial course led by Greg. The scope and breadth of Greg's business knowledge is only exceeded by his patience, compassion, and understanding with fellow inmates, some having less than basic business skills. Greg's class is equally enjoyed by high school drop outs, GED Graduates, and graduates of Top MBA programs. Greg makes all comers feel welcome and all questions asked equally important. Greg takes a personal interest in his student inmates' ideas, dreams, plans, i.e., their path toward a successful future. He ensures that each student inmate leaves each week with a knowledge and understanding of their own unbridled possibilities and capabilities.

It is unfortunate that my and Greg's paths have crossed in this less than pleasant circumstance, however, I consider myself grateful and blessed not only for his knowledge, but his friendship as well. Whether in Greg's structured class or simply "walking miles on the track", there is always something to be learned from Greg Lindberg. It is my sincere hope that this brief communication portrays Greg in an unfiltered, raw light -- as a great hybird -- successful business titan and compassionate teacher.

Best Regards,

John Monroe
20742-035

A forever read that continues the lineage of mindfulness book written by the likes of Napoleon Hill, Deepak Chopra and Nietzsche, but Greg Lindberg adds a welcomed wrinkle to the genre by spreading meticulous and digestible business cues to readers searching for practical strategies on how failing early and often can lead one to a fulfilling life - if they dare to do the work.

Lindberg's book, Failing Early and Failing Often provides quick, concise and beneficial ancedotes for those looking to achieve their highest desires. According to Lindberg, Jim Collins calls it your, "Big Hairy Audacious Goal" (BHAG). So whether you're the altruistic individual who gives to your soul is at ease - it's practical insight for you. Lindberg says, "at the core of every one of us is a desire for freedom." This book encourages everyone to identify what freedom means to them and fail toward it relentlessly.

Or if you're an entrepreneur striving to blaze your path to billions - he details a set of examples that highlight the very consequential do's and dont's of it all. He quotes C.S Lewis saying, "Integrity is doing the right thing when no one is watching." Lindberg hangs his hat on this code, because he broadly lays this out while discussing his impending incarceration. He does this in a bite size fashion that doesn't dig into the minutia of it all. He does a great job of not wrapping the reader into a tale about him specifically, but he weaves his story in and out of each chapter to serve as an exclamation point to the chapters theme.

The opening of the book is dedicated to principles set forth by some of his literary inspirations such as Descartes, Socrates and Hegel to name a few. The roots of the book are anchored in thinking, questioning, learning, adjusting, adapting and thinking through it all again. Throughout the first part of the book you see Lindberg turning into a mindful "maniac" questioning all things and leaping to find failures at every turn. The repetitive nature of the first part of the book became a bit of an irritant, because he drummed the point home of being fearless and mentally tough no matter the circumstance; COVID 19, impending prison sentence or divorce. He even encouraged the reader "to find a challenge within peace", if your life was peaceful. These points were met with more understanding within the context of the entire book.

Out of context parts of the manuscript struck me as a billionaire out of touch with the disadvantage reality that everyone faces. "Billionaires and the 1% (percent) have become a persecuted class attacked for having vision, conviction and determination to persist." says Lindberg. Which may be a truism indeed, but the aforementioned persecution that he speaks of happens at every class level.

To his credit he sprinkles some of these examples throughout the book and after digesting the entire book you can see that his philanthropic endeavors highlight this.

That is why I recommend this book is read whole at first and on the second and third I suggest the reader nibbles on the parts that serve them best.

This work starts to stretch and becomes universal when he begins to speak heavily on the "tentacles of the Levithan."

Which for me was extremly reminiscant to what Rastafarians refer to Babylon—(the oppressive social, political, economic and cultural system that is found in Western society) He spoke of the Levithon in a myriad of ways, but what resonated the most is when he spoke through the gaze of law. He noted that their has been "more than 4,200 new federal laws enacted and 88,000 federal regulations enacted between 1995 and 2014."—but in 1927 all federal laws fit in one volume.

This significant data sprinkled throughout these pages shows the ways that these tentacles can suffocate nearly every American pursuing a dream if the Levithon wanted to. In spite of these horrid circumstances Lindberg insists on "turning adversity into advantage with an undying commitment to yourself."

After setting a solid foundation for which ones mental must be wired he details a value system that preps the reader for success while detailing every nuance of winning in business. Lindbergh's business prowess shows in magnonimous portions in the latter part of the literature he gets into the weeds of everything that allows a business to run efficient. He even gives a long range view of his personal business with a 30 plus page spread of pictures, and charts and his growth areas. However, a lot like his personal profile he is not boastful in his wins, so in order to understand his make up, it's in between the lines of his book. Visualization, planning and having the mental fortitude to grow through failures are the consistent lines that Lindberg sets in order to find success.

However his most poignant line after Lindberg gives the reader the foundation, background, business values, poses questions, he simply tells the reader to

"Be careful once you decide on your "burning desire" because once you set the wage you must bear the task. This is someone who is speaking the power of his conviction — he has the federal prison number to prove it —

Yet this won't be his last time failing early, besides that is the only way Greg Lindberg knows how to grow.

In Kind

Markuetric Stringfellow

— I've already recommended it to several people.
— Truly enjoyed the read.